Separation of Church and Sex

Free at Last! Free at Last!

FELIX CLAIRVOYANT

Foreword by
International Spiritual Leader
and Founder of the
Raelian Movement
Maitreya Rael

WORLD
Publishing Company

Felix Clairvoyant
Permissions and rights inquiries may be directed to:
felixclairvoyantauthor@gmail.com

World Publishing Company
17325 Euclid Avenue
Cleveland, Ohio 44112
www.worldpublishingcompany.com

eBook ISBN: 979-8-29586-604-3
Paperback ISBN: 979-8-90427-022-3
Hardcover ISBN: 979-8-90427-023-0

Printed in the United States of America
Advance Review Copy
This manuscript is being distributed prior to publication for review purposes only. Content may be revised before final publication. Please do not reproduce, distribute, or share this material without authorization.

Contents

Dedication

I offer this book, *Separation of Church and Sex—Free at Last! Free at Last!* (SOCAS) as an expression of love, solidarity, and reverence for all those, past and present, who have dared to reclaim the right to exist fully, love freely, and express themselves authentically in a world that too often vilifies difference and sanctifies conformity. This work is dedicated to the courageous individuals who have persistently struggled, and who continue to struggle to this day, for the inherent human right to live and love without shame, fear, or persecution.

To every individual who has suffered under the crushing weight of religious dogma[1], who has endured rejection from their families, exclusion from their communities, violence from institutions, and the torment of believing they were flawed simply for existing, you are the beating heart of this book. Your endurance is a living testament to the indomitable human spirit—unyielding in courage or strength despite opposition or adversity. Your very existence is a powerful refutation of every doctrine that attempts to reduce love to sin, gender diversity to pathology, and sensual pleasure to spiritual danger.

Throughout history, this most intimate of human rights has been not only denied but systematically vilified, through grotesque distortions of sacred texts, especially those rooted in the Abrahamic religious traditions. Cloaked in the language of righteousness, these distortions have served to justify exclusion, violence, and spiritual colonization[2]. These dogmas have scarred generations through conversion therapies—practices that attempt to change or suppress sexual orientation or gender identity based on discredited pathology claims—excommunications, celibacy mandates, arranged marriages, moral policing, and genocidal silences[3]. This book stands in open defiance of those wounds. It refuses to bow to the sanctimonious authority[4] of outdated creeds, and it asserts the inalienable right of every human being to live in harmony with their body, their identity, their pleasure, and their truth.

This dedication also extends to the brave hearts within religious, academic, political, and spiritual institutions who have chosen truth over tradition, compassion over complacency, and justice over silence. To the scholars who reinterpret ancient texts through the lens of love; to the priests and imams who embrace their queerness; to the theologians who center empathy over exclusion; and to every whistleblower who exposes the hypocrisy of systems that preach love while practicing harm, your courage is sacred. May your voices echo through temples, mosques, synagogues, churches, and classrooms, opening doors for others to walk through unashamed and whole, and may your efforts hasten the dawn of an era where love is never weaponized, and where diversity is celebrated rather than feared.

Above all, I dedicate this book with deep humility, immense gratitude, and unwavering love to you, my spiritual guide and teacher, Rael—without whom this work would never have seen the light of day. Thank you, you who are the Maitreya, the Mahdi, the New Paraclete, the Mashiach. Blessed be your name, you who are the Messiah[5] and final Messenger of our creators, the Elohim of the original Bible written in ancient Hebrew. For more than thirty-five years, your teachings have illuminated my path and expanded my consciousness. In a world that demands conformity, you teach self-liberation. In a culture obsessed with guilt, you champion happiness. In the shadow of dogma, you offer the clarity of science, the beauty of reason, and the freedom of universal love. Your fearless voice has helped me reimagine not only what it means to be spiritual, but what it means to be truly human: to live without shame, to love without conditions, to question with courage, and to blossom without apology. Through your wisdom, I have come to understand that spiritual evolution is inseparable from sexual liberation. That pleasure is sacred. That happiness is a responsibility. And that peace on Earth will only be possible when love—in all its consensual, diverse, and erotic expressions—is no longer feared, suppressed, or judged, but celebrated as the very force that animates the universe.

May this book serve as a guiding light for those still navigating the dark corridors of shame, guilt, and repression instilled by sanctimonious traditions. May it bring warmth and comfort to those wounded by the contradictions and hypocrisies of their inherited faiths. May it whisper hope into the ears of those still afraid to be who they are. And may it invite every reader into a life of joyful authenticity, radiant self-discovery, and unapologetic freedom[6]. To all those who have chosen to walk the path of liberation from the confines of sexual repression, suppression, and oppression, I applaud your journey toward true freedom and the beautiful gift of **being** while being *Free at Last!* May you find enduring inner peace and happiness as you continue your life's profound journey of self-discovery and truth.

Acknowledgments

Writing *Separation of Church and Sex—Free at Last! Free at Last!* has been nothing short of a profound and transformative journey—intellectually, emotionally, and spiritually. This book was not born in isolation; it is the result of years of spiritual growth, life's experiences, learning, activism, dialogue, encouragement, reflection, and the unwavering presence of the few who stood by me with patience, compassion, and faith in the importance of this work.

To these few cherished friends, I say 'thank you' for being my pillars of strength throughout this creative and often vulnerable process. Your steady encouragement, thoughtful perspectives, and unshakable belief in the significance of this work gave me the motivation to continue, even during moments of doubt. Whether you offered a listening ear, a challenging question, a word of comfort, or a timely reminder of why this book matters, you have each contributed in ways that are immeasurable and unforgettable. You are part of its very fabric.

I wish to express my heartfelt appreciation to the esteemed members of my Ph.D. thesis committee, whose guidance during my graduate studies helped lay the intellectual foundation for much of what is explored in these pages. To Chairperson Dr. David Wohlsifer, Dr. Clint Gould, and the late Dr. Janice Epp, your mentorship, critical insights, and unwavering support not only sharpened my academic rigor[1] but also encouraged me to explore bold, boundary-challenging ideas with both clarity and integrity. I carry your knowledge and wisdom with me on every page of this book.

To the gifted publishing professionals who lent their time, craft, and care to this manuscript—thank you. Your thoughtful suggestions, meticulous attention to detail, and deep respect for the spirit of this work made the refining process both fruitful and rewarding. Your dedication to excellence helped ensure this book reaches readers in its most impactful form.

A special and deeply personal expression of gratitude goes to Maitreya Rael—a radiant source of peace, wisdom, and loving rebellion. Your teachings have been a compass for my own journey of self-liberation and conscious awakening. Thank you for illuminating the path toward a new humanity, one rooted in science, love, freedom, and respect for all forms of life. Your bold vision of a world free from dogma, fear, and sexual repression has been a foundational influence on this book. I am also profoundly grateful for your heartfelt contribution in writing the foreword and for your lifelong example of courage, compassion, and cosmic consciousness[2].

To you, the reader—thank you. Your willingness to engage with this book speaks volumes about your openness, curiosity, and courage. In a world where sexuality and religion are still too often pitted against each other, your choice to read these pages is itself a radical act of hope. I am honored by your presence. May this book serve not only as an exploration but as a mirror, a challenge, and a sanctuary. May it invite you to reflect, to question, to feel and, above all, to grow. And may it inspire deeper conversations, more expansive love, and a commitment to justice that transcends old boundaries.

Finally, to everyone—named and unnamed—who has ever dared to break free from inherited shame and reclaim their divine right to live authentically, know that this book was written with you, for you, and because of you. May its pages honor your courage, celebrate your truth, and accompany you on your path toward joyful and unrestrained self-expression[3].

Foreword by Maitreya Rael[1]

Humanity stands at a pivotal moment in its evolutionary journey. The choices we make today will determine not only our individual and collective happiness but the very future of our species. We are witnessing a time when the spiritual, the scientific, and the sexual must no longer be obstructed by archaic institutions clinging desperately to their power—nor torn apart by centuries of ignorance, fear, and domination—but instead reunited, harmonized, and elevated. This unification is not only possible but also necessary. For too long, religious institutions, particularly those rooted in the Abrahamic traditions[2], have weaponized morality and erected walls between these essential dimensions of human existence. They have declared war against what is most natural: the pursuit of knowledge, the celebration of pleasure, the right to love freely, to express our sexuality in whatever form we choose, and the happiness of simply being human. The result has been centuries of repression, shame, and confusion.

Chief among these institutions, the Catholic Church[3] has led one of the most enduring, harmful, and systematic campaigns against both sexual liberation and scientific truth. It has positioned itself as the moral authority over billions of lives, dictating not only how people should live, but how they should love, how they should explore their own bodies, and how they should understand the world around them. This institution, claiming to represent divine will, has been a relentless enemy of scientific progress and sexual freedom—two pillars essential to humanity's evolution.

Throughout history, the Catholic Church has shown a clear resistance to scientific progress. Not only did it condemn Galileo—placing him under house arrest for asserting that the Earth revolves around the Sun, a fact now taught to children—but its opposition to science extended to the rejection of evolution, reproductive health research, and any knowledge that challenged its literal interpretations of ancient texts. Even Copernicus, who first proposed the heliocentric model of the solar system, faced significant opposition from the Church, which upheld the geocentric view for centuries. In effect, the Church silenced groundbreaking truths that conflicted with its established doctrines.

Giordano Bruno, a philosopher and astronomer, expanded upon Copernicus' ideas by proposing an infinite universe filled with countless worlds, boldly challenging the Church's dogma. Condemned for his heretical views—which not only embraced heliocentrism but also questioned theological notions of the cosmos—Bruno refused to recant and was ultimately executed, burned at the stake in 1600. In its tireless effort to suppress scientific thought that conflicted with its scriptures, the Church didn't just silence brilliant minds—it destroyed them, epitomizing its fear of knowledge that threatened its ideological monopoly. These historical episodes serve as stark reminders of the Church's long-standing attempts to stifle progress whenever it posed a threat to the religious status quo.

Science—the very tool that allows humanity to understand the universe and our place within it—was treated as heresy. Why? Because with knowledge comes power, and with power comes independence from the manipulative grip of religious institutions. The Church fears a humanity that no longer relies on myth and superstition, one that sees beyond the veils of fear and guilt strategically woven over centuries. But science is not just about discovering the laws of physics or the origins of life. It's about understanding ourselves, our desires, and our capacity for love and connection.

The suppression of science is only one part of this tragic story. Perhaps nowhere has the Catholic Church's authoritarian influence been more damaging than in its war on sexuality. Sexual energy is the most powerful creative force in the universe. It is the very essence of life, of pleasure, of intimacy, and of connection. It is sacred not because it is rare, but because it is natural. Yet, for centuries, the Church has branded it as sinful, teaching generations to associate sexual desire with shame, guilt, and sin—while confining it to rigid, patriarchal, heteronormative templates[4] that erase the full spectrum of human experience.

From the baseless notion of "original sin"[5]—which absurdly posits that humanity is inherently flawed from birth due to an early act of disobedience—to the mandatory imposition of celibacy on its clergy, the Church has cultivated a culture of repression that has inflicted extensive psychological harm and, tragically, contributed to numerous cases of sexual abuse within its own ranks.

Its opposition to comprehensive sexuality education[6] is not merely a misguided stance; it has far-reaching, potentially criminal consequences. By systematically denying young people access to accurate, holistic information about their bodies, emotions, and relationships, the Church has created an environment of ignorance and vulnerability. Without proper education, youth are left unprepared to make informed decisions about their sexual health, leaving them exposed to higher risks of unwanted pregnancies, sexually transmitted infections[7], and abuse. Ignorance is not innocence—it is a breeding ground for suffering. This deliberate withholding of critical knowledge is less about upholding morality and more about maintaining control over personal autonomy and social norms. It perpetuates a cycle in which authority dictates the most intimate aspects of life, rather than empowering individuals with the tools they need to live safely, authentically, and joyfully.

Moreover, the Church's rigid stance against contraception[8], abortion, and LGBTQ+ rights further exemplifies its fear of sexual freedom. By dictating not only who we can love but also how we may express that love, it enforces a suffocating framework that restricts autonomy. Once again, this control is not about morality—it's about institutional power. In effect, its doctrines limit personal choice and stifle the diversity of human relationships, prioritizing conformity over blossoming.

This restrictive approach not only marginalizes those whose identities and desires deviate from religious norms but also perpetuates systemic inequality. It imposes a binary view of gender and sexuality that fails to reflect the complexity of the human experience. Rather than fostering empathy and inclusion, the Church's policies fuel discrimination and isolation. In doing so, it sacrifices the celebration of love and personal expression at the altar of power and dogma.

True enlightenment requires not only the liberation of the mind but also the honoring of the body. I envision a future in which science, sexuality, and religion are not enemies, but allies—fully integrated. In this reimagined world, people are encouraged to explore their sexual desires freely, without shame. Children are taught about their bodies with honesty and respect, so they may grow into adults who embrace communication, consent, and authentic connection. Love, in all its forms—whether between a man and a woman, two men, or two women—is celebrated as an essential part of the human experience and as vital to personal and collective well-being.

This is a call for a sexual revolution[9], one that reclaims the natural and liberating aspects of human sexuality. By fusing science and progressive values, we can build a world in which sexuality is not feared or suppressed but honored as a source of creativity, happiness, and fulfillment. While the ideal of separating church and state was a critical milestone in the evolution of our modern democracies, in practice, this separation remains incomplete—especially when it comes to sexuality, where religious morality still shapes laws, policies, and cultural attitudes. Secularism[10] must now take center stage if we are to build a truly inclusive society. The time has come to dismantle the chains that have enslaved our minds and bodies for millennia, and to embrace the joyful, natural diversity of human expression.

In *Separation of Church and Sex—Free at Last! Free at Last!* the author confronts one of the most enduring and damaging taboos[11] of modern society: religious control over sexuality. For centuries, religious institutions have preserved outdated doctrines at the expense of their followers' well-being. From censoring science to opposing sexuality education, their goal has been control—not compassion. This book exposes that legacy and challenges the very foundation of a moral system rooted in the suppression of natural human desires and intellectual curiosity.

But it goes further. It offers a vision of liberation. It imagines a world in which reason, compassion, and love—not shame and fear—guide our personal and collective growth. A world in which sexuality is free, diverse, and celebrated.

This happiness is the path to true liberation, and it is the essence of my teachings for more than fifty years. More than anything else, happiness is what unites Raelians. Why? Because at the core of my message is radical freedom: the freedom to live without guilt—especially about our bodies and desires. Sexuality is not something to fear or repress. It is something to honor. A joyful, liberated sexuality is not only natural but also necessary. Pleasure is not a temptation to resist; it is a gift of life to be celebrated. And yet, for centuries, religions have invented sin to dominate minds, instill fear, and suppress pleasure and sexuality. But fear is not a path to awakening—it is a tool of oppression.

True spirituality does not oppose science, it embraces it. True love does not come with rules, it flows freely. True education does not indoctrinate, it liberates. The future of humanity will not be written by those who chant empty prayers, but by those who unite their minds and bodies in joy, curiosity, and empathy. It is through comprehensive sexuality education, through the liberation of desire, and through the celebration of pleasure, sensuality, and consent that a new world will be born. This is why I teach sensual meditation—to repair and strengthen the mind-body connection so we can better appreciate the pleasures of life. Why I launched Clitoraid—to restore stolen pleasure. Why we celebrate GoTopless Day—to end body shame and promote gender equality[12]. Why we champion science, human rights[13], and truth-based sexuality education for children. This book is a testimony to those values. It is not just a critique of religious authoritarianism[14] but a blueprint for justice, freedom, and peace.

To all who have suffered under religious oppression, to all whose desires have been called unnatural, to all who have been taught to be ashamed of their bodies: know this—you are perfect just as you are. No scripture can invalidate your existence. No religious law can erase your right to pleasure, to love, and to live freely.

May this book shine like a torch for future generations, and inspire many to walk the path of liberation, to separate church and sex once and for all, and to co-create a world where love is never a sin and freedom is never feared.

With infinite love and cosmic hope,

Maitreya Rael
Founder of the Raelian Movement
Messenger of the Elohim

September 2025 (80, aH – year 80 after Hiroshima)

Preface

This book has been two decades in the making, with the past five years dedicated to writing it with renewed focus and consistency. From the outset, I wish to openly declare my affiliation with the Raelian Movement—an international, non-profit spiritual organization to which I have remained steadfastly devoted for the past 36 years. Despite public misperceptions and sensationalized portrayals by dishonest and deceitful media[1] outlets, I continue to identify as a Raelian with pride. That pride is rooted in the profound transformation that Maitreya Rael's teachings have brought to my life. His philosophy, visionary yet grounded in science and humanism, has gifted me with a set of 21st-century values (**see Appendix E**) that I believe, if embraced, could transform not only individuals but the whole of humanity.

As the author, I have been compelled by an inner force to undertake this journey of exploration and understanding of the complex landscape where religion intersects with sexuality, and where the most intimate aspects of human sexual identity are too often subjected to religious control. The genesis of the book *Separation of Church and Sex—Free at Last! Free at Last!* is rooted in a profound conviction, curiosity, and concern regarding the nexus between religion and human sexuality.

My inspiration can be distilled into several key elements. First and foremost, it emerges from a deep sense of empathy and a commitment to social justice[2]. Throughout the centuries and continuing today, countless individuals have been denied their fundamental human right to express their sexual differences freely. This denial, perpetuated by traditional religious teachings, has inflicted immense suffering and, tragically, has led to the loss of many human lives. Conscience demands that we confront this legacy, and affirm the rights and dignity of every human being, regardless of sexual orientation[3] or gender identity[4].

In this effort, I find resonance with voices like that of Christopher Hitchens[5], who unflinchingly exposed how religion can treat our bodies not as vessels of joy and agency, but as battlegrounds of shame. "This life is treated as a mere prelude," he once noted, "a veil of tears." His warning was clear: religious guilt is not incidental—it is intentional, encoded into doctrine to subdue the human spirit and demonize pleasure. My own path, by contrast, begins with a simple and radical affirmation: this life is not a rehearsal. It is the stage upon which dignity, love, and human blossoming must be fully lived.

Similarly, Sam Harris[6] has called out the moral confusion that arises when "divine commands" are treated as immutable truth, even when they justify oppression. He reminds us that defending religion in the name of tolerance must never come at the expense of those it victimizes—especially women, LGBTQ+ individuals, and the sexually curious. The cost of blind reverence[7], Harris insists, is too often paid with human dignity[8].

My intention is not to vilify belief but to challenge its unchecked authority over human sexuality. The relationship between religion and sexuality has long been fraught with misunderstanding, prejudice, and rigid dogma—producing not only personal suffering but also deep societal divides across communities, generations, and cultures. Rather than framing this as a conflict between believers and non-believers, I invite a more compassionate inquiry—one that encourages open, honest dialogue as a means to dismantle stereotypes, challenge inherited biases, and make space for both spiritual depth and sexual authenticity[9].

This is another driving force behind this work: the desire to foster dialogue and deepen understanding. By engaging with this complex terrain, I hope to contribute to a more nuanced and respectful discourse—one that transcends entrenched boundaries and recognizes the full spectrum of the human experience. My goal is to cultivate a space where differing perspectives can be acknowledged without judgment, ultimately fostering a more inclusive understanding of sexuality that upholds individual freedom and embraces the many ways people find meaning, both spiritually and sexually, in their lives.

At its core, this book is also fueled by intellectual curiosity and a quest for truth. Religion, with its intricate tapestry of beliefs, commandments, and traditions, has profoundly shaped human societies and continues to influence our moral and cultural landscapes. However, the consequences of religious doctrine on marginalized groups—

especially for women, queer people, and young people navigating their identities—remain insufficiently scrutinized.

Marty Klein[10], a pioneering sex therapist and political advocate, has chronicled how religious ideology seeps into policy, education, and even medicine—waging what he calls "America's war on sex." His insights expose how moral panic, cloaked in piety, becomes weaponized to erode sexual rights under the guise of virtue. It's not only about what people believe privately—it's about how those beliefs are legislated into public law and cultural norms. This book joins that resistance by laying bare how sexual repression is not neutral; it is enforced, normalized, and deeply political.

These are not abstract issues. They have real-life consequences that affect the dignity, rights, and even the survival of individuals in these communities. If this book can help save even one life—by challenging destructive ideologies[11], by offering solace and clarity, or by inspiring a more inclusive worldview—then every hour spent writing it will have been worthwhile.

I want to emphasize that this work is not intended to ridicule or denigrate religious beliefs. Rather, it serves as an invitation—a call to reflect critically on the impact of certain doctrines, particularly those that have marginalized individuals for being different, sexually diverse, or simply human. My hope is that it opens space—a safe, courageous, and compassionate space—where difficult truths can be named, diverse experiences acknowledged, and healing dialogue possible. In doing so, it seeks to advocate for justice and equality, challenging oppressive norms while inviting both believers and non-believers to consider how a more inclusive perspective can enrich society as a whole.

As you journey through SOCAS, I invite you to reflect on how religion and sexuality have shaped not only society, but your own life. I hope these pages serve as both mirror and catalyst—revealing internalized beliefs[12], sparking conversation, and illuminating new possibilities. Yes, this book critiques systems of oppression. But more than that, it offers a vision for the future—a future where liberation is both spiritual and sexual, where education is grounded in truth, and where the dignity of all human beings is upheld.

Ultimately, I hope this book contributes to the movement for a more compassionate world—one in which the separation of church and sex is not merely an abstract ideal, but a lived reality that upholds and affirms the dignity, rights, and identities of all individuals. May it serve as a steppingstone toward a future where every person is free to define their own identity and pursue the fullness of their human experience without fear, shame, or prejudice.

May this book reach many—young and old, curious and cautious, devout and doubting—and offer something transformative. Whether it plants a seed, opens a door, soothes a scar, or sparks a quiet revolution within, may it accompany you on your journey toward greater freedom, deeper self-love, and unapologetic joy[13].

The world we long for is possible. And it begins with the courage to heal.

With unwavering commitment to truth, freedom, and justice.

Felix Clairvoyant, Ph.D.

San Francisco, January 2025

Introduction

Confronting the Shackles of Sanctimony

In exploring the intricate relationship between religion and sexuality, it is essential to confront one of the most daunting obstacles to human self-development: sanctimony[1]. Humanity, I believe, stands at a defining crossroads—a pivotal moment in our collective history where the bright promise of progress collides with the lingering grip of antiquated dogma[2]. For centuries, sanctimony—this veneer of pious moral superiority—has been wielded by powerful religious institutions to police thought, behavior, and desire. Cloaked in righteousness, it has dictated how people should live and love, while suffocating intellectual inquiry, emotional authenticity, and self-expression.

But what, precisely, is sanctimony? At its core, sanctimony is moral self-righteousness—an excessive and often hypocritical display of piety, virtue, or moral superiority. Within religious contexts, it often manifests as an unwavering conviction in one's own moral correctness, accompanied by judgment and condemnation of those who deviate from prescribed norms. The consequences are profound. Sanctimony has long created hostile environments in which individuals—particularly those whose sexual orientation or gender identity falls outside rigid frameworks—are subjected to shame, guilt, exclusion, and rejection. These experiences leave deep psychological, emotional, and social scars that often endure for a lifetime.

Queer theologian Marcella Althaus-Reid[3] powerfully challenges this legacy in her work on queer theology—a field that resists heteronormative hierarchies and exclusionary interpretations of religious tradition. She explores "how reimagining theology can empower marginalized sexual identities by offering a modern perspective on deconstructing the oppressive narratives tied to sanctimony" (**Althaus-Reid, 2005**). Her work underscores a vital truth: sanctimony is not an inevitable expression of spirituality, but a constructed mechanism of control.

There is little doubt that the oppressive legacy of sanctimony has long shackled the human spirit, constraining the pursuit of truth and authentic existence. In SOCAS, the reader embarks on an unflinching examination of these chains—an exploration of the historical and contemporary mechanisms through which sanctimony has been deployed to suppress intellectual freedom, emotional depth, and sexual liberation.

For centuries, religious leaders wielding moral authority have enforced rigid sexual norms at the expense of individual autonomy and human dignity. Religious institutions, deeply embedded in the regulation of social life, have cloaked themselves in sanctimony to legitimize their power and preserve control. This posture has systematically marginalized individuals and communities whose sexual identities or practices diverged from doctrinal prescriptions. Sexual minorities[4]—particularly LGBTQ+ individuals—have borne the brunt of this moral violence. Many religious traditions have condemned same-sex relationships and non-binary gender identities, citing sacred texts as justification, thereby fueling discrimination, ostracism[5], and, in extreme cases, physical violence.

The Catholic Church, in particular, has historically positioned itself as the ultimate arbiter of morality, intertwining divine authority with the governance of human behavior. This carefully constructed narrative has been meticulously crafted to instill fear and obedience, using sanctimony to delegitimize dissent and suppress deviation. By rigidly defining what is deemed "acceptable," the Church has not only hindered scientific inquiry and rational thought but also demonized natural expressions of human sexuality. The result is a legacy of repression—one that has left enduring wounds across generations, depriving countless individuals of the freedom to explore the full breadth of their humanity.

Even in our modern era—despite remarkable advances in science, technology, and social awareness—the shadow of sanctimony remains deeply embedded in cultural and political life. Ancient moral codes are frequently resurrected to contest emerging understandings of love, gender, and identity. This resurgence often manifests subtly yet persistently: in the politicization[6] of sexuality education, the stigmatization of gender diversity, and the suppression of scientific research that challenges entrenched beliefs. Sanctimony has evolved, adapting its strategies to contemporary contexts while perpetuating the same mechanisms of control. It continues to negotiate human freedom against conformity, tradition, and fear.

At the heart of the struggle against sanctimony lies the urgent necessity to reclaim intellectual, emotional, and sexual sovereignty. To confront these shackles is to challenge the deeply embedded narratives that have long confined us to a limited view of our potential. This confrontation is not merely an act of defiance; it is a profound affirmation of the human spirit's resilience and its unquenchable thirst for knowledge and genuine connection. By deconstructing the myth of sanctimony, we begin dismantling the structures that have long stifled growth—structures that function not as moral guides, but as instruments of control rather than catalysts for liberation. Liberation requires a holistic approach—one that honors scientific inquiry alongside the rich diversity of love, desire, and sexuality that define the human experience.

Envisioning a future free from the oppressive grip of sanctimony demands a radical rethinking of cultural values and institutional authority. Imagine a world where education is untainted by fear, where knowledge is celebrated rather than censored, and where sexual diversity is recognized as a natural and enriching dimension of life—free from the judgment and repression of outdated doctrines. Recognizing that every individual's journey is unique and that love and desire are fundamental aspects of our humanity allows us to approach the intersection of religion and sexuality with humility rather than judgment. Such a future is grounded in the conviction that truth, reason, empathy, and compassion—not dogma or superstition—must guide our collective evolution.

Religious individuals and communities, too, can play a role in this transformation by embracing a more expansive ethic of care—one that seeks to uplift rather than oppress. This means moving beyond the limited injunction[7] "to love thy neighbor," traditionally understood as those who are close or familiar, and embracing the deeper imperative instead "to love the outsider, the foreigner, the other." Such an ethic transcends geographic, cultural, and ideological boundaries, affirming the dignity and rights of all people regardless of race, nationality, sexual orientation, or gender identity.

As you engage with the pages that follow, may you find the courage to question inherited certainties, the strength to resist oppressive norms, and the inspiration to break free from the shackles of sanctimony. This journey is one of transformation—toward reclaiming the fullness of our intellectual, emotional, and erotic selves, and toward envisioning a future defined by freedom, diversity, and boundless possibility. In challenging the legacy of sanctimony, we do more than advocate for change—we affirm our collective commitment to a world in which every human being can blossom in the light of truth, dignity, and love.

The Role of Religious Texts in Shaping Sexual Norms and Behaviors

Religious texts have long served as foundational sources of moral authority and ethical guidelines within societies, shaping not only spiritual guidance but also the most intimate dimensions of human life, including sexuality. Across cultures and centuries, these texts have delineated what is deemed acceptable, permissible, or forbidden in matters of sexual behavior. In *Separation of Church and Sex—Free at Last! Free at Last!* I examine the complex and multifaceted ways in which religious scriptures—emerging from ancient traditions and historically interpreted through patriarchal structures of power[8]—have profoundly shaped sexual norms that continue to influence contemporary cultures. From explicit prescriptions embedded within sacred writings to the elaborate interpretive traditions that have grown around them, religious texts have exerted a sustained influence over personal conduct, social customs, and public policy related to sexuality, often privileging heteronormative frameworks[9] while marginalizing alternative sexual identities and expressions.

Historically, the scriptures of major religious traditions—including Christianity, Islam, Judaism, and Hinduism—have been interpreted as conveying divine mandates governing sexual conduct. Many of these texts contain explicit passages addressing sexuality, purity, reproduction, and gender roles. For example, biblical passages found in the *"Book of Leviticus"*[10] and the *"Pauline Epistles"*[11] have long been cited as authoritative declarations of sexual morality, defining what is considered pure, lawful, or acceptable, and conversely, what is labeled deviant or sinful. These texts were not regarded merely as spiritual teachings but as comprehensive moral codes[12] regulating both individual behavior and social order. Over time, they established normative frameworks that elevated heterosexual, procreative unions while relegating nonconforming sexualities to the margins. This codification of sexual norms[13] became deeply embedded within cultural consciousness, shaping legal systems, social expectations, and moral judgments in ways that persist into the modern era—often framing deviation not only as social nonconformity[14] but as transgression against divine law itself.

The influence of these texts has been significantly amplified by centuries of interpretation conducted by religious scholars, clerics, and theologians. These interpretive traditions have frequently prioritized the preservation of institutional authority and social control over a more expansive or contextual understanding of spiritual meaning. Through selective exegesis—critical interpretation of a text through analysis of its historical and linguistic context—doctrinal formulations, and the reinforcement of particular readings deemed orthodox, religious authorities have constructed moral systems that serve political, cultural, and hierarchical interests. Within these systems, certain sexual behaviors are exalted as virtuous while others are condemned as immoral, unnatural, or sinful. This process has entrenched rigid sexual norms that privilege heterosexuality and reproductive sexuality while stigmatizing identities and practices that fall outside prescribed boundaries. As a result, moral frameworks derived from religious interpretation have exerted profound control over individual autonomy, framing dissent not only as moral failure but as existential deviation.

In their article *Forbidden Conversations: A Comprehensive Exploration of Taboos in Sexual and Reproductive Health,* Nor Faiza Mohd Tohit and Mainul Haque[15] examine the pervasive influence of cultural and religious taboos on sexual and reproductive health. Drawing on a decade of interdisciplinary literature, they demonstrate how deeply ingrained beliefs have rendered discussions surrounding menstruation, contraception, fertility, sexual orientation, and gender identity both marginalized and stigmatized across diverse societies. Their analysis "highlights the far-reaching consequences of these taboos on individual well-being, community health, and public policy, and calls for a critical reassessment of the narratives that continue to suppress open discourse" (**Tohit & Haque, 2024**). By documenting how these prohibitions shape behavior and norms, the authors underscore the urgent need for more inclusive, informed, and transparent conversations capable of challenging and transforming restrictive frameworks governing sexual and reproductive health.

In an era marked by rapid scientific advancement and evolving social values, the enduring influence of religious texts on sexual norms is increasingly being scrutinized and contested. Contemporary debates surrounding sexuality education, marriage equality, gender identity and gender equality, and reproductive rights reveal a persistent tension between progressive understandings of human sexuality and traditional doctrinal positions. Despite growing acceptance of more inclusive interpretations, religious texts are still frequently invoked in public discourse to legitimize discriminatory policies and practices. This dynamic underscores the need to critically reassess the role these texts play in shaping contemporary moral and legal frameworks. At the heart of this tension lies the broader struggle between faith and modernity—a struggle that remains central to ongoing efforts toward sexual liberation. The challenge, therefore, is not merely to critique these texts within their historical context, but to reclaim their interpretive possibilities in ways that affirm human dignity, diversity, autonomy, and fundamental human rights.

In response to restrictive religious interpretations, scholars, activists, and spiritual thinkers have increasingly turned to alternative frameworks such as queer theology[16], feminist theology[17], liberation theology[18], and secular humanism[19]. These perspectives seek to dismantle exclusionary narratives embedded in traditional readings of sacred texts and to foreground interpretations rooted in lived experience, justice, and compassion. Additional approaches—including progressive Christianity, Raelism, interfaith pluralism, and ethical non-theism—a moral framework grounded in reason and human responsibility rather than divine command—further challenge entrenched assumptions by offering inclusive, human-centered models of spirituality and morality. Through critical re-readings of scripture, these movements emphasize liberation, empathy, and the inherent worth of every individual—values that have often been obscured by centuries of doctrinal rigidity[20]. Such efforts are not merely academic in nature; they are integral to the broader project of disentangling sexual ethics from systems of domination and control. Acknowledging the historical significance of religious texts while rejecting the limitations and condemnations they have imposed is a necessary step toward genuine emancipation[21].

Ultimately, religious texts have played a pivotal role in establishing and perpetuating sexual norms that have constrained personal expression and reinforced heteronormative ideals across generations. The effort to separate these sacred prescriptions from secular life remains an ongoing and essential endeavor—one aimed at liberating human sexuality from the oppressive weight of dogma. As you continue your journey through SOCAS, I invite you to engage critically with these texts, to question inherited assumptions[22], and to participate in the collective pursuit of a more just and liberated future. By confronting and deconstructing the sanctimony long associated with religious authority, we can move toward a more inclusive, rational, and emancipatory understanding of human sexuality—one in which every individual is free to define their own identity, behavior, and destiny.

Chapter One:
Historical Perspectives on Religious Beliefs and Sexuality

Eroticism and Sexual Ethics in Antiquity: The Sexual Practices of Ancient Societies

Throughout human history, the dynamic interplay between religious beliefs and sexuality has shaped a complex and often tumultuous narrative. To understand this intricate relationship, we must embark on a historical journey that traverses diverse epochs, cultures, and spiritual traditions. This section offers a broad and foundational overview, reaching back into the annals of early civilization to examine how ancient societies approached sex, pleasure, and procreation—not as taboo subjects, but as vital, often sacred, dimensions of human life. Through mythologies, rituals, and cultural practices, sexuality was integrated into the fabric of communal and spiritual existence. These early expressions were transmitted orally and later documented in rudimentary texts, laying the groundwork for how intimacy and eroticism were understood and valued.

In antiquity, sexuality was not relegated to the private sphere. Rather, it was deeply embedded in public life, religious rites, and ethical frameworks. Eroticism and sexual ethics were seen as central to the cohesion of society and the cultivation of personal and communal well-being. Contrary to modern perspectives that often frame sexuality in binary terms—purity versus sin, sacred versus profane—many ancient cultures embraced a far more fluid and multifaceted understanding of erotic expression.

As societies evolved and organized religions emerged, a significant shift in the regulation of sexual behavior began to unfold. Religious texts gradually transitioned from descriptive accounts of human sexuality into prescriptive, rigid codes that defined acceptable sexual conduct. These scriptures became the authoritative source for moral and ethical guidelines, and increasingly positioned chastity, purity, and procreation as moral ideals, while alternative expressions of sexuality—non-procreative, queer, or gender-nonconforming—were marginalized or outright condemned. In doing so, these texts redefined not only private morality but public order, establishing normative frameworks that would shape identity, family, gender roles, and social belonging for centuries.

This transformation did not occur in isolation. It was intertwined with broader socio-political changes, including the consolidation of religious authority, the stratification of social classes, and the formation of centralized laws and institutions. As doctrines solidified, they began to inform not only personal ethics but also legal codes, educational systems, and public policy—extending the reach of religious sexual morality into nearly every aspect of civic life. Thus, sacred texts became instruments of governance, shaping both spiritual consciousness and political power.

By examining the historical evolution of religious texts and their interpretations, we uncover the mechanisms by which these documents were used to legitimize hierarchies and regulate intimate human experiences. These narratives reflect the cultural values of their time while also actively constructing enduring systems of control—systems that continue to influence contemporary debates around gender, sexuality, bodily autonomy, and human rights. Critical analysis allows us to peel back layers of interpretation and uncover more inclusive, liberatory readings that were often buried beneath centuries of theological dogmatism.

Ultimately, this inquiry challenges us to revisit long-held assumptions about the relationship between faith and sexuality. By tracing the historical trajectory of sacred narratives, we begin to see how religion has alternately constrained and catalyzed human expression. This awareness is vital for cultivating a more inclusive and respectful discourse—one that acknowledges human diversity while interrogating the structures that have suppressed it.

In the end, this exploration of sexuality in ancient societies provides a revealing lens into the intertwined forces of spirituality, eroticism, and social order. It shows how early civilizations navigated the complex terrain of sexual ethics, often in ways that were celebratory, integrative, and life-affirming. These traditions laid the groundwork for contemporary discussions around sexual freedom, moral authority, and the possibilities for reimagining the future of erotic justice. Indeed, the attitudes and practices of the ancient world reflect deeply embedded cultural values that continue to shape—explicitly and implicitly—how we think about sex, power, and the sacred.

Mesopotamia: Ancient Mythologies and Fertility Cults

In ancient Mesopotamia—the cradle of Sumerian, Babylonian, and Assyrian civilizations—the intimate connection between sexuality, reproduction, and spirituality permeated every aspect of religious life. Sexuality was not viewed as a private or merely physical act, but as a vital, sacred force woven into the fabric of myth, ritual, agriculture, and cosmology. Mythological narratives and ceremonial practices reflected a worldview in which human sexuality aligned with divine powers governing fertility, creation, and cosmic balance.

Central to this belief system were deities like Inanna (later known as Ishtar) and her consort Tammuz (Dumuzid), whose mythic cycles of union, death, and rebirth embodied the rhythms of nature and human life. Their stories portrayed eroticism as a conduit for divine blessings, agricultural renewal, and the maintenance of both social harmony and universal order. As Thorkild Jacobsen[1] observes, "For the Mesopotamians, fertility rites were not peripheral but lay at the heart of cosmic and social stability" (**Jacobsen, 1976**). In this holistic cosmology[2], the erotic was deeply sacred, with sexuality playing a central role in ensuring the flourishing of both land and people.

Religious festivals and temple rituals often revolved around honoring these fertility deities. Temples dedicated to Inanna/Ishtar and Dumuzi served as spiritual and social centers where elaborate ceremonies marked seasonal transitions, agricultural hopes, and mythic reenactments. Earlier scholarship often described some of these rituals as involving "sacred prostitution"[3]—a term suggesting sexual acts were performed in the temple to embody or provoke divine creative energy. However, contemporary scholarship has increasingly questioned this interpretation. As Stephanie Budin[4] points out, "Despite pervasive myths, there is scant reliable evidence for institutionalized sacred prostitution in Mesopotamian temples" (**Budin, 2008**). Rather than focusing on literal enactments, these rites—recorded in chants, administrative texts, and art—should be understood as symbolically rich practices that revered sexuality as a generative, cosmic force.

Fertility cults[5] were not merely symbolic but essential to the survival of agricultural societies whose prosperity depended on successful harvests. Rituals celebrating fertility were inseparable from agricultural rhythms and communal well-being. As Samuel Noah Kramer[6] notes of Sumerian mythology, "Inanna embodies the dual aspects of love and war, but foremost she represents the fecundity that ensures life's renewal" (**Kramer, 1963**). These mythologies reinforced the view that sexual union was sacred—central not only to reproduction but to the continual regeneration of life. Erotic expression, when performed in ritualized contexts, was not stigmatized but honored as a sacred act mirroring divine creativity. This reverence did not imply unrestrained license; instead, sexuality was integrated into a larger spiritual and communal framework that honored its power to mirror divine creative processes.

The integration of sexuality into everyday life is further reflected in Mesopotamian art, literature, and legal-administrative records. Cylinder seals[7], mythological poems, and temple hymns feature rich erotic imagery and fertility symbols alongside practical matters such as inheritance rights, marriage contracts, and temple offerings. These cultural artifacts reveal a society that did not compartmentalize the erotic but understood it as an essential element of existence—a reflection of the cosmic order itself. Sexual union was revered as a fundamental expression of the forces that governed nature and ensured continuity of life—a perspective that continues to offer insight into ancient worldviews that embraced, rather than suppressed, erotic vitality.

By examining the religious and cultural practices of ancient Mesopotamia, modern scholars gain a deeper understanding of how early civilizations balanced bodily impulses with spiritual imperatives. Far from being repressive or moralizing, Mesopotamian culture celebrated sexuality as indispensable to both physical survival and spiritual harmony—a legacy that challenges contemporary assumptions and invites a reexamination of the sacred dimensions of erotic life.

Medieval Europe: The Age of Asceticism

During the medieval period, the Christian Church exerted immense authority over European society, shaping norms, laws, and personal conduct that extended into every aspect of daily life, including sexual behavior. Asceticism[8] emerged as a hallmark of that era, with both clergy and devout laypeople encouraged to embrace celibacy[9], continence[10], and the renunciation[11] of bodily pleasures as pathways to spiritual purity[12]. Sexual abstinence[13] was exalted as a marker of holiness, while desire was treated with suspicion or outright condemnation. As Augustine of Hippo[14] famously writes, "Lord, grant me chastity and continence, but not yet" (**Louth, 1996**), capturing the internal struggle between human desire and the pursuit of divine grace. This ascetic ideal cast a long shadow over sexual expression: sex was endorsed only within the sacrament of marriage—and even then, primarily for procreation—while other forms of sexual expression were often demonized as sources of sin and moral corruption[15].

Central to this worldview was the doctrine of original sin, deeply shaped by Augustine's interpretations. Although the Genesis account of the Fall does not explicitly mention sex, medieval theologians saw Adam and Eve's sudden awareness of their nakedness as evidence of a tainted sexual nature marking the loss of sexual innocence[16]. Augustine argues that original sin was transmitted through lustful reproduction, "casting sexual desire itself as a consequence of humanity's fallen nature" (**Louth[17], 1996**). This interpretation fueled a theological framework in which sexual acts, if not explicitly ordered toward procreation, were seen as requiring strict regulation and moral scrutiny. Over time, this fusion of sin and sexuality laid the foundation for a culture of restraint that profoundly influenced Christian teachings and the lived experiences of both clergy and laity.

Despite the Church's official stance, medieval interpretations of scripture sometimes betrayed a deeper complexity. The *Song of Songs*[18]— originally a frank celebration of erotic love—was recast by mystics and theologians as a metaphor for the soul's union with God. This allegorical reading—an interpretive method that seeks symbolic meanings beneath a text's literal narrative—reflects the era's central tension: a fervent call to chastity juxtaposed with a tacit recognition of erotic longing as part of the human condition. This duality also surfaced in the arts. Though the Church promoted sexual repression, illuminated manuscripts[19], sculptures, and poetic texts often contained veiled or symbolic references to sexuality, revealing a persistent fascination with erotic themes. As John Boswell [20] notes, "Medieval Christian teaching invested sexuality with an aura of sinfulness, leading to an obsessive concern with regulating every aspect of sexual behavior" (**Boswell, 1980**). Ironically, the intense regulation of sexuality by the Church produced a cultural environment in which erotic themes persisted, reemerging through metaphorical, symbolic, and artistic forms.

Modern scholarship continues to uncover the contradictions embedded in medieval sexual ethics. For example, Dyan Elliott's[21] research on marital continence reveals how even within marriage—the one socially sanctioned setting for sexual relations—many couples pursued abstinence as a spiritual aspiration. "The concept of spiritual marriage[22] allowed medieval couples to assert devotion to God through renunciation of sexual relations, reflecting the era's valorization of purity over natural impulse" (**Elliott, 2021**). In this framework, sexual restraint was not merely a moral requirement but a profound act of religious devotion. Yet this renunciation never fully eclipsed human desire. Rather, it fostered a climate in which erotic expression was both repressed and sublimated, and therefore transformed into religious allegory[23], artistic nuance, or disciplined self-denial.

Ultimately, the medieval period bequeathed a legacy of sexual anxiety and moral rigidity, but also one of rich symbolic interplay and cultural negotiation. Its legacy endures not only in religious teachings but also in Western art, literature, and philosophy, where the tension between spiritual aspiration and human desire continues to echo. By examining this era, we gain insight into the historical roots of moral discourse around sexuality—and the enduring human struggle to reconcile faith with the body's innate longing for connection and pleasure.

The Renaissance: Reawakening the Body and the Self

Emerging between the rigid asceticism of the medieval period and the rational critiques of the Enlightenment, the Renaissance marked a subtle yet significant cultural shift in the Western understanding of the human body, desire, and individuality. Drawing inspiration from classical Greek and Roman antiquity, Renaissance humanism re-centered attention on human experience, artistic expression, and the beauty of the physical form. This renewed interest is vividly reflected in the visual arts, where the nude body—once a source of moral suspicion—was reintroduced as a subject of aesthetic admiration and philosophical inquiry (Burke, 2014).

Yet this reawakening did not dismantle the moral authority of the Church. Religious doctrine continued to regulate sexual behavior, and institutions maintained considerable influence over law, education, and social norms. Rather than a rupture, the Renaissance represents a period of tension—where emerging ideals of individual expression and embodied experience coexisted with enduring frameworks of restraint and moral discipline (Wiesner-Hanks, 2010). Erotic themes, though more visible, were often mediated through mythology, allegory, or classical reference, allowing artists and thinkers to explore desire without directly confronting ecclesiastical boundaries.

In this sense, the Renaissance functioned less as a revolution than as a reorientation. It reopened intellectual and cultural space for considering the body not solely as a vessel of sin, but as a site of meaning, beauty, and inquiry. While it stopped short of fundamentally redefining sexual ethics, it laid important groundwork for the more explicit challenges to religious authority that would emerge during the Enlightenment. By restoring attention to human dignity, sensory experience, and the legitimacy of earthly life, the Renaissance helped initiate a gradual shift toward a more nuanced and human-centered understanding of sexuality.

The Enlightenment and Secularism

Following the Scientific Revolution, the late seventeenth and eighteenth centuries witnessed the sweeping dismantling of traditional systems of authority, belief, and scientific thought. Pioneered by the new philosophy and Enlightenment thinkers such as Voltaire[24], Diderot[25], and

Rousseau[26], this intellectual upheaval challenged the very foundations of monarchy, aristocracy, and religious power (**Israel[27], 2001**). The Radical Enlightenment, in particular, played a decisive role in this transformative epoch, rejecting not only political and ecclesiastical hierarchies, but also the subjugation of women, the theological control of education, and the institution of slavery.

The Enlightenment[28] ushered in a transformative era of intellectual and cultural revolution that profoundly redefined the relationship between religion and sexuality. Spinoza[29] played a profound and pioneering role during the early Enlightenment, particularly in shaping ideas about freedom of thought, secularism, and the critique of religious authority. His critique of organized religion as a tool of political control was revolutionary for its time and helped lay the foundation for the separation of church and state. Spinoza also championed freedom of thought[30] as essential to human happiness, insisting that individuals must be able to reason freely without fear of persecution. His bold defense of intellectual freedom would later resonate deeply with Enlightenment thinkers who built on his ideas to advocate for secularism and freedom of thought.

Philosophers such as Voltaire, Rousseau, and Kant[31] advanced this philosophical current by promoting empirical observation, rational inquiry, and the intrinsic worth of the individual. They rejected the moral absolutism[32] of religious dogma and proposed a worldview in which ethical norms—including those relating to sexuality—should arise from reason rather than divine decree. This period signaled a decisive break from theological interpretations of human behavior, ushering in a secular framework that emphasized human dignity, critical thought, the right to self-determination[33], and the belief in inherent human rights. As a result, these shifts laid the groundwork for modern understandings of sexual ethics, rooted not in religious prescription but in personal freedom and rational thought.

Denis Diderot and Jeremy Bentham[34] were among the Enlightenment thinkers who took these ideas further, applying them to the realm of sexual norms and personal behavior. Though Diderot never publicly acknowledged Spinoza as a core influence—due to the risks of persecution— his embrace of materialism, pantheism[35], and the rejection of divine providence clearly reflects Spinoza's influence. In his satirical novel *Les Bijoux indiscrets* (*The Indiscreet Jewels*), Diderot critiqued the sexual hypocrisy of his time by "promoting sexual transparency and free expression. His literary satire functioned not just as entertainment but as a vehicle for advancing Enlightenment ideals regarding the rational critique of societal norms" (**Beeharry-Paray[36], 2000**).

Equally groundbreaking was Bentham's unapologetic defense of same-sex relationships. In his unpublished essay *Paederasty (Offences Against One's Self)*, Bentham "condemned both legal and religious persecution of homosexuality, calling such punishment irrational and harmful. He argued for the decriminalization of consensual homosexual acts, positioning himself well ahead of his time in advocating for the moral legitimacy of diverse sexual orientations" (**Bentham & Crompton, 1978**). Together, the contributions of Diderot and Bentham reveal how Enlightenment ideals extended beyond abstract philosophy to challenge entrenched social mores and advocate for greater personal freedom and dignity in matters of sexuality.

One of the most enduring outcomes of the Enlightenment was the gradual separation of church and state. This shift enabled secular governments to assume greater control over laws and education, thereby diminishing the direct influence of religious institutions on public policy. Although contemporary concepts of sexual orientation and identity had not yet been articulated, the philosophical foundations laid during this era—especially the emphasis on liberty, dignity, and reason—paved the way for future movements advocating sexual rights, reproductive freedom, and bodily autonomy. The impact of these changes was neither immediate nor absolute, but as Enlightenment ideals gained influence, they opened space for new, more inclusive approaches to understanding human sexuality.

The impact of the Enlightenment on sexual morality was also reflected in literature, art, and public discourse. Writers and artists of the time began to question the strictures imposed by religious morality, using literature, visual art, and public discourse to explore desire, intimacy, and erotic expression. Such works often pushed boundaries, signaling a broader cultural movement toward self-expression and critical reflection. By promoting the idea that human experience could be understood through reason and scientific inquiry, the Enlightenment laid the intellectual groundwork for modern secular societies, where sexual freedom is increasingly recognized as a fundamental human right.

The enduring legacy of this transformative period underscores the vital importance of separating religious doctrine from public policy and ensuring that individual autonomy remains central to modern governance. By advocating for reason, individual rights, and the separation of church and state, Enlightenment thinkers set in motion a gradual relaxation of sexual norms that has paved the way for modern reforms in sexual education, contraception, and LGBTQ+ rights. This transformative period remains a critical reference point for understanding how rational thought and secular governance can challenge and ultimately reshape deeply entrenched cultural and religious norms.

Ancient Egypt: The Celebration of Life and Afterlife

In Ancient Egypt, sexuality was deeply interwoven with its cosmology and mythology, embodying a celebration of both life and the promise of the afterlife. Far from being viewed as shameful or merely physical, sexuality was considered a divine expression—central to creation, social order, and cosmic balance. Egyptian myths, religious rituals, and artistic depictions abound with sexual symbolism and imagery that celebrate fertility and the creative power of the gods. Among the most emblematic myths is the union of Isis and Osiris[37]—an act of sacred sexual union symbolizing the regenerative power of love, fertility, and divine order, thus reinforcing the belief that sexuality was essential not only for human procreation but for sustaining the rhythms of nature and the cosmos itself.

As historian Lise Manniche[38] explores in *Sexual Life in Ancient Egypt*, sexuality permeated "all aspects of the intimate life of Egyptians, including prostitution, concubines[39], adultery, homosexuality, intercourse with animals, necrophilia[40], incest and polygamy[41], from the Old Kingdom to the start of the Graeco-Roman period" (**Manniche, 2013**). Egyptian society, while grounded in religious ritual, was pragmatic and open in its acknowledgment of sexual diversity and behavior. Pleasure was not inherently sinful—it was a sacred and life-affirming force.

Pharaohs[42] were expected to embody virility as part of their divine mandate, with procreative success serving not only dynastic continuity but also as a signal of alignment with divine will. This cultural expectation extended beyond royalty to the general population, where fertility was revered, and family life was upheld as a religious and social cornerstone. The Egyptians held a positive view of sexual desire and pleasure, considering them divine gifts that contributed to the balance and harmony of the universe. Temples dedicated to gods and goddesses of fertility[43], often served as centers for sexual and agricultural rituals. While the popular image of sacred temple prostitution has been challenged by modern scholars (**Budin, 2008**), others suggest that certain temples may have hosted symbolic or ritualized sexual rites—such as hierogamic ceremonies[44] (sacred marriage rites)—linking erotic expression to divine fertility and cosmic renewal (**Assante[45], 1998**).

Furthermore, while the celebration of sexuality was prominent, the sanctity of marriage and family life was equally emphasized. Marriage was regarded as a sacred covenant, essential for both social stability and religious order. Laws and cultural norms were established to regulate sexual behavior within this framework; adultery was discouraged, and strict rules governed inheritance and property rights within the family. The Egyptians also demonstrated a pragmatic approach to sexual health by practicing contraception and fertility control, reflecting their sophisticated understanding of the practical implications of sexual activity. This duality—celebrating sexual vitality while also upholding the virtues of fidelity and marital sanctity—illustrates the complex social and cultural fabric of Ancient Egyptian society.

Even in death, sexuality retained its sacred significance. Egyptian funerary practices reflected the belief that sexual regeneration mirrored cosmic renewal. Tomb art and funerary texts often depicted intimate scenes, fertility symbols, or union with the divine as metaphors for rebirth in the afterlife. The continuity between life, sexuality, and resurrection was not metaphorical alone—it was embedded in ritual, language, and sacred art. To the Egyptians, the physical and spiritual worlds were not separate domains but intertwined realms where sex was both a source of earthly joy and a key to eternal life.

By embracing sexuality as a natural, divine, and regenerative force, Ancient Egyptian culture offers a striking contrast to later religious systems that would pathologize or repress erotic expression. Their integrated worldview—affirming pleasure, honoring procreation, and embedding sexuality within the rhythms of cosmic and spiritual life—continues to inspire scholars seeking to understand how ancient societies wove eroticism, ritual, and metaphysics into a unified cultural fabric. In the Egyptian vision, to honor the body was to honor the divine; to engage in sexuality was to participate in the sacred cycles of life, death, and eternal renewal.

Ancient Greece: Eros and the Pursuit of Beauty

Ancient Greece cultivated a nuanced and multidimensional understanding of sexuality, one in which Eros—the god and concept of desire—was seen not merely as carnal appetite but as a vital, unifying force linking body, soul, and civic life. Sexuality, in this context, was not divorced from ethics or aesthetics; rather, it was integrated into broader pursuits of beauty, wisdom, and personal excellence. Among the most emblematic expressions of this ideal was pederasty[46], a socially sanctioned bond between adult men and adolescent boys, particularly in Athens. Far from being viewed as solely erotic, these relationships were infused with educational and civic purpose, serving as vehicles for mentorship, character formation, and preparation for full participation in public life. Sir Kenneth James Dover[47] notes, "The Greeks regarded homosexuality in general to be natural, normal, and salutary, subject only to certain social conventions governing age, status, and decorum" (**Dover, 1978**). Such bonds were structured by codes of reciprocity and restraint, reinforcing the idea that Eros—desire—could be a path to self-discipline and moral elevation.

Greek art, philosophy, and literature reflected and reinforced this worldview. Sculpture and vase-paintings celebrated the male and female form as embodiments of ideal proportion and inner virtue, linking physical beauty to metaphysical truth. The *kouros statues*[48], for instance, exemplify this synthesis: youthful male figures captured in perfect balance, symbolizing the harmony between physical grace and moral strength. Erotic desire was not repressed but ritualized, explored through poetry, drama, and myth. The Symposium by Plato[49] remains a seminal philosophical meditation on love's role in guiding the soul from sensual pleasure toward the contemplation of eternal truths. As John J. Winkler[50] eloquently summarizes, "Eros in Greek thought was not a mere appetite to be repressed or indulged in isolation, but a dynamic force that united body, mind, and polis in the pursuit of beauty, knowledge, and ethical self-formation" (**Winkler, 1990**).

While Rome inherited many of these ideals, it adapted them to fit its own rigid social stratifications. Roman men were afforded greater sexual freedom, especially with enslaved persons or partners of lower status, whereas women's sexuality was tightly controlled within patriarchal marriage norms. Still, among the educated elite, Greek conceptions of erotic beauty endured in literature and art. However, as Christianity spread across the Roman Empire, the open celebration of Eros came under increasing scrutiny. Early Christian teachings introduced new moral paradigms that emphasized chastity, celibacy, and the renunciation of fleshly desires in favor of spiritual purity. What had once been seen as a source of moral and aesthetic growth was redefined as temptation or sin, eventually leading to the suppression of many classical sexual ideals through ecclesiastical doctrine[51] and legal codes.

Despite this transformation, the legacy of Greek erotic philosophy endured. Renaissance humanists[52] and Enlightenment thinkers rediscovered and reinterpreted classical texts, rekindling conversations about the role of beauty, love, and sensuality in the good life. In contemporary debates on sexual ethics, Ancient Greece offers a provocative counterpoint to the asceticism that shaped Western religious tradition. Its model of Eros—honoring sexual desire not as shameful but as a catalyst for personal development, interpersonal connection, and civic virtue—invites modern readers to reconsider the place of sexuality in ethical and philosophical life. The Greek tradition thus stands as a compelling historical example of how societies might harmonize desire, morality, and identity, offering enduring insights into the complex role of sexuality in human blossoming.

India: The Kama Sutra and the Quest for Pleasure

In the richly layered spiritual and philosophical traditions of India, sexuality has historically been approached not with shame or suppression, but with a complex and often celebratory sensibility. Rather than being relegated to the margins of moral discourse, sexual expression was integrated into the broader framework of human purpose, encompassing dharma (duty), artha (prosperity), kama (pleasure), and moksha (liberation)—the four aims of life (*purusharthas*[53]) in classical Hindu philosophy. As Ruth Vanita and Saleem Kidwai[54] emphasize in their influential anthology on Indian sexualities, "Ancient Indian societies often displayed a remarkable pluralism[55] in attitudes toward desire, gender, and erotic expression, resisting any monolithic view of sexuality" (**Vanita & Kidwai, 1996**). This pluralism underscores how Indian civilization offered space for both the embrace and the transcendence of sensual desire, depending on one's path, social role, or stage of life.

Among the most iconic expressions of this integrated worldview is the Kama Sutra[56], traditionally attributed to the sage Vatsyayana[57]. Often mischaracterized in the modern West as a mere manual of sexual positions, the text is in fact a sophisticated treatise on eroticism, aesthetics, courtship, companionship, and the ethical cultivation of pleasure. In their definitive translation, Wendy Doniger and Sudhir Kakar[58] clarify that the Kama Sutra "frames erotic intimacy as an essential component of human well-being, provided it is pursued with mutual respect, consent, and an awareness of one's social and moral obligations" (**Doniger & Kakar, 2002**). Pleasure, far from being frivolous[59] or sinful, is treated as an essential dimension of a well-lived life, provided it is harmonized with dharma. The Kama Sutra thus exemplifies a cultural ethos in which sexual fulfillment, aesthetic sensibility, and ethical conduct are mutually reinforcing—a vision in which the sacred is not found in the denial of desire, but in its mindful and artful expression.

Yet this celebration of pleasure existed alongside other spiritual traditions that emphasized renunciation. Early Buddhist and Jain teachings, particularly within monastic contexts, advanced an ascetic path in which sensual desire was to be overcome as a source of attachment and suffering. Peter Harvey[60] notes, "In Buddhism, renunciation of sexual activity in the monastic code is seen as vital for cultivating mindfulness and overcoming attachment, reflecting a belief that sensual pleasures can impede spiritual progress" (**Harvey, 2000**). The coexistence of such seemingly opposing perspectives—the householder's embrace of kama and the monk's pursuit of detachment—is not contradictory within Indian philosophy but rather reflective of its inherent pluralism, allowing for multiple spiritual trajectories within a shared cosmology.

This pluralism also extended to gender and sexual diversity. Pre-modern Indian texts, legal codes, and devotional poetry often reflect acknowledgment of third-gender identities, same-sex relationships, and non-normative sexualities, indicating a far more expansive view of erotic life than what later colonial narratives allowed. Ruth Vanita and Saleem Kidwai[61] point to numerous historical sources affirming that "pre-colonial Indian cultures frequently acknowledged gender fluidity and a spectrum of erotic possibilities, long before modern identity categories emerged" (**Vanita & Kidwai, 1996**). These inclusions were neither anomalies nor aberrations, but part of a cosmological acceptance of human variation as natural and divinely inspired. Temples with erotic carvings, such as those at Khajuraho and Konark[62], visually reaffirm this integration of sexuality, spirituality, and aesthetic sensibility within the public sacred sphere.

However, the British colonial period, influenced by Victorian moral codes[63], introduced legal and cultural repressions that sought to sanitize and pathologize Indian erotic traditions. The criminalization of same-sex relations (via Section 377 of the Indian Penal Code[64]) and the censoring of erotic art redefined ancient expressions of kama through the lens of sin and shame. Yet, in recent decades, there has been a revival of interest in the precolonial sexual ethos, prompting scholars and activists to reclaim India's more inclusive and holistic sexual heritage.

Ultimately, the Kama Sutra and related traditions reveal a worldview in which sexuality was not separated from the sacred but was embraced as one of its most vital, beautiful, and ethically significant expressions. It calls into question the binary of sacred versus profane and reminds us that, in ancient Indian thought, pleasure and liberation were not mutually exclusive but, when pursued with awareness, profoundly intertwined.

China: Taoism and Sexual Harmony

Ancient Chinese understandings of sexuality were profoundly influenced by Taoist philosophy[65], which emphasizes balance, harmony, and the interconnectedness of all things. At the heart of Taoist cosmology lies the concept of Yin and Yang[66]—opposing yet complementary forces present in every aspect of the cosmos, including human sexuality. Kristofer Schipper[67] explains in *The Taoist Body*, "The harmonious union of yin and yang within the individual is essential to the free flow of qi, and sexual energy is viewed as a primary manifestation of this interplay" (**Schipper, 1993**). In this view, sexual union is not merely a biological act but a microcosmic expression of cosmic equilibrium[68], through which the individual aligns with the Dao—the Way of nature. The masculine (yang) and feminine (yin) are not fixed genders but energetic principles whose integration is essential for maintaining vitality, fostering emotional resonance[69], and cultivating spiritual awareness. Sexual union thus transcends mere procreation; it is celebrated as a pathway to physical health, emotional equilibrium, and spiritual cultivation, reflecting Taoism's broader aim of aligning the individual with the natural order.

This integration forms the basis of Taoist sexual cultivation—a system of practices designed to refine and direct sexual energy (*jing*) for both health and transcendence. Rather than viewing sex as a mere outlet for desire or a reproductive necessity, Taoist teachings regard it as a sacred technology capable of alchemical transformation—a symbolic process of profound inner change involving dissolution, purification, and rebirth. According to Catherine Despeux and Fabrizio Pregadio[70] in *The Encyclopedia of Taoism*, "Taoist internal alchemy regards sexual energy as a precious substance: through controlled breathing, visualization, and specific exercises, practitioners seek to transmute jing into qi, reinforcing vitality and opening pathways toward higher realization" (**Despeux & Pregadio, 2008**). Techniques often include meditative visualization of energy circulation, Qigong movements that stimulate the lower dantian[71] (the body's energy center), and partner exercises that emphasize mindfulness, synchrony, and mutual respect. These disciplines aim to conserve and redirect sexual essence, transforming it into shen—spiritual consciousness.

As Livia Kohn[72] elaborates in *Daoist Body Cultivation*, such practices are rooted in a holistic vision that views sexuality as an interdependent relationship between body, mind, and spirit. She writes, "The Taoist approach to sexuality integrates body, mind, and spirit: sexual harmony is not merely a private pleasure but a means to cultivate life force, deepen interpersonal connection, and realize one's place within the cosmic pattern" (**Kohn, 2006**). Sexual activity, in this context, is neither repressed nor indulged heedlessly—it is ritualized and moderated, framed by ethical principles and attunement[73] to natural rhythms. For men, this often involves regulating ejaculation to preserve vital energy, while women are encouraged to align sexual activity with energetic and lunar cycles, honoring the wisdom of their own bodies. The underlying ethic is one of intentionality and balance, where pleasure serves as a gateway to vitality, intimacy, and transcendence.

This Taoist sexual ethos continues to resonate in contemporary discourses on holistic health, somatic awareness[74], and integrative medicine[75]. Isabelle Robinet[76] notes, "Taoist sexual practices reflect the broader Taoist principle of balancing yin and yang for harmony within the individual and the cosmos, underscoring that sexuality can be a path to both health and spiritual realization rather than a mere source of desire or reproduction" (**Robinet, 1997**). In modern contexts, these teachings have inspired mindfulness-based intimacy practices, Qigong[77]-infused relationship workshops, and psychophysiological research into the health benefits of conscious sexuality. At a time when sexuality is often reduced to either mechanical function or moral taboo, Taoism offers an ancient yet remarkably contemporary vision—one in which erotic experience becomes a sacred art of living, cultivating both inner equilibrium and cosmic alignment.

Indigenous Cultures: Celebrating Life and Nature

Indigenous cultures[78] around the world have long embraced a holistic worldview that places human sexuality within a broader web of interdependence—linking people, land, spirit, and cosmos. Far from being seen as a mere physical act or private matter, sexuality is often understood as a sacred force mirroring the creative energies of the earth. In this worldview, sexuality is not separate from ecology but an extension of nature's regenerative rhythms. Fertility rites, seasonal ceremonies, and rites of passage[79] are frequently embedded within ecological cycles, celebrating human sexuality as a vital expression of life's continuity, a marker of cultural identity, and a homage to the earth's creative powers.

Beyond this connection to nature, many Indigenous societies historically cultivated inclusive and expansive understandings of gender and sexual diversity—long before Western frameworks introduced binary norms or pathologized nonconformity. Will Roscoe[80] observes that "numerous Native North American communities recognized roles for individuals embodying both masculine and feminine spirits, integrating them into social, ceremonial, and healing functions" (**Roscoe, 1998**). Such recognition reflects an inclusive ethos[81]: diversity in gender identities and sexual orientations was often accepted, even revered, rather than stigmatized, as they were woven into the moral and cosmological fabric of the community, grounded in principles of respect, reciprocity, and relational ethics.

Elders played a crucial role in teaching youth about relational boundaries, emotional intelligence, and respect for others' autonomy. Sexuality was viewed not only through the lens of desire but through responsibility to the community, the ancestors, and the land. This ethic extended to all relationships—human, animal, and ecological—reinforcing the idea that intimacy must be practiced with care and awareness of its ripple effects on the collective. As Vine Deloria Jr.[82] reminds us, "Indigenous spirituality teaches that all life is connected; human actions, including those of intimacy, resonate through the community and the natural world" (**Deloria, 2003**).

Such integrative views offer a stark contrast to the often fragmented and moralistic approaches introduced during colonialism. Colonial powers[83] imposed rigid gender hierarchies, Christian sexual mores, and punitive legal codes that undermined Indigenous sexual traditions[84]. The result was not only the criminalization of non-normative identities but also the erosion of spiritual systems that honored sexuality as sacred. In this context, reclaiming Indigenous sexualities becomes an act of cultural survival and epistemological resistance[85]—a restoration of knowledge systems in which desire, identity, and ecology are not compartmentalized but coalesce into a unified whole.

In contemporary discourse, revisiting these Indigenous perspectives offers valuable insights for addressing modern challenges in sexuality, consent, and environmental stewardship. Robin Wall Kimmerer[86] writes, "When we honor the land as teacher and kin, our understanding of relationships deepens, including how we relate to one another in love and intimacy" (**Kimmerer, 2013**). This counter-narrative[87] challenges fragmented modern approaches by linking sexual well-being to ecological health and cultural continuity. Learning from Indigenous wisdom[88]—celebrating balance, respect, and harmony with nature—can inform more inclusive, empathetic, and sustainable models of sexuality today. By acknowledging the diverse traditions that have historically integrated sexuality with spirituality and environment, we cultivate a richer discourse that honors cultural diversity and the intricate connections between humanity and the natural world.

This section reminds us that the reconciliation of deeply held religious convictions with evolving sexual norms has always been a dynamic process, one in which societies continuously reexamine and redefine the relationship between the sacred and the sexual. By delving into the sexual practices of ancient civilizations, we uncover a rich tapestry of experiences in which desire was not merely a biological drive but a complex interplay of spirituality, morality, and social order. These ancient perspectives illuminate how sexuality was integrated with rituals, art, and even political structures, serving as a bridge between the physical and the divine.

The historical context provided by these ancient societies is invaluable for understanding contemporary debates surrounding religion and sexuality. In an era grappling with issues of sexual freedom, gender identity, and equality, and bodily autonomy, our current challenges are not entirely novel. They echo age-old questions about the nature of desire, the limits of moral authority, and the sacred meaning of intimacy. By acknowledging the diversity of sexual expression in antiquity—from the celebratory rituals of fertility cults to the strict ethical codes imposed by emerging monotheistic traditions[89]—we gain a more nuanced perspective that respects the multiplicity of human experiences across different times and cultures.

To these ancient civilizations, sexuality was not simply a biological necessity but an essential aspect of life deeply intertwined with the natural world, the divine order, and the fabric of society itself. Their approaches to eroticism and ethics demonstrate that the interplay between sexuality and religion is as old as civilization, continuously evolving yet always significant. This enduring dialogue invites us to embrace a more holistic understanding of human sexual desire—one that honors both our biological impulses and our higher aspirations for meaning and connection.

Ultimately, the insights gleaned from ancient sexual beliefs and practices challenge us to look beyond binary thinking and simplistic moral judgments. They invite us to reexamine the roots of our sexual ethics— not as fixed doctrines but as evolving dialogues shaped by culture, consciousness, and compassion. They urge us to remember that a liberated sexuality is not separate from holiness but can be its most intimate expression. By listening to their echoes across time, we are reminded that to love, to desire, and to seek connection are not deviations from the sacred but, as in many traditions, the very path to it. As we move forward into a future increasingly defined by the need to balance tradition with progress, these ancient perspectives offer timeless wisdom and urge us to cultivate empathy, celebrate diversity, and continually explore the profound and intricate relationship between sexuality and the sacred.

The Influence of Religious Beliefs and Institutions

Throughout history, religious beliefs and institutions have profoundly shaped societal attitudes toward sexuality, providing moral frameworks that have guided both private behavior and public norms. From antiquity to modern times, these frameworks have not only defined what constitutes acceptable sexual behavior but also have played a critical role in shaping legal and cultural institutions. Early religious narratives and rituals— whether in the context of fertility cults or sacred mythologies—served to integrate sexuality into the broader cosmic order, offering a way to understand human desire in relation to divine forces and natural cycles.

However, with the rise of monotheistic religions, especially Judaism, Christianity, and Islam, sexual norms became increasingly codified and prescriptive. Religious scriptures outlined explicit guidelines that confined sexual activity to the sanctity of marriage, emphasizing ideals such as chastity[90], fidelity, and procreation. These guidelines were institutionalized and enforced by religious authorities who had spiritual and political influence over communities. In medieval Europe, for example, the Church not only dictated personal morality but also influenced legal systems and societal structures, embedding religious sexual ethics into the very structure of society, thus reinforcing a culture that revered sexual restraint and regulated behavior through strict moral codes.

Religious institutions thus came to serve as custodians of moral authority, regulating not only what individuals could do with their bodies but also how entire communities understood the moral implications of intimacy and desire. In doing so, they created powerful dichotomies—sacred versus profane, pure versus impure—that often marginalized those whose identities or behaviors did not conform. These distinctions endure into the present, informing contemporary debates on issues such as contraception, abortion, same-sex relationships, and gender identity. Even in secular societies, the influence of religious morality persists in laws, policies, and cultural norms. Therefore, the interplay between religious doctrine and social control remains a critical lens through which to examine the ongoing evolution of sexual ethics in modern society.

At the same time, religious responses to sexuality have never been monolithic[91]. Within and across traditions, there exists a wide spectrum of interpretations—from rigid orthodoxies to more inclusive and fluid theologies. This diversity reveals that the relationship between religion and sexuality is not fixed but dynamic, constantly negotiated in response to changing social, historical, and cultural contexts. Some religious teachings have served to liberate sexual expression and honor the sacredness of human intimacy, while others have constrained it under the weight of moral control.

Studying these variations allows us to critically assess how religious institutions have functioned both as gatekeepers of sexual repression and as potential sources of liberation. As we continue to examine the evolving discourse around sexuality and faith in modern society, this historical lens becomes essential. It reminds us that today's tensions between spiritual beliefs and sexual freedoms are not new—they are part of a long and complex legacy.

In essence, this section explores how religious doctrines and institutions have shaped, restricted, and at times sanctified human sexuality. By understanding this legacy, we are better equipped to question inherited moral frameworks, foster inclusive conversations, and envision a more compassionate and informed approach to the intersection of spirituality and sexual ethics.

The Judeo-Christian Influence: The Transition to Monotheism

The transition from ancient fertility cults to monotheistic traditions marked a profound religious and cultural transformation that reshaped human attitudes toward sexuality and religions. Karen Armstrong[92] describes this transformation as one in which "religion moved from a celebration of nature's fecundity to a concern with ethical obedience to a single, transcendent deity" (**Armstrong, 1994**). In polytheistic societies[93], sexuality was often revered as a sacred, life-giving force—interwoven into seasonal rituals, communal celebrations, and mythologies that honored the earth's creative abundance. Fertility rites were not merely symbolic but experiential, reflecting a deep reverence for the natural cycles of birth, growth, death, and renewal.

With the rise of monotheistic worldviews, however, this celebratory embrace of eroticism was gradually replaced by frameworks that subordinated sexuality to moral law. The emerging monotheistic traditions—Judaism, Christianity, and later Islam—introduced a divine authority that was not just powerful but singular and absolute. Within this evolving paradigm, sexuality became subject to divine commandments, moral restrictions, and theological interpretations that sought to govern desire as a potential threat to spiritual purity and social order.

The Hebrew Bible's account of Adam and Eve in the Garden of Eden became a foundational narrative that linked sexuality to disobedience and shame. As Elaine Pagels[94] explains, this myth "recasts the body's sexual knowledge not as a force for communal well-being but as the origin of sin"

(**Pagels, 2011**). The consequence was a moral framework that positioned human sexuality as something to be controlled, confined within the institution of marriage, and directed primarily toward procreation. Concepts such as chastity, monogamy, and sexual restraint became virtues, while nonconforming expressions of desire were increasingly pathologized or condemned—a dramatic departure from the more permissive attitudes of earlier cultures.

The process of transitioning to monotheism was neither immediate nor uniform. It unfolded over centuries through theological reinterpretation, political consolidation, and evolving social norms. Yet its impact was far-reaching. Over time, the once-celebratory view of sexuality found in ancient fertility cults gave way to a more controlled and ascetic approach during the medieval period. The rigorous moral codes that accompanied the rise of monotheistic religions deeply impacted the development of Western thought. Mircea Eliade[95] notes, "The codification of sexuality under a single god entailed an elaborate system of prohibitions and taboos, reflecting the new religion's need to assert control over both individual bodies and communal life" (**Eliade, 1959**). This shift not only redefined sexual norms but also established long-lasting cultural narratives—valorizing chastity, stigmatizing adultery[96], and criminalizing non-procreative acts—that continue to influence modern debates on sexuality and morality. The transformation underscored the tension between celebrating human fertility as a divine gift and constraining it within the bounds of religious doctrine—a duality that still resonates in contemporary discussions of sexual ethics and human rights.

Even today, the legacy of these ancient transformations continues to shape contemporary attitudes toward sexuality. Debates around abortion, LGBTQ+ rights, and reproductive freedom are frequently colored by centuries-old religious doctrines that still inform modern legal systems and cultural values. Yet in parallel, there has been a resurgence of interest in pre-monotheistic spiritualities—particularly among neo-pagan[97], feminist, and queer movements—which reclaim the erotic as sacred and challenge the rigid binaries imposed by traditional religious frameworks.

By revisiting the transition to monotheism, we gain a deeper understanding of how religious ideologies have historically shaped, and often restricted, human sexual expression. This critical reflection invites us to imagine new possibilities—ones that honor the full spectrum of human desire, restore dignity to diverse identities, and reestablish the body as a site of pleasure, connection, and spiritual meaning. In doing so, we take a vital step toward healing the centuries-old divide between the sacred and the sexual, thereby fostering a more inclusive, empathetic, and progressive approach to human sexuality.

A Transformative Era

The emergence of Judaism, Christianity, and Islam ushered in a transformative era that redefined religious and sexual norms across civilizations. In Judaism, the Torah[98] not only serves as a spiritual guide but also delineates a comprehensive set of laws governing sexual behavior— "from strict prohibitions against adultery, incest, and premarital relations to intricate prescriptions for marital intimacy and family purity, these rules served to maintain a distinct covenantal relationship between God and the people of Israel" (**Masterson**[99] *et al.,* **2014**). Scholar David Biale[100] adds that "the regulation of sexual conduct functioned as a declaration of communal solidarity, affirming the inseparability of daily life and covenantal commitment[101]" (**Biale, 2023**). In this context, sexuality was not a private affair but a sacred expression, deeply interwoven with the collective life of the community.

With the rise of Christianity, a new paradigm emerged—one that both built upon and departed from Jewish precedent. While Jesus of Nazareth[102] taught a message grounded in love, compassion, and forgiveness— challenging many of the restrictive sexual norms of his time—early Christian theologians reinterpreted sexuality through the lens of asceticism and spiritual purity. Thinkers such as St. Augustine reframed sexual desire as a site of struggle between the flesh and the spirit, promoting celibacy and chastity as paths to transcendence, and arguing that "sexual renunciation is the highest form of Christian self-mastery" (**Brown, 1990**). This shift reoriented sexual ethics, emphasizing that intimacy should be confined within the sacred boundaries of marriage—a stark contrast to the more permissive practices of earlier cultures.

Islam, emerging in the 7th century, introduced its own theological and legal frameworks for sexual conduct. Rooted in the Qur'an and

Hadith, Islamic sexual ethics emphasize modesty, marital fidelity, and the sanctity of the family unit. But unlike the ascetic extremes of certain Christian interpretations, Islam views sexuality as a natural and even blessed part of life—provided it is expressed within lawful bounds. According to Kecia Ali[103], "Islamic sexual ethics, grounded in Qur'anic injunctions and prophetic traditions, seek to balance individual rights with communal responsibilities, emphasizing that sexuality should be exercised within a framework of mutual respect and social harmony" (**Ali, 2016**). Through a complex and evolving body of jurisprudence, Islamic traditions developed sophisticated rules governing not only marriage and divorce but also issues such as consent, menstruation, and sexual pleasure—often with remarkable nuance, yet still within a patriarchal framework.

Together, these three monotheistic religions laid the groundwork for a moral framework that came to dominate the spiritual and social lives of billions. Their influence extended far beyond the private realm, shaping public institutions, educational systems, and legal doctrines. But this shift from ancient, celebratory views of sexuality to moralistic, highly regulated frameworks did not occur in isolation. It was the result of centuries of political consolidation, theological debate, and cultural negotiation.

As these religions expanded their influence, they redefined sexual ethics in ways that resonated with broader societal values—often promoting control, hierarchy, and discipline under the guise of divine order. The enduring legacy of these religious traditions is evident today in contemporary debates over gender roles, sexual freedom, contraception, abortion, and LGBTQ+ rights. These legacies reveal not only the historical depth of religious influence but also the powerful role of faith in constructing the boundaries of sexual morality.

Understanding how deeply embedded these religious systems are in shaping contemporary sexual norms allows for a more compassionate and contextualized dialogue. By examining how the Abrahamic religions have shaped attitudes toward sexuality over the centuries, scholars can trace contemporary ethical frameworks back to their religious roots, revealing how doctrines have both constrained and defined sexual behavior. It also opens the door to reimagining a future where religion and sexuality need not be in opposition, but rather in dynamic, evolving conversation.

Moreover, the ongoing dialogue between ancient religious traditions and modern perspectives is vital for addressing current issues of sexual liberation and gender inclusivity. Revisiting the historical influence of the Abrahamic religions clarifies the origins of many enduring attitudes, fostering an inclusive and informed discourse that acknowledges the complex interplay between faith, culture, and human sexual desire while advocating for the evolution of sexual ethics in a rapidly changing world.

Pauline Christianity and Celibacy

Pauline Christianity[104], as articulated in the letters of the Apostle Paul, played a pivotal role in shaping early Christian attitudes toward sexuality, celibacy, and spiritual devotion. Among these, 1 Corinthians 7 stands out as a foundational text, in which Paul famously writes, *"It is good for a man not to marry,"* advocating celibacy as a path to spiritual purity and divine focus. For Paul, abstaining from sexual relationships was not simply a private lifestyle choice but a theologically significant orientation toward God. As John M. G. Barclay[105] explains, Paul viewed celibacy as a unique charism, a spiritual gift enabling "undivided devotion to the Lord" (**Barclay, 2015**). This vision positioned celibacy as a higher calling—one that offered believers an opportunity to transcend the distractions of earthly attachments in pursuit of greater spiritual depth.

Yet Paul was no idealistic ascetic disconnected from the realities of human desire. He acknowledged the strength of sexual impulses and offered marriage as a moral and pragmatic solution: *"If they cannot exercise self-control, they should marry. For it is better to marry than to burn with passion."* (1 Corinthians 7:9). Ben Witherington[106] notes that "Paul recognized human sexual desire—he counseled marriage 'to avoid burning with passion'—yet esteemed celibacy as superior when the gift is present" (**Witherington, 2024**). This tension between acknowledging natural impulses and elevating religious dedication became a cornerstone of early Christian moral frameworks.

As Christianity evolved from a persecuted sect to a state-supported institution, the Pauline teachings on celibacy were elevated to a normative ideal, especially within the Catholic Church. Celibacy became a symbol of radical devotion—codified through vows taken by monks, nuns, and priests. Asceticism, particularly sexual renunciation, came to be seen as a superior expression of holiness. Historian Peter Brown[107] emphasizes that in early Christian thought, "sexual renunciation was celebrated as a means of spiritual perfection," (**Brown, 1988**), reinforcing the idea that the denial of bodily pleasure could lead to a more elevated communion with God. This theological shift transformed celibacy into an institutionalized standard for clerical life, shaping the Church's structure and moral authority for centuries.

However, the idealization of celibacy also generated ongoing debates regarding its practical and ethical consequences. Critics—both historical and contemporary—have questioned whether such a rigorous ideal is psychologically sustainable or theologically necessary for spiritual fulfillment. The Church's insistence on celibacy, particularly for clergy, has often resulted in unintended consequences, including emotional repression, secrecy, and scandal. Scholars such as Dale Martin[108] (1996) contextualized Paul's teachings within the Greco-Roman world, where early Christians were negotiating a complex terrain between pagan sexual permissiveness and Jewish moral strictness: "Paul's insistence on celibacy reflects early Christian attempts to navigate between pagan permissiveness and Jewish moral rigor" (**Martin, 2006**). Understanding this cultural climate helps illuminate why celibacy was so powerfully elevated at the time—and also why it may require reassessment today.

In our contemporary context, Pauline teachings on celibacy remain both influential and contested. While many still honor celibacy as a noble spiritual path, others call for a more expansive sexual theology—one that encourages critical reflection on tensions between spiritual ideals and human sexual desires. Theologians, pastors, and ethicists increasingly advocate a voluntary, life-giving reinterpretation of celibacy, rather than a mandatory, repressive one. This evolving conversation reflects a broader shift in Christian thought: a movement toward integrating sexual honesty, psychological health, and relational fulfillment within the spiritual journey.

The legacy of Pauline Christianity thus presents a dual challenge and opportunity: to honor the sincerity and spiritual aspirations behind celibacy, while also recognizing the importance of reimagining sexual ethics in ways that embrace the full spectrum of human experience. In this ongoing dialogue, Paul's writings continue to serve as a vital reference point—not as static commands, but as historical insights ripe for reinterpretation in light of changing understandings of love, intimacy, and spiritual maturity.

Christianity: Sin, Purity, Marriage, Virginity and Chastity

Christianity, in its various denominations, has played a pivotal role in shaping Western perspectives on sexual morality. Doctrines concerning sin, purity, marriage, virginity, and chastity—rooted in biblical texts and centuries of ecclesiastical tradition—have deeply influenced societal norms, legal frameworks, and personal attitudes toward sexuality, especially in the Western world. As Peggy Sanday[109] observes, "the Christian valorization of virginity and sexual purity has historically contributed to systemic gender inequality, framing women's bodies as sites of moral contest" (**Sanday, 1981**). These teachings wove moral restraint into the fabric of Christian life, aligning personal conduct with communal identity and religious devotion.

Sin, in Christian theology, is broadly defined as any thought or act that violates God's will. This concept has deeply influenced sexual ethics, categorizing a wide range of behaviors—such as premarital sex, adultery, and homosexual acts—as sinful, particularly under traditional interpretations. This view has fostered a moral framework emphasizing restraint, repentance, and adherence to divine commandments. Purity, meanwhile, extends beyond physical cleanliness to encompass religious and moral integrity. Historically, the emphasis on sexual purity has been disproportionately imposed on women, idealizing virginity before marriage and leading to cultural practices such as "purity balls"—ceremonies where young girls publicly pledge abstinence until marriage—where young girls pledge to remain virgins until marriage. Jessica Valenti[110] notes, "Purity culture in contemporary America often positions young women as moral gatekeepers, burdening them with unrealistic expectations and deep-seated guilt over natural sexual development" (**Valenti, 2010**).

Marriage occupies a central role in Christian theology as the only legitimate context for sexual activity. It is regarded as a sacred union, a covenant reflecting the relationship between Christ and the Church, ordained by God for both procreation and mutual support. Saint Thomas Aquinas[111] writes that "marriage is willed by God for the procreation of children and the mutual assistance of the spouses" (**Aquinas, 1952**). This theological ideal has long influenced Christian advocacy for abstinence before marriage, opposition to premarital cohabitation, and the resistance to legal recognition of same-sex unions in many Christian-majority societies.

Virginity and chastity stand as twin pillars in Christian teachings on sin, purity, and marriage. Across centuries, virginity—especially in women—has been extolled as a symbol of purity, self-control, and closeness to the divine, epitomized by the veneration of the Virgin Mary. Jaroslav Pelikan[112] writes, the Cult of the Virgin[113] "institutionalized the ideal of chastity, making it the supreme feminine virtue" (**Pelikan, 1996**). Yet chastity encompasses more than abstaining from sex; it represents an enduring moral discipline that governs both thought and behavior. The unmarried are called to celibacy, while the married are expected to express their sexuality faithfully and responsibly within the sacred bounds of marriage. These ideals have deeply shaped Christian cultural narratives around honor, shame, and personal worth, echoing across literature, media, education, and personal identity.

In recent decades, however, society has moved toward more inclusive understandings of sexuality, embracing a broader spectrum of identities, relationships, and expressions of personal autonomy. Yet traditional Christian teachings on sin, purity, and sexual ethics continue to influence contentious debates over reproductive rights, LGBTQ+ inclusion, and sexuality education. Melissa Wilcox[114] notes, "LGBTQ+ Christians often find themselves negotiating a faith tradition that upholds chastity while seeking recognition of diverse sexual identities and loving commitments" (**Wilcox, 2003**). Despite growing social acceptance of premarital sex, cohabitation, and same-sex marriage, the legacy of Christian moral teachings remains embedded in laws, curricula, and cultural norms.

The increasing presence of sexual content in media and the adoption of comprehensive sexuality education—which includes discussions of contraception, consent, and orientation—stand in marked contrast to abstinence-focused models still promoted by many Christian institutions.

Feminist scholars (**Sanday, 1981; Blank, 2008; Valenti, 2010**) have critiqued purity doctrines for perpetuating gender-based double standards, calling for a reexamination of ecclesiastical teachings through the lens of gender equity. Meanwhile, LGBTQ+ believers continue to advocate for theologies that affirm their dignity and relationships, challenging traditional definitions of chastity as inherently heterosexual and procreative.

Ultimately, the evolving dialogue between Christian faith and contemporary values reflects a dynamic moral landscape. In striving to reconcile tradition with compassion, Christian communities are called to reimagine a sexual ethics grounded not only in doctrine, but also in love, justice, and the affirmation of human dignity in all its diversity.

Islamic Views on Sexuality

Islam places strong emphasis on modesty, family values, and marital fidelity, with its sexual ethics deeply rooted in the teachings of the Qur'an and Hadith. These foundational texts establish a clear moral framework that continues to shape the lives and relationships of Muslim individuals and communities around the world. As John Esposito and Yvonne Haddad[115] observe, "Islam views modesty (haya) as an all-encompassing ethic, extending beyond dress to behavior, speech, and interpersonal interactions, thereby safeguarding individual dignity and social harmony" (**Esposito & Haddad, 1998**). The promotion of modest clothing, such as the hijab[116], symbolizes privacy, piety, and respect, underscoring the broader ethical vision of Islamic life.

Marriage is held in the highest regard within Islamic teachings, not only as a social contract but also as a sacred institution ordained by God. Sexual relations are viewed as a source of spiritual and emotional fulfillment within marriage and as a legitimate means for procreation. Premarital and extramarital sexual activities are generally prohibited, reflecting the Qur'anic vision of sexual intimacy as a blessing to be enjoyed within the bounds of marital commitment. This framework serves to strengthen the family unit, which is seen as the cornerstone of social stability and moral order in Islamic society.

While classical Islamic jurisprudence has traditionally deemed same-sex acts impermissible, contemporary scholarship has begun to interrogate and reinterpret these positions. Kecia Ali notes that although "the majority of Muslim scholars deem same-sex relations impermissible, the range of interpretive approaches within the Islamic legal tradition suggests the potential for more inclusive readings" (**Ali, 2016**). This ongoing diversity of opinion highlights how religious doctrines continue to shape contemporary debates over sexuality, personal freedom, and the separation of mosque and state in Muslim-majority societies.

In *Homosexuality in Islam: Critical Reflection on Gay, Lesbian, and Transgender Muslims*, Scott Siraj al-Haqq Kugle[117] offers a groundbreaking reassessment, arguing that "the Qur'anic ethos of mercy and 'no compulsion in religion' supports a broader understanding of sexual diversity as part of God's creation" (**Kugle, 2010**). His work marks a critical turning point in Islamic discourse, illustrating how scripture, Hadith, and legal traditions can be read through lenses of compassion, dignity, and inclusivity. Kugle's scholarship, along with the work of others such as Amina Wadud[118] (1999) and Kecia Ali (2016), is part of a growing intellectual movement aimed at reconciling traditional teachings with contemporary understandings of justice, human rights, and personal autonomy.

This evolving discourse extends beyond sexual orientation to encompass broader questions of gender equity, bodily integrity, and individual freedom. Reform-minded scholars and activists within the Muslim world are increasingly challenging patriarchal interpretations and advocating for a sexual ethics grounded in mutual respect, spiritual equality, and personal identity and freedom. The dynamic tension between preserving religious tradition and embracing modern sensibilities reflects a larger, ongoing process of ijtihad—independent scholarly reasoning in Islamic law when foundational texts provide no explicit ruling—shaped by historical experience, cultural diversity, and the impact of globalization, all of which continue to influence how sexuality is understood and practiced in contemporary Muslim societies.

Understanding this complexity is essential for navigating the intersection of religion, sexuality, and human rights in Muslim-majority and Muslim-influenced societies. Islamic teachings on sexuality should not be viewed as static or monolithic, but rather as representing a living dialogue that is constantly negotiated by communities, scholars, and believers as they confront new realities. Examining these views within that evolving framework fosters more meaningful discussions about the interplay of religion, culture, and autonomy—especially in debates over the separation of mosque and sex—by revealing how historical and social forces shape contemporary attitudes toward intimacy.

Looking ahead, Islamic sexual ethics stands at a crossroads where tradition meets transformation. Emerging voices—particularly among younger Muslims, feminist theologians, LGBTQ+ advocates, and forward-thinking spiritual leaders—are calling for renewed engagement with scriptural texts and legal traditions in ways that honor both religious heritage and the dignity and inherent rights of diverse identities. This evolving dialogue holds the potential to reshape societal attitudes and influence legal and cultural institutions, advancing a more inclusive and nuanced understanding of sexuality that remains faithful to core Islamic principles while embracing the evolving human experience.

The Devastating Effects of Christian and Muslim Colonization on Indigenous Sexualities

Erotic Freedom Before Colonization

Before the arrival of missionaries and imperial powers, many Indigenous societies across Kama[119] (Africa), the Americas, Asia, and the Pacific Islands maintained complex, life-affirming, and deeply spiritual relationships to eroticism. Sexuality was not isolated from the sacred; it was its very expression. The body was honored as a divine vessel, and pleasure—far from being condemned—was a pathway to understanding nature, self, and cosmos. In Kama, as detailed in Uriel Nawej's[120] *Erotic Africa* (**Nawej, 2012**), nudity was common, not scandalous. Communities celebrated fertility rites, sensual dances, and multi-gender expressions without fear of sin. These practices were not 'primitive' but deeply symbolic: embedded with cosmological meaning, social unity, and ancestral reverence. Erotic knowledge was transmitted through generations, often led by women—matriarchs, priestesses, or sacred dancers—who held honored positions in society. Such erotic autonomy and gender fluidity existed in the Americas as well, with the revered Two-Spirit[121] identities among Indigenous nations, while Polynesian and Melanesian cultures embraced sexual openness. This global tapestry of diverse sexualities formed a beautiful counter-narrative to the binary, repressive moral codes that would soon be imposed by colonial religion.

Moral Colonization Through Religion

The introduction of Christianity and Islam into Indigenous territories marked more than a religious shift—it initiated a campaign of cultural and moral colonization[122] that redefined gender and sexual norms in colonized societies. Churches, especially under European rule, often served as colonial outposts, and Christian missionaries operated as moral soldiers of the empire. In some regions, Islamic expansion also reshaped local sexual and social norms through mosque-centered religious reforms, typically through trade, Sufi influence, and scholarship rather than formal colonization. As Manuela Picq and Josi Tikuna[123] argue, "The colonial project often translated into a spiritual and sexual conquest that delegitimized Indigenous knowledge systems, gender diversity, and erotic expression" (**Picq & Tikuna, 2019**). Both traditions, at times, imposed foreign moral codes in the form of heteronormativity and sexual restraint that disrupted Indigenous understandings of eroticism, gender, and spiritual expression.

Missionary institutions, such as the monjeríos of Spanish California[124], exemplify how religious authorities sought to control Indigenous sexuality directly by segregating and disciplining girls and women according to Christian moral standards. Valeria Rivera[125] writes, "Franciscans placed girls of about eight years and up, together with young, unmarried women and widows, in a shared room, or dormitory called the monjerio (dormitory)… the monjerio also served to train the Indian women and girls in skills befitting their new lifestyle" (**Rivera, 2013**). Christian influence also contributed to the erosion of traditional gender roles and sexual autonomy, reshaping Indigenous power structures and suppressing cultural expressions of sexuality and gender variance. As documented for Native North American communities, gender-fluid and same-sex roles once integrated into Indigenous societies were marginalized, leading to long-term impacts on gender relations and expressions.

Uriel Nawej, in *White Poison*, describes this process as a mental occupation: "They colonized our minds by shaming our pleasures" (**Nawej, 2007**). African matrilineal systems—social structures tracing descent and inheritance through the mother's line—once rooted in respect for women's reproductive autonomy—the right to decide whether and when to have children without coercion—were dismantled. Priestly roles held by women were disbanded or demonized. Circumcision rites[126], formerly seen as rites of passage or sexual empowerment, were rebranded as tools of moral correction. Erotic art was destroyed. Dances were banned. The naked body became scandalous. Desire became dangerous. And pleasure, once sacred, became a source of guilt. In North and South America, gender-diverse individuals were forced into conversion camps and "civilizing" schools, erasing centuries of tradition and ancestral respect. Missionaries taught Indigenous children that their very desires were demonic and that salvation required self-denial. This wasn't merely spiritual conversion—it was psychosexual disarmament[127].

The Silent Shadow of Islam

While Christian colonization has been widely scrutinized for its overt repression of Indigenous sexualities, the expansion of Islam across North, West, and East Africa also contributed to significant transformations in erotic and gender norms—though often through subtler forms of cultural and religious assimilation. Along with the spread of monotheism came a legalistic and moral framework rooted in Sharia[128], which emphasized modesty, patriarchal authority, and gendered behavioral codes. In many societies where sexuality had been sacred, communal, and celebrated—especially through matriarchal customs, nude rituals, or sensual rites—the adoption of Islamic norms introduced new ideals of veiling (hijab), sexual discipline, and gender segregation.

Although conversion to Islam often occurred through trade, intermarriage, and religious conviction, its effect on Indigenous conceptions of the body, desire, and gendered power was profound. Scholars have shown how "Islamic interpretations of modesty and family law gradually displaced older traditions, restructuring both public and private life." (**Syed**[129], **2010**). Though less violent than European Christian colonization, the Islamic reordering of erotic life still severed many communities from ancestral practices that once honored fluidity, sensuality, and female leadership in sexual and spiritual domains.

Judaism: The Proto-Scripture of Erotophobia[130]

Although Judaism did not engage in colonization or seek to impose its views through conquest, it played a foundational role in shaping religious sexual prohibitions that were later adopted and expanded by Christianity and, to some extent, Islam. The Torah, especially the book of Leviticus, sets forth specific commandments regulating sexual behavior, such as the injunction in **Leviticus 18:22**: "Do not lie with a male as with a woman; it is an abomination," echoed again in **Leviticus 20:13**. Within Jewish legal and theological traditions, these verses have been interpreted as prohibitions against certain same-sex acts and as broader prescriptions for maintaining ritual purity and upholding divine law. These early codes of sexual conduct helped establish enduring moral paradigms that would go on to influence the development of Christian sexual ethics and Islamic legal traditions. In doing so, Judaism provided a foundational scriptural framework for the religious regulation of erotic life, situating sexuality as a domain governed by divine command and communal norms.

Global Patterns of Erotic Suppression

What is most striking is the uniformity of this moral violence across colonized territories. The same mechanisms—shame, fear, sin, obedience—were deployed globally to dismantle Indigenous erotic systems. In Asia, colonial authorities reinterpreted Taoist and Tantric texts, reducing centuries of refined sexual wisdom to exotic curiosities or outright taboos. In Oceania, where entire communities once engaged in sensual rituals as communal bonding practices, missionaries demanded enforced monogamy and sexual silence[131]. The body was no longer a site of joy but became a battlefield for purity. Uriel Nawej describes this as a form of global psychosexual genocide[132]: a targeted eradication of erotic consciousness[133]. He argues that colonial religion did more than seize land and resources; it undermined Indigenous spiritual and erotic traditions, replacing them with doctrines of shame and moral constraint that, in his view, damaged people's capacity to experience sex and pleasure freely.

The uniformity of repression was not accidental. It was engineered. Religious authorities, allied with colonial governments, knew that breaking the erotic spirit of a people made them easier to dominate politically and economically. A sexually liberated population is harder to control. But a people paralyzed by guilt, isolated in shame, and confused about their own desires—such a people becomes governable.

Sexual Violence as a Tool of Colonization

Sexual violence was not merely an unfortunate byproduct of colonization—it was a deliberate and systemic instrument of domination. In settler colonial contexts such as North America, Sarah Deer[134] argues that "rape and sexual assault were routinely used to assert power, humiliate Indigenous communities, and dismantle traditional kinship systems" (**Deer, 2015**). The bodies of Indigenous women were treated as symbolic battlegrounds upon which the myths of racial and moral superiority were enacted. Entire generations of children were born from acts of colonial sexual violence, often stripped of their mother tongues, cultural identities, and erotic traditions.

In both Christian missions and Islamic colonial expansions, sexual control was woven into religious dogma and civilizing ideologies. Catherine McKinley and Hannah Knipp[135] write, "Christian boarding schools imposed enforced chastity and shamed bodily pleasure, while some Islamic colonial systems institutionalized gender segregation and polygynous domination through religious justifications" (**McKinley & Knipp, 2022**). These forms of violence were more than physical—they represented a systematic rewriting of erotic scripts through shame, trauma, and erasure.

As scholars have shown, this legacy continues today: Indigenous women remain among the most vulnerable populations for sexual exploitation, a reality rooted in centuries of dehumanization and state-sanctioned violence. The normalization of such abuses has contributed to modern gender-based violence, human trafficking, and cultural disconnection. As Sarah Deer notes, "the beginning of rape against Native women was the beginning of colonization itself" (**Deer, 2015**).

Erotic Decolonization

From a Raelian perspective, this global repression of sexual pleasure is one of the greatest tragedies of human history. Human beings were designed to live in harmony with their desires and pleasures. Sensuality, happiness, and sexual fulfillment are not sins—they are sacred expressions of life itself. Monotheistic religions—particularly those that seek dominion over sexual behavior—function as control mechanisms rather than spiritual paths. This book stands in direct opposition to these dogmas. It calls for a radical re-evaluation of inherited sexual guilt, and a commitment to reclaiming ancestral erotic wisdom. Uriel Nawej's work invites us to undertake an erotic decolonization[136]—a process of healing that involves remembering, restoring, and reclaiming the sacredness of pleasure. This is not merely a return to the past, but a forging of a new erotic ethos: one that blends science, spirituality, sensuality, and human rights. It's a call to unlearn shame, to critique missionary morality, and to restore the right of every person to love, feel, explore, and rejoice in their body without fear.

Healing Through Erotic Memory and Cultural Revival

The path to healing begins with memory. Erotic memory[137]—the collective remembrance of sensual wisdom, ancestral freedom, and embodied cultural practices—must be reclaimed if communities are to fully recover from the sexual repression imposed by colonial religion. Across the globe, movements for sexual liberation are reviving ceremonies, languages, and creative expressions that colonial systems once sought to erase. Among Indigenous peoples of Turtle Island, Two-Spirit and queer scholars describe this process as the recovery of a *sovereign erotic*[138], in which reclaiming sexual and gender diversity becomes inseparable from cultural resurgence, spiritual wholeness, and healing from historical trauma (**Driskill, 2004; Reardon-Smith, 2023**). Likewise, research on Indigenous cultural health highlights that "reconnecting with traditional teachings, ritual life, and embodied ways of knowing strengthens well-being and restores relational balance disrupted by colonization" (**Biles *et al.*, 2024**). Sarah Reardon Smith[139] writes, "In Oceania, revitalized concepts such as takatāpui[140] affirm longstanding Māori understandings of sexuality and intimacy as relational, spiritual, and culturally grounded—challenging colonial binaries and shame-based norms" (**Reardon-Smith, 2023**). These revivals demonstrate that erotic healing is not merely about sexual acts; it is about restoring integrity to cultures, realigning values with nature, and honoring the sexual as sacred. Through literature, film, ceremony, activism, and digital storytelling, Indigenous creators are reclaiming erotic joy as a form of resistance and renewal. In this sense, erotic memory becomes both healing and revolutionary—echoing contemporary spiritual visions, including the Raelian affirmation of sexuality as a pathway to happiness, freedom, and human blossoming. By reawakening what was nearly extinguished, humanity rediscovers a timeless truth: that our bodies are not sites of sin, but vessels of pleasure, connection, and love without fear.

Chapter Two:
Contemporary Challenges

Abstinence vs. Sexuality Education: *When Silence Replaces Science*

Traditional religions have significantly shaped global policies and attitudes toward sexuality education, often prioritizing abstinence-only education over comprehensive sexuality education[1] (CSE). This has resulted in programs offering limited information on crucial topics such as contraception, sexual health, and relationship management. Rooted in doctrines emphasizing purity, virginity[2], and the sanctity of marriage[3], many religious frameworks portray pre- and extra-marital sexual activity as morally suspect—if not sinful—fostering environments steeped in shame, guilt, secrecy, and misinformation.

Religious groups frequently advocate abstinence until marriage as the only morally acceptable path, based on interpretations of sacred texts. This perspective often casts sexual pleasure in a negative light while adopting anti-science and anti-medical stances. In essence, these programs trade knowledge for fear. As John S. Santelli *et al.*[4] observe, "Abstinence-only-until-marriage programs generally have not been shown to delay initiation of sex, reduce the number of sexual partners, or reduce teen pregnancy rates," (**Santelli *et al.*, 2006**), underscoring how moral prescriptions disconnected from evidence fail to prepare young people for real-life sexual decision-making. Sloan Caldwell[5] goes further, arguing that "such programs not only fail to meet their stated goals but also violate human rights standards" (**Caldwell, 2015**). These are not fringe findings; studies consistently show that schools and families investing solely in abstinence-based curricula discover that students still become sexually active, but uninformed, unprepared, and vulnerable.

As a result, sexuality education has become a battleground between moral doctrine and empirical evidence. The downstream consequence of these doctrinally driven curricula is a generation of youth who are often insufficiently informed about critical dimensions of sexuality—such as contraception, consent, relationship dynamics, and sexual orientation—leaving them vulnerable to unintended pregnancies, sexually transmitted infections[6] (STIs), and emotional harm. In contrast, comprehensive sexuality education treats sexual development as a normal part of adolescence. Programs that integrate accurate information on anatomy, contraception, relationships, and diverse identities have consistently shown superior outcomes. As Douglas Kirby[7] summarizes: "Programs that provide comprehensive, accurate information about contraception and condom use do not increase sexual activity; instead, they increase condom and contraceptive use and reduce teen pregnancy and STIs" (**Kirby, 2007**).

Moreover, abstinence-only education[8] systematically excludes vulnerable populations. LGBTQ+ youth, sexually active teens, and those from diverse cultural backgrounds often find no place in such curricula, which marginalize their realities and health needs. Many traditional religious perspectives exclude or stigmatize LGBTQ+ individuals, worsening health disparities and reinforcing isolation. The *UNESCO International Technical Guidance on Sexuality Education*[9] emphasizes that effective curricula must be "age-appropriate, scientifically accurate, culturally relevant and inclusive of diverse sexual orientations and gender identities" (**UNESCO, 2018**). Without this inclusive lens, sexuality education reinforces heteronormativity and fails those who most need support, thus perpetuating cycles of vulnerability.

The moral, emotional, and societal costs of silence are steep. Denied accurate education, adolescents turn to peers, media, or experimentation—raising the risks of unsafe sex, unplanned pregnancy, and psychological distress linked to shame and confusion.

Guilt & Shame: *The Emotional Residue of Religious Morality*

Religious teachings have long weaponized guilt and shame as tools of control—especially in matters of the body and sexuality. As Christopher Hitchens observed, "Religion will never be able to live down the shame with which it has stained itself for generations" (**Hitchens, 2008**). His critique underscores that guilt is not an incidental byproduct of faith, but a deliberate mechanism of dogmatic submission. It illuminates how guilt is not an unfortunate side effect but a deliberate instrument of dogmatic submission—a moral toxin passed down in the name of virtue. Such moral framing doesn't merely suppress bodily joy or sensuality; it burdens even innocent experiences of pleasure with suspicion and fear. The result is a cultural inheritance in which sexual curiosity is equated with spiritual failure, and desire itself becomes a site of internalized struggle.

To this end, the long-standing entanglement between religious tradition and human sexuality has produced a cultural landscape in which guilt and shame often emerge as default emotional responses to natural sexual desires and behaviors. Major world religions have historically advanced conservative sexual ethics, framing sexuality within strict moral codes and confining its legitimacy to heterosexual, marital contexts oriented toward procreation. This rigid framework has prompted generations to internalize such judgments, interpreting their desires or identities not as natural expressions of self, but as moral failures or evidence of impurity or unworthiness.

Brené Brown[10] explains that shame induces a uniquely painful form of self-evaluation: "Shame is the intensely painful feeling or experience of believing that we are flawed and therefore unworthy of love and belonging" (**Brown, 2015**). As a result, rather than being a site of pleasure and connection, sexuality becomes entangled with self-reproach, repression, and emotional burden.

Religious rituals that promise moral redemption[11]—such as confession, repentance, and purity practices—often reinforce rather than relieve this guilt. Moreover, religious teachings have long weaponized guilt and shame as tools of control, especially concerning the human body and sexuality. Michel Foucault[12], in his study of Western sexuality, demonstrates how confession transformed desire into an object of extended scrutiny and self-policing, thus deepening internalized guilt and reinforcing normative control. He writes, "The confession… underscores the individual's obligation to produce truth about oneself, making sexuality a site of control rather than simple repression" (**Foucault, 1990**). Similarly, anthropologist Mary Douglas[13] shows how purity systems frame sexual transgression[14] as a symbolic violation of social order rather than merely personal misbehavior. She notes, "The idea of impurity is altogether a matter of classification: something is polluting because it does not fit the pattern and thus reminds us of the possibility of disorder" (**Douglas, 2003**).

These dynamics exert an especially acute toll on sexual and gender minorities. When religious condemnation combines with social stigma, it generates what Ilan Meyer[15] terms "minority stress," which is a chronic psychological strain caused by internalized shame, external prejudice, and the erasure of identity. He writes, "such stress produces adverse health outcomes, in part because individuals internalize negative societal attitudes, leading to shame and self-rejection" (**Meyer, 2003**). When non-heteronormative identities are pathologized by religious teachings, shame becomes embedded in the very process of self-discovery—making the reconciliation of desire and identity a difficult, often traumatic, journey.

Overcoming this legacy demands both individual healing and systemic transformation in the ways religious traditions engage with human sexuality. Rather than relying on guilt and shame as tools of moral enforcement, emerging frameworks must affirm human dignity, reduce stigma, encourage open dialogue, and recognize sexuality as a natural, multifaceted aspect of being. This is precisely what this book seeks to contribute: a reimagining of sexuality education and spiritual ethics that liberates rather than condemns, and nurtures the conditions for emotionally healthy, guilt-free sexual expression.

Reproductive Rights: *Bodies Battling Doctrine*

Historical religious practices have profoundly influenced societal norms and public policy surrounding reproductive rights[16]. This influence has often functioned to limit reproductive choices, especially for women, through a combination of cultural authority and institutional power—from shaping public attitudes to lobbying for restrictive laws. Faye Ginsburg and Rayna Rapp[17] articulate this dynamic clearly: "Control over reproduction is fundamentally a site where cultural, religious, and political forces intersect to regulate bodies and define citizenship" (**Ginsburg and Rapp, 1995**). In this context, citizenship[18] extends beyond legal status—it encompasses whose bodies, choices, and familial structures are validated or subordinated in the social order.

Sam Harris openly challenges the Christian fixation on controlling women's reproductive choices. In *Letter to a Christian Nation*, he critiques the idea that a fertilized egg has the same moral status as a conscious human being, calling it "an astonishing claim." His argument helps dismantle religious reasoning behind anti-abortion laws and underscores the absurdity of prioritizing theological belief over scientific understanding and women's autonomy (**Harris, 2008**).

Religious frameworks have long served as legitimizing tools, establishing boundaries around what kinds of reproductive decisions are deemed morally acceptable—or even allowed to be discussed. This suppression extends not only to services such as abortion and contraception, but also to the public discourse itself, making it difficult for women to openly discuss their bodies, desires, and needs without fear of judgment or backlash.

In his book, *America's War on Sex*, Marty Klein observes in his critique of the religious right's sexual politics, "The goal of this war is to control sexual expression, colonize sexual imagination, and restrict sexual choices" (**Klein, 2012**). Moreover, evangelical Christian mobilization in the U.S. has been central to anti-abortion politics, embedding opposition to abortion into state and federal policy through lobbying, judicial appointments, and public campaigns. Mary Ziegler[19] further notes that "the politicization of abortion in America was significantly driven by religious conservatives who transformed a medical procedure into a moral crusade—a collective effort to impose or defend specific moral norms in public life—reshaping the legal landscape and stigmatizing those seeking reproductive care" (**Ziegler, 2020**).

The Roman Catholic Church's enduring opposition to artificial contraception provides another prominent example of religious doctrine and interference encroaching on reproductive freedom. Rooted in natural law theory[20], the Church's teachings have shaped national policies and everyday practices in countries, regions, and communities with a strong Catholic influence. Agata Ignaciuk and Laura Kelly[21] write that the Vatican's stance "has remained essentially unchanged since the publication of the encyclical *Humanae Vitae*[22] (1968), which solidified a ban on all 'artificial' contraceptive methods for Catholic spouses" (**Ignaciuk & Kelly, 2020**). In these contexts, public health priorities are often subordinated to theological dictates[23], restricting access to family planning and contraception even where evidence-based medical need is clear.

This interference extends beyond borders. According to Catholics for Choice[24] **(2018),** the Vatican has used its unique diplomatic status—the Holy See's recognition as a sovereign entity with international diplomatic influence—at the United Nations to block global family planning initiatives and promote its Humanae Vitae-centered vision of sexuality. Through funding channels and moral pressure, it has sought to defund or delegitimize comprehensive reproductive care efforts across both domestic and international platforms. The result is a rhetorical framework that conflates reproductive freedom with moral decay—transforming health decisions into battlegrounds over authority, virtue, and bodily sovereignty.

Beyond law and international policy, religiously inflected cultural norms also play a critical role in producing stigma around reproductive decision-making. In conservative religious environments, many women internalize the belief that using contraception or seeking abortion constitutes a moral failure. This internalized shame often leads to silence, isolation, and the avoidance of essential healthcare. Institutions that promote abstinence-only education or moralistic messaging, further crowd out fact-based reproductive literacy, compounding misinformation and fear. The cumulative impact of these dynamics is a multi-dimensional erosion of reproductive autonomy—legal, psychological, and cultural. It fosters enduring myths about contraception and abortion, restricts public discourse, and perpetuates the policing of bodies through doctrine rather than care. Disentangling religion from reproductive health is not merely a political project—it is an ethical imperative central to the fight for sexual freedom, gender equality, and bodily justice.

LGBTQ+ Rights: *Faith Versus Freedom of Identity*

Religious condemnation of queer identities has produced some of the most violent and enduring forms of cultural erasure. Hitchens does not mince words when exposing this cruelty: "The Bible and the Qur'an both condemn homosexuality, sometimes with the death penalty" (**Hitchens, 2008**). He questions how believers can claim moral authority while defending texts that incite hatred, violence, and spiritual invalidation. These ancient proscriptions continue to echo in modern laws, school policies, and the self-hatred of queer individuals raised in conservative faiths. Secular humanists call for a radical moral clarity—one that refuses to tolerate bigotry merely because it is wrapped in the robe of tradition.

The influence of traditional religions on LGBTQ+ individuals has been both far-reaching and deeply personal, thereby shaping societal norms, legal frameworks, and private lives across cultures. Major world religions—Christianity, Islam, Judaism, Hinduism, and Buddhism—have historically upheld conservative doctrines that frame non-heteronormative sexual orientations and gender identities as sinful, deviant, or unnatural. These moral frameworks often become the lenses through which followers evaluate LGBTQ+ existence, institutionalizing exclusion and stigma.

As John Boswell[25] emphasizes in his landmark historical study, earlier Christian perspectives on same-sex love were not uniformly hostile but evolved over time into moral and legal condemnation. He observes: "Homosexual behavior came to be classified as a sin and a crime, and same-sex desires were constructed as inherently aberrant," a transformation that merged ecclesiastical authority with societal marginalization (**Boswell, 1980**). This stigmatization, when legitimized by religious doctrine, has justified criminalization and sanctioned violence against LGBTQ+ people in numerous countries, with punishments ranging from social ostracism to imprisonment and, in extreme cases, execution.

Pippa Norris and Ronald Inglehart[26] note that "religious traditionalism is strongly correlated with opposition to gay rights," adding that "societies with pluralistic or secular religious cultures tend to enact more inclusive policies and protections" (**Norris & Inglehart, 2011**).

However, doctrinal rejection often extends beyond legal structures and penetrates the personal realm, especially for those raised in conservative faith communities. Many LGBTQ+ individuals experience internalized homophobia—the internal absorption of anti-LGBTQ+ stigma resulting in self-directed shame, spiritual dissonance[27], and a painful alienation from their religious communities. This alienation can manifest as depression, anxiety, self-harm, or suicidal ideation—exacerbated by the absence of affirming familial or communal support. Empirical studies indeed confirm these mental health outcomes. Ryan, Huebner, Diaz, and Sanchez[28] report that "LGB young adults who experienced high levels of family rejection during adolescence were 8.4 times more likely to report having attempted suicide," also facing elevated rates of depression and substance abuse (**Ryan *et al.*, 2009**). Religious condemnation was frequently a significant driver of such familial rejection.

Yet, alongside these challenges, there is growing resistance and reform. Some religious and spiritual movements have begun to reinterpret sacred texts and reshape moral teachings in favor of inclusivity. Progressive religious groups—such as the United Church of Christ[29], Muslims for Progressive Values[30], Reform Judaism[31], and the International Raelian Movement—publicly affirm LGBTQ+ dignity and advocate for their rights. In a historic response to anti-LGBTQ+ violence, Maitreya Rael issued a "Fatwa[32] of Love" in 2005, denouncing Iranian Ayatollah Al-Sistani's[33] incitement to violence and offering unconditional spiritual support to LGBTQ+ people worldwide.

Religious institutions also wield considerable influence in the political arena, particularly in shaping legislation related to LGBTQ+ rights. In the United States, for example, religious lobbies have played central roles in debates over marriage equality, gender-affirming care, and anti-discrimination laws. Whether these forces work to expand or restrict rights depends largely on how theological traditions are interpreted and enacted in the public sphere. Although traditional doctrine has often hindered LGBTQ+ acceptance, many faith communities now recognize the importance of affirming identity over dogma. The growing call to decouple religious morality from civil and sexual rights reflects an urgent need to honor the inherent dignity of every person, regardless of whom they love or how they identify.

Gender Roles & Gender Inequality: *Religious Constructs and Patriarchal Control*

Religious traditions across cultures have long played a pivotal role in shaping, reinforcing, and legitimizing gender norms, particularly in relation to human sexuality. Rooted in patriarchal ideologies, these traditions have codified binary gender constructs and prescribed rigid roles for men and women—roles that often elevate male authority while relegating women to spheres of domesticity, obedience, and sexual purity. Framed as divine mandates, these prescriptions have profoundly influenced not only individual behavior but also the broader architecture of law, education, and social expectations, serving as the ideological backbone of what many societies describe as "traditional family values." Within this framework, religious texts across traditions have encoded misogyny into divine law, positioning women as subordinate in both domestic and spiritual spheres. As Christopher Hitchens writes in his critique of religious patriarchy, "All the major religions have expressed contempt for the female and insisted upon her subjugation" (**Hitchens, 2008**). Whether through commandments that silence women, restrict their autonomy, or reduce them to vessels for male desire and lineage, sacred texts have consistently reinforced a gender hierarchy falsely sanctified as eternal truth, a reality that—when viewed through a secular lens—reveals patriarchy not as sacred, but as political, historical, and fully subject to critique, dismantling, and reimagining.

Sacred texts—such as the Bible, Qur'an, Torah, and others—contain explicit passages that reinforce gender hierarchies and prescribe sexual norms. For example, in Christianity, Ephesians 5:22–24 commands wives to submit to their husbands, casting men as the spiritual and social heads of households. While defenders may argue these are theological or historical expressions, such interpretations often carry profound sociopolitical weight, particularly when institutionalized into legal systems or wielded in policymaking. Within these frameworks, sexuality is heavily regulated: chastity, heterosexual marriage, and procreative sex are elevated as moral ideals, while any deviation—such as same-sex relationships, premarital sex, or child-free lifestyles—is pathologized or condemned.

Religious influence has shaped laws that restrict bodily autonomy and civil liberties. Examples include the criminalization of homosexuality, the limitation of reproductive rights, and the exclusion of women from leadership roles. These legal manifestations of religious doctrine uphold the belief that deviation from heteronormative, binary gender expectations is not only immoral but also socially destabilizing. As a result, individuals who diverge from prescribed norms often face stigma, reduced life opportunities, mental health challenges, and violence in many cases. Women, in particular, encounter barriers to autonomy and decision-making power, both within religious institutions and in secular society. At the same time, men are burdened by expectations of emotional stoicism[34] and dominance, making vulnerability a form of transgression.

Yet amid these constraints, change is underway. Progressive religious voices and movements are challenging traditional interpretations, urging a reexamination of sacred texts through inclusive, justice-oriented lenses. Feminist theologians in Christianity, Islam, Judaism, and other faiths are reclaiming interpretive authority and advocating for gender equality within spiritual life. These scholars question the theological underpinnings of patriarchal control[35] and reframe the divine in more expansive, egalitarian terms.

As Rosemary R. Ruether[36] warns, "If God is male, then the male is God," a stark critique that exposes the theological roots of male dominance and its societal consequences (**Ruether, 1983**). This insight continues to inspire theologians across faiths to examine how divine representations translate into power structures. In the Islamic tradition, Amina Wadud[37] advances egalitarian interpretations of the Qur'an, stating: "The Qur'an must be read with a consciousness of the historical marginalization of women in interpretive authority. Only then can we move toward a just gender ethic in Islam" (**Wadud, 2013**).

While many religious institutions continue to cling to restrictive gender ideologies, others are evolving. Progressive spiritual communities and reformist scholars are building momentum toward more inclusive, pluralistic understandings of gender and sexuality. This theological shift reflects a broader cultural awakening—one that recognizes the fluidity of gender, the diversity of sexual expression, and the universal right to dignity, equality, and self-determination.

Marriage & Family Norms: *Sanctifying the Nuclear Ideal*

Traditional religious teachings have long elevated marriage beyond a mere social contract, casting it as a sacred covenant with spiritual, moral, and reproductive significance. Rooted in centuries of clerical authority and sacred texts, this view tightly regulates sexuality—sanctioning it only within the bounds of heterosexual marriage and linking it almost exclusively to procreation. At the heart of this framework lies the nuclear family: a heterosexual couple, bound by marital vows, fulfilling predefined gender roles. This model has been upheld not just as a religious ideal but as the presumed foundation of societal stability.

Across religions such as Christianity, Islam, Judaism, and Hinduism, marriage is imbued with sacred meaning and celebrated through formal religious rites, reinforcing its legitimacy as a cultural and religious institution. Teachings within these faiths often dictate that sexual activity must be reserved for marriage, with any deviation cast as immoral or sinful. As historian Stephanie Coontz[38] explains, "Marriage has served as a linchpin[39] for organizing sexuality, parenthood, and inheritance in most cultures for centuries" (**Coontz, 2006**). In this way, religious doctrine has functioned not only to define the moral boundaries of sexual behavior but also to embed them in the legal and cultural fabric of societies.

Indeed, religious definitions of marriage have profoundly shaped legal frameworks governing marital relationships, parental rights, and inheritance. These theological constructs have historically been written into law—privileging heterosexual unions and marginalizing all others. As Lucy Robinson[40] notes, "Religion continues to exert a profound influence over the legal and social regulation of family life, often to the exclusion of those who do not conform to the dominant heterosexual marital ideal" (**Robinson, 2013**). The effects are tangible: non-traditional families, such as single parents, LGBTQ+ couples, and cohabiting partners, often find themselves stigmatized or denied legal recognition.

This exclusion is frequently justified through appeals to divine order or fears of social instability. Religious authorities have resisted reforms to expand the definition of family, arguing that such changes threaten moral cohesion. But as Sara Ahmed[41] observes, "Heteronormativity is sustained through repeated citation of religious and moral norms that mark other forms of intimacy as deviant" (**Ahmed, 2013**). These norms do more than structure law; they shape personal aspirations, instilling in individuals—especially those raised in devout environments—a belief that fulfillment and legitimacy come only through heterosexual marriage and biological parenthood. The psychological toll can be profound, leading many to repress authentic identities in pursuit of religiously sanctioned ideals.

Yet even beyond theological critique, contemporary evolutionary research further destabilizes the framing of desire as moral deviation. Biological anthropologist Helen E. Fisher[42] has demonstrated that romantic love, sexual attraction, and long-term attachment are governed by distinct but overlapping neurochemical systems shaped by evolutionary pressures—not divine command or moral failure. In *Anatomy of Love*, she writes, "Romantic love is one of the most powerful emotions on earth," describing it not as a weakness but as a biologically embedded drive (**Fisher, 1982**). Her earlier work, *The Sex Contract*, challenges the assumption that lifelong monogamy is a universal moral constant, suggesting instead that serial bonding and relational transitions are recurrent features of human social organization (**Fisher, 1982**). When desire is understood as an evolved human capacity rather than a spiritual defect, the moral architecture built upon guilt, repression, and purity begins to lose its authority. The issue is not that human beings are flawed—but that certain religious systems have misdiagnosed biology as sin.

Nevertheless, transformation is underway. Progressive movements within numerous faith communities are challenging restrictive doctrines around family and marriage. Denominations such as the United Church of Christ, the Episcopal Church[43], Reform Judaism, and the International Raelian Movement have taken bold steps toward inclusivity—celebrating same-sex unions, ordaining LGBTQ+ clergy, and redefining marriage beyond heterosexual norms. The Raelian Movement, for instance, rejects the very premise of marriage as a binding legal contract. As Rael often says, "Marriage, whether religious or civil, is useless. You cannot sign a contract to unite living individuals, who are bound to change because they are alive… Any contract can only destroy [over time] the harmony existing between two individuals. When we feel loved, we feel free to love, but when we have signed a contract, we feel like prisoners who are forced to love each other, and sooner or later we begin to hate each other" (**Rael, 1974**).

In this vision, authentic love thrives not through obligation but through freedom, fluidity, and mutual choice. These emerging spiritual paradigms do more than reinterpret sacred texts—they push back against the notion that love, care, and commitment must conform to narrow theological frameworks. By embracing chosen families, gender equity, and inclusive understandings of sexuality, these voices affirm that spiritual depth can coexist with modern notions of identity, freedom, and human rights.

Same-Sex Marriage: *The Clash Between Tradition and Equality*

The debate over same-sex marriage sits at the crossroads of religious tradition, civil liberties, and evolving cultural norms. For centuries, dominant religious doctrines have framed marriage as a sacred covenant—exclusively between a man and a woman—anchored in procreation and the maintenance of social order. This framing embeds heteronormative marriage deep within both theological and societal consciousness, rendering any challenge to its definition as a perceived threat to moral stability.

Yet over the past few decades, public values have shifted decisively toward greater recognition of individual rights and equality. A pivotal moment came in 2015, when the U.S. Supreme Court, in *Obergefell v. Hodges*, held that "the Fourteenth Amendment... requires States to license a marriage between two people of the same sex" on equal terms with opposite-sex couples (**Hermann, 2015**). This landmark ruling reframed marriage not simply as a religious or cultural institution, but as a constitutionally protected civil right. It affirmed that same-sex couples, like heterosexual ones, possess the fundamental freedom to marry, thereby grounding marital rights in equal protection under the law[44].

Public opinion quickly evolved in tandem with legal progress. Data from the Public Religion Research Institute[45] (PRRI) showed that, by 2016, a majority of adherents in several religious groups—including white mainline Protestants (63%), white Catholics (63%), and Jews (73%)—expressed support for same-sex marriage. Even within traditionally conservative communities such as Orthodox Christians, support reached 59%. This data signaled an emerging cultural reconciliation between faith and equality in some circles.

However, resistance persists. In 2025, conservative efforts continue to challenge marriage equality under the banner of religious freedom. One high-profile example is former Kentucky clerk Kim Davis, who filed a 90-page petition asking the U.S. Supreme Court to overturn *Obergefell*, calling the decision a "legal fiction" and claiming it violated her First Amendment rights to religious expression and free speech. Although such efforts are widely regarded as unlikely to succeed legally, they reflect an ongoing political strategy: to recast religious liberty as a justification for undermining anti-discrimination protections. These challenges keep the culture war around marriage equality alive, emphasizing that legal victories do not necessarily equate to cultural resolution.

Empirical research helps explain the root of this resistance. In a landmark study spanning five datasets from the U.S. and Canada (N = 1,673), Van der Toorn *et al.*[46] applied *system justification theory*[47] to analyze the relationship between religiosity and opposition to same-sex marriage. They concluded that "the relationship between religiosity[48] and opposition to same-sex marriage was mediated by sexual prejudice and resistance to change, rather than by benevolent motives or theological interpretations per se" (**Van der Toorn *et al.*, 2017**). This finding suggests that resistance to marriage equality is less about doctrine and more about preserving traditional hierarchies and resisting social transformation.

Thus, the conflict over same-sex marriage extends beyond legal rulings or theological interpretations. It represents a deeper cultural tension between inclusion and exclusion, between dynamic social progress and the inertia of longstanding power structures. In this context, the battle for same-sex marriage rights continues not only in legislatures and courtrooms but also within the hearts and minds of societies learning to reconcile freedom with tradition.

Censorship: *Protecting Virtue and Policing Thought*

Religious institutions have long used censorship[49] not only as a means of regulating behavior but as a powerful tool for shaping thought, especially in matters of sexuality. While such efforts are frequently justified as necessary to protect moral virtue, in practice they suppress expressions of identity, curtail intellectual freedom, and restrict the flow of knowledge. As the Free Speech Center[50] cautions, "by restricting information and discouraging freedom of thought, censors undermine one of the primary functions of education: teaching students how to think for themselves" (**MTSU Free Speech Center, 2023**).

The reach of religion-based censorship extends far beyond places of worship, infiltrating public policy, school curricula, media representation, and even family structures. Traditional religious groups have frequently supported laws that codify their sexual ethics—prioritizing abstinence, heterosexuality, and binary gender roles. The result has often been the censorship of any discourse that deviates from these norms: bans on discussing sexual orientation in schools, the removal of books reflecting LGBTQ+ experiences, and restrictions on access to reproductive healthcare and sexuality education. In many countries, these religiously motivated policies go so far as to criminalize homosexuality, effectively extinguishing the right to self-expression for entire segments of the population.

Censorship also takes a visible toll on artistic expression and media. Works that portray nontraditional families, gender diversity, or sexual autonomy are frequently targeted for exclusion through book bans, content restrictions, and funding withdrawals. These acts not only stifle creative freedom but also silence public conversations around vital human experiences. As Rev. Walter Raushenbush[51] argues, "Censorship is a religious freedom issue—book banning is a political strategy that could silence diverse religious voices and traditions that are a major part of the rich social fabric of America" (**Raushsenbush, 2024**).

Education is particularly vulnerable. When religious doctrine infiltrates public school policy, comprehensive sexuality education is often replaced with abstinence-only curricula that fail to address consent, contraception, gender identity, and sexual orientation, and thereby fostering a climate of ignorance, stigma, and shame. Students are left unequipped to make informed decisions or understand themselves. In *Bantam Books, Inc. v. Sullivan* (1963), the U.S. Supreme Court warned that even informal efforts to pressure booksellers or educators into moral conformity could amount to unconstitutional censorship. Justice Brennan wrote that such tactics "constitute a system of informal censorship," which can be just as dangerous as overt repression.

Despite these enduring challenges, resistance to censorship continues to gain strength. Artists, educators, activists, and inclusive spiritual leaders are actively reclaiming the right to speak openly about sexuality and identity. Movements advancing LGBTQ+ rights, academic freedom, and comprehensive sexuality education reflect the growing cultural awareness that censorship rooted in religious orthodoxy is increasingly seen as incompatible with pluralism, democracy, and human dignity. This evolution signals the gradual unraveling of long-standing taboos and underscores the persistent tension between religious conservatism and the universal right to self-expression. More and more, society is recognizing that the protection of so-called 'virtue' must not come at the expense of truth, identity, or human dignity. At its core, the fight against censorship is a battle for the soul of democracy, one in which diverse voices must be heard, not silenced.

There remains, however, one notable and ethically compelling exception to the general condemnation of censorship, and that is the suppression of content that incites hatred, violence, or discrimination. To this end, Rael, founder of the International Raelian Movement, was the first and only spiritual leaders to call upon the United Nations to take formal action. As early as 1992, Rael proposed the creation of an international body tasked with evaluating all religious texts and doctrines to identify and censor elements that promote violence, misogyny[52], homophobia, or ethnic hatred. He emphasized that such censorship was not an attack on religious freedom, which is enshrined in the Universal Declaration of Human Rights, but a necessary safeguard against the misuse of sacred authority. Rael's proposal emphasized the need for moral responsibility that transcends misplaced scriptural intolerance. In his words: "We must prevent religions from hiding behind freedom of belief to justify oppression, war, violence, discrimination, or sexual abuse" **(Rael, 1992)**.

This groundbreaking proposal called for a distinction between freedom of belief and freedom to harm. Its purpose was not to abolish religion or suppress spiritual traditions, but to challenge and reform those doctrines that undermine human rights while masquerading as divine command. As Rael argues, true spiritual evolution demands moral accountability, and no scripture, however revered, should be exempt from scrutiny if it incites hatred or violence.

In this context, censorship becomes not a weapon of repression but a mechanism for protection—an ethical imperative in the face of ideologies that seek to dehumanize others. A peaceful and just global civilization cannot tolerate the unchecked spread of doctrines that advocate for the subjugation or extermination of entire groups. By calling for the cleansing of hate from religious texts, Rael was not rejecting religion itself but urging its alignment with the universal values of peace, dignity, human rights, and love.

Interfaith Relationships: *Love Across Doctrinal Borders*

Interfaith relationships—romantic partnerships between individuals of different religious backgrounds—exist at the intersection of love and doctrine, where emotional bonds encounter theological boundaries. While such unions have long existed throughout history, they continue to provoke controversy in many religious communities, where marriage is regarded not merely as a personal choice but as a sacred covenant intended to preserve and perpetuate shared beliefs and values. Traditional religious teachings often advocate for endogamy, or marrying within one's own faith, on the grounds that religious homogeneity ensures marital harmony, moral continuity, and the proper religious upbringing of children. This emphasis creates significant social, familial, and institutional barriers to interfaith unions.

Endogamy, however, functions as more than a theological preference—it serves as a powerful mechanism of group cohesion and boundary maintenance. As Michael Rosenfeld[53] explains, "Sociologists have long recognized that endogamy[54], or marriage within the group, is a fundamental indicator of group cohesion and solidarity, and also of social isolation from other groups" (**Rosenfeld, 2008**). Religious doctrines concerning marriage, gender roles, and sexuality often reinforce these boundaries by either restricting or outright prohibiting unions across faith lines. In many Islamic contexts, for example, Muslim women are generally forbidden from marrying outside the faith, while Orthodox Judaism does not typically recognize marriages between Jews and non-Jews. Such restrictions often reflect anxieties over conversion, dilution of doctrine, and the potential erosion of community identity, especially when children are raised outside the dominant faith.

These theological tensions often play out in intimate, daily realities. When one religion prescribes strict gender hierarchies and the other promotes egalitarian ideals, relational dynamics can become strained. Disagreements over marital roles, spiritual obligations, or expectations of obedience may pressure one partner to compromise deeply held beliefs or personal autonomy. As Muluneh Animut Tilahun *et al.*[55] observe in their study of Muslim–Orthodox Christian marriages in South Wollo, interfaith couples must often "build relational resilience through adaptive strategies such as practicing mutual respect and prioritizing shared values despite their religious differences" (**Tilahun *et al.*, 2025**). This dynamic of identity negotiation becomes essential to both the survival and the deepening of the relationship.

The challenges intensify when factoring in traditional religious views on sexuality. Many faiths continue to promote sexual abstinence outside of marriage, define morality in heteronormative terms, and restrict expressions of sexuality to narrow doctrinal frameworks. As a result, interfaith couples may face moral condemnation, familial rejection, or even spiritual excommunication[56]. They are often excluded from religious rituals, denied access to community support systems, or pressured to conform through conversion or separation. In environments where religious conformity is socially enforced, such ostracism can have severe psychological consequences—creating a climate of secrecy, guilt, and emotional alienation. Individuals may be forced to choose between romantic love and religious loyalty, a decision fraught with internal conflict and social risk.

In some countries where religious law shapes civil codes, these pressures are codified into legislation. Interfaith marriages may face legal restrictions, a lack of official recognition, or discriminatory provisions in areas such as inheritance, divorce, and child custody. Nancy Foner and Richard Alba[57] insightfully note that "when religious homogeneity underpins social cohesion, interfaith marriages frequently emerge as contested sites where the boundaries of national belonging are redrawn and enforced" (**Foner & Alba, 2008**). In such contexts, love across faiths becomes a political act—one that challenges not only personal belief systems but national ideologies and legal frameworks.

Despite these barriers, change is on the horizon. Progressive religious leaders and reformist voices within various faiths have begun to embrace a more inclusive view of love and partnership. Interfaith dialogues, ecumenical movements[58], and evolving theological interpretations are slowly reshaping rigid norms. Some communities now recognize the spiritual value of interfaith unions, especially when they are rooted in mutual respect, shared ethics, and compassion.

And yet, despite these enduring barriers, signs of transformation are emerging. Across various faith traditions, progressive religious leaders and reformist theologians are reexamining the rigidity of doctrinal exclusivity. Interfaith dialogues, ecumenical initiatives, and inclusive interpretations of sacred texts are giving rise to new paradigms of partnership—ones rooted not in conformity, but in mutual respect, ethical alignment, and spiritual curiosity. Some communities now embrace the possibility that interfaith unions, far from threatening religious identity, can in fact model a deeper kind of compassion, tolerance, and coexistence.

As Jürgen Habermas[59] contends, "A post-secular society must make room for both religious and secular reasoning in the public sphere, including the deeply personal space of love and family" (**Habermas, 2008**). Interfaith relationships embody this possibility. They challenge tribalism[60], expand empathy, and offer blueprints for living together in a pluralistic world. Ultimately, these relationships are more than romantic commitments—they are courageous acts of spiritual bridge-building. They call for a reimagined understanding of love, one that transcends doctrinal borders and honors the human capacity to connect across difference.

Moral Dilemmas: *When Conscience and Doctrine Collide*

One of the most profound ethical tensions in contemporary life emerges when personal conscience comes into conflict with religious doctrine. As individuals navigate complex questions around sexuality, gender identity, reproductive autonomy, and family structure, they are often caught between an internal moral compass and the external dictates of their faith. These are not hypothetical or abstract tensions—they are deeply personal, often existential dilemmas, where the cost of either choice can feel unbearably high.

By definition, a moral dilemma involves competing ethical imperatives, where choosing one path necessarily entails violating the other. Within religious contexts, this tension is frequently heightened by fear: fear of divine punishment, social ostracism, or eternal damnation, and can become paralyzing. As Howard Mason[61] puts it, moral dilemmas constitute "a genuine ontological conflict," in which all available options require some form of betrayal—either of one's faith or of one's inner sense of truth (**Mason, 1996**).

Traditional religious teachings, particularly within monotheistic faiths, have long claimed exclusive moral authority over sexuality, gender roles, and family structures. But conscience often charts a different course. Many believers find that their intuitive sense of justice, empathy, or love clashes with doctrines that condemn homosexuality, prohibit contraception, or uphold rigid gender hierarchies. Centuries ago, Thomas Aquinas acknowledged this fundamental tension, asserting that "a man is bound to follow his conscience even if it is erroneous, for to do otherwise is to sin" (**Aquinas, 1947**). That radical insight still resonates today. As Cecil Coady[62] notes, in modern ethical discourse, conscience is understood as "a deeply personal, complex faculty—not merely a reflection of indoctrination but a capacity for moral reasoning that can evolve beyond religious authority" (**Coady, 2023**).

These conflicts come into sharp focus in matters of sexual and reproductive rights. Consider a devout Catholic woman who chooses birth control to preserve her health but is told by her church that this choice is morally wrong. Or a gay man raised in a conservative religious community who must decide between living authentically and being accepted by his faith. Such individuals are not rejecting morality—they are striving to live it more fully, reconciling moral integrity with lived experience.

When religious institutions claim moral supremacy, they demand that adherents suppress their inner ethical voice in favor of rigid submission. But this model is ill-suited to the moral complexity of modern life. As Stephen Genuis[63] argues in the context of medical ethics, "conscience-based refusals may in fact represent the highest form of integrity when institutional expectations conflict with deeply held moral convictions" (**Genuis, 2013**). This perspective holds broader relevance: true morality cannot be reduced to compliance.

The clash between conscience and ideology also raises critical questions about the limits of religious freedom in pluralistic societies. When religious doctrines are codified into law—shaping policies on abortion access, LGBTQ+ rights, or sexuality education—they often override individual autonomy and marginalize those whose consciences diverge from dominant theologies. In doing so, they risk turning religion into an instrument of coercion rather than a source of moral insight.

In a world marked by diversity of belief and evolving moral awareness, the role of conscience must be reclaimed. Ethics grounded in empathy, critical thought, and personal experience often offer a more humane and just moral compass than doctrines rooted in antiquated hierarchies that no longer resonate with evolving understandings of dignity and human rights. Following one's conscience in the face of religious condemnation is not rebellion—it is moral courage. As this book affirms, true ethical growth lies not in blind obedience but in the fearless pursuit of authenticity, accountability, and justice.

Sexual Prohibitions: *Religious Control in the Name of Morality*

Throughout history, organized religions—especially the monotheistic traditions of Judaism, Christianity, and Islam—have played a central role in constructing and enforcing sexual prohibitions under the guise of upholding moral order. These prohibitions have shaped not only personal behavior but also influenced civil laws, educational systems, and broader societal norms. From regulating premarital sex to condemning masturbation, homosexuality, and non-procreative acts, religious institutions have long positioned sexuality as something to be monitored, disciplined, restricted, and controlled.

Rooted in ancient scriptures and patriarchal interpretations, many of these prohibitions emerged as mechanisms for maintaining authority over bodies, reinforcing gender roles, and sustaining rigid social structures. As Michel Foucault explains in *The History of Sexuality*, religion reframed sexuality as a moral issue—one requiring confession, surveillance, and discipline. "Sexuality was carefully confined; it moved into the home. The conjugal family took custody of it and absorbed it into the serious function of reproduction" (**Foucault, 1978**). This moral architecture upheld heterosexual marriage as the sole legitimate context for sexual activity, casting all other expressions as deviant, impure, or sinful.

The Catholic Church, for example, has long prohibited both premarital sex and contraception, asserting that the primary function of sex is procreation. Similarly, many Islamic scholars and evangelical Christian leaders have denounced homosexuality as sinful or unnatural, reinforcing heteronormativity through theological condemnation. These doctrines have not only policed private conduct but have also justified political and legal actions—from anti-sodomy laws [64] and abortion bans to restrictions on LGBTQ+ rights. Far from being abstract teachings, such prohibitions shape real-world policies and inflict lasting psychological harm. As sociologist Linda Woodhead[65] observes, "religions have sacralized certain sexual norms, embedding them in a sacred order that makes questioning or deviating from them not just rebellious but blasphemous" (**Woodhead, 2008**). This sacralization of sexuality has fostered guilt, shame, and internalized stigma, particularly among those whose identities or desires diverge from religious ideals.

These sexual controls are deeply gendered as well. Religious prohibitions have historically imposed far stricter expectations on women than on men, reinforcing patriarchal power both within religious communities and in secular societies. Emphasis on female virginity, modesty, and obedience reflects a broader logic in which women's bodies are viewed as symbols of family and communal honor. As scholar Leila Ahmed[66] explains in *Women and Gender in Islam*, sexual ethics rooted in religious doctrine have often served to "perpetuate male authority and define women's moral worth in terms of sexual purity" (**Ahmed, 2021**). In this context, sexual control becomes not only a matter of individual morality, but also a strategy of social containment—particularly for women.

Despite the persistence of these doctrines, global shifts are challenging the theological underpinnings of sexual control. Increasingly, both secular movements and progressive religious voices are calling attention to the harm caused by repressive sexual norms. The growing visibility and acceptance of diverse sexual orientations, the movement for comprehensive sexuality education, and the call for bodily autonomy are part of a broader cultural shift toward affirming sexual expression as a human right rather than a moral peril. Still, the legacy of religious sexual prohibitions remains deeply entrenched in many societies, and efforts to dismantle them often meet fierce resistance. In this context, examining the origins and functions of these prohibitions is not only a historical inquiry but a critical step toward liberating human sexuality from centuries of religiously sanctioned repression.

Yet despite the enduring power of these doctrines, cultural and theological shifts are challenging the foundations of religious sexual repression. Progressive theologians[67], feminist scholars, LGBTQ+ advocates, and human rights organizations are exposing the harms inflicted by rigid moral codes and calling for a reimagining of sexuality as a dimension of human dignity rather than moral peril. The increasing visibility of diverse sexual identities, the global movement for comprehensive sexuality education, and renewed calls for bodily autonomy reflect a broader awakening: one that reclaims sexual expression as a fundamental human right.

Still, the legacy of religious sexual prohibitions remains deeply embedded in laws, traditions, and collective consciousness. As such, dismantling these doctrines requires more than critique—it demands historical understanding, cultural courage, and the affirmation of pleasure, love, and desire as worthy dimensions of the human experience. To liberate sexuality from centuries of religious control and sanctioned repression is not to forsake morality, but to reclaim it in the service of freedom, dignity, and truth.

Female Genital Mutilation (FGM): *The Blade of Patriarchy*

Female Genital Mutilation[68] (FGM) stands as one of the most egregious violations of bodily autonomy—an enduring expression of patriarchal control masked by appeals to religion, culture, and morality. Defined as the partial or total removal of the external female genitalia for non-medical reasons, FGM is internationally recognized as a human rights abuse. Yet despite decades of global advocacy, over 200 million girls and women alive today have been subjected to this practice, primarily in parts of Africa, the Middle East, and Asia (**UNICEF[69], 2021**).

The roots of FGM lie not in theology but in deeply entrenched patriarchal ideologies that conflate a woman's worth with her chastity, obedience, and reproductive function. In many communities, an uncircumcised girl is stigmatized as impure, promiscuous, or unfit for marriage. These perceptions are often reinforced by religious leaders or cultural gatekeepers, even though no major religion explicitly mandates FGM. As Ellen Gruenbaum[70] observes, "FGM is not about religion—it is about power, control, and the regulation of female sexuality" (**Gruenbaum, 2001**). Though framed as a rite of passage or a symbol of family honor, the practice is a cultural construct and ultimately about suppressing female sexual autonomy and the right to pleasure. Women's bodies become repositories of communal morality, with their compliance serving to uphold familial reputation and social cohesion. In this framework, sexuality is not a private experience but a public matter subject to surveillance and discipline.

Ironically, it is often women themselves—mothers, grandmothers, midwives—who perform or perpetuate FGM. Some critics argue that this complicity weakens the patriarchal critique. However, a deeper analysis reveals that these women operate within rigid systems where their social legitimacy, economic security, and moral identity are bound to the maintenance of tradition. As Patricia Akweongo *et al.*[71] explain, "Circumcised women are the main source of social support for the practice, which they exercise through peer pressure in concert with co-wives" (**Akweongo *et al.*, 2021**). In this context, participation in FGM is not a free choice, but a survival strategy within a tightly regulated moral economy.

The physical and psychological consequences of FGM are devastating. The procedure frequently leads to chronic pain, infection, complications during childbirth, infertility, and heightened risk of neonatal death. Psychologically, it can result in trauma, anxiety, depression, and a disconnection from one's own sexuality. The World Health Organization[72] emphasizes that "FGM has no health benefits, and it harms girls and women in many ways. It is a violation of their rights to health, security and physical integrity." Beyond these clinical harms, FGM perpetuates a broader culture of silence, shame, and bodily dissociation—a form of gendered violence that cuts not only the body but also the spirit.

While legislation banning FGM exists in many countries, enforcement remains inconsistent. Deeply rooted social norms, religious customs, and the threat of ostracism continue to sustain the practice. Therefore, eradication requires more than criminalization; it demands a holistic approach that includes education, community-led dialogue, survivor-centered advocacy, and the empowerment of women and girls. Essentially, interventions must be culturally sensitive and locally driven, led by local voices and survivors—those most affected and most equipped to inspire change from within.

FGM epitomizes the dangerous convergence of religion, tradition, and patriarchal power—the mutilation of the female body in the name of morality. It illustrates how sacred texts and cultural customs, when filtered through the lens of control, can justify systemic violence. As this book repeatedly affirms, ending such practices necessitates more than reforming laws—it requires transforming consciousness. We must replace the blade of patriarchy with the voice of liberation, reaffirming that morality should never be built on the subjugation of bodies or the silencing of pleasure.

The Sacrament of Reconciliation: *Absolving Sin and Dodging Accountability*

The Sacrament of Reconciliation[73] (also known as Confession or Penance) occupies a central role in many Christian traditions, particularly Catholicism. Framed as a sacred rite, it offers the faithful an opportunity to confess sins, express contrition, perform penance, and receive absolution from a priest, thereby restoring their communion with God and the Church. According to Catholic doctrine, "through the sacrament, the faithful are absolved of sins committed after Baptism" and reintegrated into the spiritual community. Yet behind this solemn ritual lies a more complex and troubling dynamic—one that reveals the interplay between institutional authority, moral control, and the evasion of public accountability.

While Reconciliation is intended to provide spiritual renewal, it can also serve as a ritualized means of avoiding consequences—particularly in cases of grave harm. Nowhere is this more evident than in the Catholic Church's response to clerical sexual abuse. In upholding the absolute confidentiality of the confessional, Church authorities have prioritized sacramental protocol over transparency, justice, and the protection of the vulnerable. As *Commonweal* magazine reported, Vatican officials have maintained that even priests who confess to the sexual abuse of minors "should be absolved and should generally not be encouraged... to disclose his acts publicly or to his superiors" (**Commonweal, 2010**). In this logic, forgiveness operates within a closed circuit, disconnected from social redress or legal consequences, and the confessional becomes not a path to transformation, but a license for continued harm and a shield for impunity.

Importantly, Christianity is not alone in confronting the ethical complexities of repentance. In Islam, the act of *tawbah* (repentance) emphasizes a sincere return to Allah, with personal remorse and the intention not to repeat the wrongdoing as key elements of divine forgiveness. Yet many Islamic scholars stress that when harm has been done to another, repentance must include restitution to the injured party—acknowledging a moral obligation that transcends personal guilt. Likewise, Jewish ethics, particularly through Maimonides[74] teachings on *Teshuvah*, insist that atonement for interpersonal harm is incomplete until the wronged individual is directly appeased: "Repentance for a sin committed against another person is not complete until one appeases the person harmed" (**Mishneh Torah, Laws of Teshuvah[75] 2:9**). These traditions highlight a key moral distinction—while some religious frameworks demand interpersonal accountability as part of spiritual reconciliation, others may allow absolution to occur in a private, introspective vacuum, thereby sidestepping broader social ethics and restorative justice.

Critics have long questioned the consequences of offering private absolution without public reckoning. As theologian Hans Küng[76] warned, institutional religion "becomes an instrument of suppression when it offers absolution without transformation" (**Küng, 2007**). In such cases, the function of confession risks becoming a bureaucratic transaction—a kind of spiritual laundering devoid of ethical reflection or restitution. Moreover, legal protections such as the seal of confession can allow individuals in positions of power to remain unchallenged, even in the face of systemic abuse. This is not merely a theological issue but a civic one. Efforts to mandate the reporting of confessed crimes, particularly child abuse, have met strong resistance from religious institutions, citing freedom of religion. Yet, as legal scholar Kent Greenawalt[77] argues, "The freedom to practice religion does not extend to shielding criminal acts under the guise of doctrine" (**Greenawalt, 2007**). The tension between sacred confidentiality and public justice remains an unresolved moral fault line in many societies.

Without accountability, there can be no justice. Redemption must be grounded not only in remorse but in the conscious effort to repair harm and restore balance through meaningful action. According to Raelian teachings, genuine atonement requires more than internal contrition—it demands full responsibility, transformative action, and tangible contributions that outweigh the harm inflicted. In this view, redemption is measured not by the ability to elicit forgiveness, but by the depth of one's commitment to healing and service.

This understanding of accountability is not retributive. It is restorative. It invites the individual not into shame, but into a deeper encounter with empathy, growth, and responsibility. As Rael reminds us, "It's always better to be kind toward others than to be right, because when you are kind, you're always right"— a reminder that true moral clarity emerges not from rigid dogma, but from compassion in action. In the end, reconciliation must never be a spiritual escape hatch. It must be a courageous moral act—anchored in transparency and oriented toward justice. For atonement to be real, it must not only demand humility but also honesty and a sincere desire to repair.

Legislating anti-Human Rights Laws: *Doctrine Over Human Dignity*

Religious traditions—once rooted in sacred texts, rituals, and the private sphere of spiritual life—have increasingly entered the legislative domain, exerting tangible, and often harmful, influence over public policy. Doctrines originally meant to guide the faithful now shape civil law, transforming moral prescriptions into state mandates. This convergence between faith and governance has led to a global crisis in human rights, where the authority of religious dogma undermines the foundational principles enshrined in international frameworks such as the Universal Declaration of Human Rights (UDHR) and the International Covenant on Civil and Political Rights[78] (ICCPR).

Across continents, religious morality is codified into law in ways that criminalize difference and curtail freedoms. From bans on same-sex relationships and gender expression to the criminalization of abortion, apostasy, and sexual autonomy, entire legal systems are being reshaped to reflect the tenets of conservative theology rather than the ethics of pluralism. These laws disproportionately target women, LGBTQ+ individuals, religious minorities, and others whose existence or choices fall outside traditionalist interpretations of scripture.

In Iran, for example, apostasy and consensual same-sex conduct are punishable by death—a stark illustration of theology weaponized by the state. In northern Nigeria, Sharia law allows for public flogging, stoning, and imprisonment for so-called moral infractions, including premarital sex and same-sex relations (**Human Dignity Trust**[79], **2024**). Uganda's 2023 Anti-Homosexuality Act—backed by American evangelical networks—imposes life imprisonment and, in some cases, the death penalty, all in the name of "biblical values." These are not anomalies. They are the logical outcome of allowing religious absolutism to become legislative authority.

The core issue is not faith itself, but the transformation of belief into coercive legal norms. What begins as a moral framework for the devout becomes a compulsory standard for the entire populace—including those who do not share those convictions. The result is a system where theological purity supersedes civic equality. As legal scholar Katherine Franke[80] notes, "When religion enters the courtroom or the legislature to define the public good, it tends to do so in ways that constrict rights, not expand them" (**Franke, 2015**).

This is especially clear in the realm of reproductive rights. In El Salvador, abortion is criminalized under all circumstances—including rape and life-threatening pregnancies—an absolutist stance rooted in Catholic doctrine. Dozens of women have been imprisoned for miscarriages, charged with aggravated homicide in a legal system that privileges fetal rights over women's autonomy (**Center for Reproductive Rights**[81], **2023**). Poland, a country with a strong Catholic identity, recently enacted sweeping abortion restrictions after sustained lobbying by religious groups. The European Court of Human Rights[82] later found the country in violation of international law, citing infringements on the right to privacy and freedom from inhumane treatment (**ECHR, 2022**).

Even in ostensibly secular democracies, creeping theocratization is on the rise. Religious lobbies exert disproportionate influence on legislation, from limiting comprehensive sexuality education to banning gender-affirming care. In such contexts, freedom of religion is not simply protected—it is weaponized, leveraged to erode the rights of others. The UDHR's Article 18 guarantees the right to freedom of religion or belief—but it is balanced by other rights: to equality before the law (Article 7), to freedom from cruel or degrading treatment (Article 5), and to personal autonomy and dignity. When religious ideology becomes the basis for civil legislation, this delicate balance is shattered. One group's theological conviction becomes another's legal oppression.

The United Nations Human Rights Committee (UNHRC) has repeatedly condemned laws that privilege one religion over others or that criminalize sexual and reproductive choices based on religious belief. In 2019, UN Special Rapporteur on Freedom of Religion or Belief, Ahmed Shaheed[83], warned: "States must refrain from using religion as a justification for laws and policies that violate human rights—especially those of women, LGBTQ+ people, and religious minorities" (**Shaheed, 2019**).

At its heart, this is more than a legal or political dilemma—it is a philosophical clash between two moral paradigms: the ethics of divine command versus the ethics of human dignity. The former insists on obedience to immutable laws believed to be God-given; the latter places the autonomy, welfare, and freedom of individuals at the moral center. When religious doctrine becomes law, the citizen is reduced to a subject, no longer a moral agent but a vessel for conformity. The consequences are dire. These are not abstract debates but lived realities. People are jailed, tortured, executed, or driven into exile because of who they love, what they believe, or how they express their identity. Legal systems rooted in religious absolutism do not protect; they punish. They do not promote virtue; they enforce submission.

These injustices are not isolated but are systemic, embedded in frameworks that elevate dogma over dignity. That is why *Separation of Church and Sex* is not only timely but necessary. This book seeks to illuminate the moral distortions and human suffering caused by the entanglement of religion and law, and to champion a future where human rights, pleasure, dignity, and freedom are no longer sacrificed at the altar of outdated dogma.

Sex for Procreation: *When Pleasure Becomes a Sin*

Across centuries and cultures, religious institutions have sought to define and restrict the purpose of human sexuality, often casting sexual pleasure as sinful unless confined to heterosexual marriage and reproduction. Within this framework, any expression of sexuality not oriented toward procreation is commonly viewed as morally suspect, spiritually dangerous, or outright forbidden. This perspective, especially prominent in Christian thought, has been enshrined in doctrine, moral codes, and law, shaping private behaviors and public policies alike. Rather than celebrate sexuality as a natural, life-affirming force, many religious traditions have cast it as a potent danger requiring strict regulation and tolerated only when it fulfills reproductive and marital roles deemed religiously acceptable.

This paradigm, deeply embedded in scripture and reinforced by centuries of theological interpretation, has profoundly shaped cultural norms, laws, and individual sexual identities. In Christian doctrine, marital sex is seen as possessing both connecting and procreative functions. The *Catechism of the Catholic Church* affirms that "conjugal love… aims at a deeply personal unity… [and] remains ordered toward the procreation of human life" (**Catholic theology of sexuality, 2025**). Pope John Paul II's *Theology of the Body* further elucidates this view, portraying sexual union as a reflection of divine design, and condemning contraception as a disruption of this sacred symbolism. The encyclical *Humanae Vitae* takes this further, declaring that any sexual act which "intentionally frustrates" procreation violates both natural and divine law.

The philosophical roots of this worldview stretch back to early Church Fathers. Augustine taught that the Fall imbued sexual pleasure with moral ambiguity, associating it with human frailty and sin. Athenagoras of Athens[84] went so far as to claim that "the purpose of marriage was the procreation and education of children," positioning pleasure as secondary, if not suspect. Over time, such interpretations hardened into doctrine, marginalizing the role of sensuality and pleasure, and reinforcing guilt-based moral frameworks.

Islamic teachings likewise frame sexuality as a divine gift, but one tightly bound to marriage and childbearing. While some schools permit contraception with mutual consent, the moral weight of sexual activity remains tied to reproduction and religious duty. In Jewish rabbinical tradition, there is more room for acknowledging pleasure—particularly through the concept of Onah[85], the husband's obligation to provide sexual satisfaction to his wife. Yet even here, the emphasis is often filtered through patriarchal and heteronormative lenses, with childbearing and lineage preservation playing central roles.

This legacy of religious teachings that have historically sought to confine sexual expression within rigid moral boundaries is profound, and its impact is far-reaching. For generations, religiously influenced policies and cultural pressures have framed sex as an act of duty rather than delight. Non-procreative sexual acts—such as contraception, masturbation, and same-sex intimacy—are condemned or shamed, even within loving, consensual relationships. These doctrines have shaped civil law, cultural education, and even global health policies, criminalizing contraception, banning LGBTQ+ intimacy, and obstructing comprehensive sexuality education.

In many countries, theological values masquerading as public morality have become state-sponsored tools of repression, regulating not only what people do with their bodies but also what they are allowed to feel and believe about them. These inherited frameworks have led to a tragic and enduring disconnection between body and mind, sensual joy and spiritual integrity. Sexual expression—especially when divorced from procreation—has been tightly regulated and subordinated to religious dogma that equates pleasure with moral corruption. Many individuals internalize these prohibitions, resulting in profound guilt, shame, and anxiety around their erotic selves. What should be a source of joy, connection, and exploration becomes a site of moral conflict and internalized repression. Policies in several countries have even criminalized contraception, LGBTQ+ intimacy, and comprehensive sexuality education under the guise of "moral preservation," revealing how theological ideals can morph into legal oppression and shape not only physical autonomy but also the very narratives people are taught to believe about their bodies.

And yet, not all religious or spiritual traditions reject pleasure. The biblical *Song of Solomon* unabashedly celebrates erotic love and bodily delight with no explicit link to reproduction (**Rainbow, 2007**). Eastern traditions such as Hinduism and Tantric Buddhism go further, presenting sexual pleasure as sacred. The *Kama Sutra* presents kama (pleasure) as one of life's four legitimate aims, viewing erotic connection not merely as carnal, but as a path to spiritual intimacy, joy, and personal balance (**Doniger, 2003**). These traditions suggest that the fear of sexuality, so deeply entrenched in Abrahamic religions, is not universal, but culturally conditioned.

Into this diverse philosophical landscape, Raelian teachings offer a bold and liberating counter-narrative. According to Rael, sexuality is not a dangerous impulse to be controlled but a sacred and life-affirming force—an essential expression of our humanity and a gateway to personal and spiritual blossoming. Raelism celebrates pleasure, sensuality, and sexual diversity not only as natural, but as ethically and spiritually vital. The body is not a vessel of sin but a temple of sensations, discoveries, pleasure, love, and transcendence. This sex-positive ethos embraces consensual sexual expression in all its forms, including masturbation, polyamory, same-sex love, and non-reproductive intercourse. In Raelian thought, true obscenity lies not in erotic exploration, but in its systematic repression—especially when used to control women, demonize LGBTQ+ individuals, or withhold life-affirming sexuality education from the young. Raelism honors the legacy of Epicurean ethics, advocating for a life rooted in pleasure, harmony, and compassion. Sexual freedom, in this context, is not a luxury but a cornerstone of peace, equality, and global happiness.

Ultimately, *Separation of Church and Sex* seeks to restore sexuality to its rightful place—not as a taboo or sin, but as a profound, life-enhancing expression of freedom and joy. It urges us to rethink sex not as a duty to fulfill or a temptation to resist, but as a dynamic, ethical, and spiritually enriching part of the human experience. When disentangled from guilt and dogma, sexuality emerges as a healing force that is capable of nurturing intimacy, expanding consciousness, and celebrating the beauty of our embodied lives. We do not need to earn the right to feel good in our own bodies. We were born with it. To reclaim sexuality is to reclaim sovereignty over our bodies, our desires, and the stories we tell about them.

It is a radical act of resistance against centuries of shame and silence, and a step toward a world where sexuality is embraced not with fear, but with reverence.

"Go Forth and Multiply": *Procreation as Doctrine in a Finite World*

The biblical injunction in Genesis to "be fruitful and multiply" has long functioned as a theological affirmation of life, continuity, and divine blessing. In ancient societies marked by high mortality rates and fragile populations, such a directive may have served practical and survival-oriented purposes. Yet in the twenty-first century, this ancient imperative intersects with radically different demographic, ecological, and political realities.

In many contemporary religious traditions, procreation remains morally elevated—sometimes subtly, sometimes explicitly—as a sacred duty. Parenthood is framed not merely as a personal aspiration but as obedience to divine command. Within this framework, contraception, voluntary childlessness, abortion access, and comprehensive sexuality education are often portrayed as threats to moral order. Sociologist Kevin McQuillan[86] notes that religion influences fertility "when religious institutions have both the authority and the means to enforce compliance with pronatalist norms" (**McQuillan, 2004**). The result is not only a theological position but, at times, a policy agenda: resistance to reproductive healthcare, opposition to family planning initiatives, and pronatalist movements that equate demographic growth with cultural or spiritual vitality.

Modern society faces unprecedented global pressures. Humanity now inhabits a planet experiencing environmental degradation, climate instability, biodiversity loss, and resource strain. Earth system scientist Will Steffen and colleagues[87] warn that human activity now operates beyond several "planetary boundaries," meaning that "human actions could push the Earth system outside the stable environmental state" that has supported civilization (**Steffen *et al.*, 2015**). While ecological crises cannot be reduced solely to population growth—since overconsumption, industrial practices, and economic inequality are central drivers—the scale and distribution of human populations remain ethically relevant. The question is no longer whether humanity can multiply, but whether multiplication without reflection is responsible within a finite biosphere.

The concept of "overpopulation" is itself contested, and its historical misuse in coercive or discriminatory policies demands caution. Population politics scholar Betsy Hartmann[88] cautions that population discourse has often "served as a convenient scapegoat for deeper structural inequalities" **(Hartmann, 1995)**. Acknowledging ecological limits does not require endorsing demographic alarmism[89]. Rather, it calls for thoughtful integration of demographic awareness with environmental ethics and social justice. When reproduction is framed as a divine mandate rather than a conscious choice, demographic expansion may outpace infrastructure, healthcare systems, and ecological resilience— exacerbating vulnerabilities already present in fragile regions.

Moreover, the fusion of theological pronatalism [90] with political power intensifies contemporary struggles around abortion rights, access to contraception, and sexuality education. Legal restrictions justified in the name of protecting life frequently coexist with inadequate support for maternal healthcare, childcare systems, and economic equity. The ethical coherence of such positions merits critical examination.

In countries shaped by Christian missionary colonization—including much of Latin America, the Philippines, parts of sub-Saharan Africa, and historically Catholic Europe—the injunction to "multiply" did not remain a private theological conviction but became embedded in social norms, legal frameworks, and public policy through enduring church–state entanglements. In Latin America, Catholic institutional authority historically influenced state regulation of family life, reinforcing restrictive regimes around contraception and abortion **(Htun[91], 2003)**. In the Philippines, prolonged ecclesiastical opposition to modern family planning significantly delayed the implementation of reproductive health legislation, even amid public health concerns **(Van *et al.*[92], 2021)**. Similar patterns can be observed in countries such as Poland and Ireland, where theological doctrine long shaped reproductive law. These dynamics are not reducible to faith itself, nor do they define the full complexity of these societies. Rather, they illustrate how missionary and colonial religious frameworks became woven into state structures in ways that continue to shape reproductive governance in the twenty-first century.

SOCAS does not position parenthood as problematic, nor does it portray religious communities as monolithic. It challenges instead the moral absolutism that renders procreation obligatory. Sexual expression is not reducible to reproductive function, and human dignity is not contingent upon biological legacy. When reproduction becomes a religious mandate rather than a freely chosen path, bodily autonomy is compromised—particularly for women, whose lives, health, and futures are often disproportionately shaped by pro-natalist expectations. As reproductive justice scholar Loretta J. Ross, writing with historian Rickie Solinger, defines it, reproductive justice affirms "the human right to maintain personal bodily autonomy, have children, not have children, and parent the children we have in safe and sustainable communities" (**Ross & Solinger**[93]**, 2017**).

Philosophically, the twenty-first century invites a shift: from reproduction as unquestioned destiny to parenthood as a mindful, informed choice. To affirm reproductive freedom is to affirm both the right to have children and the right not to. It requires recognizing that autonomy, ecological awareness, and social responsibility must inform discussions about population, sustainability, and human blossoming.

In this light, the command to "multiply" cannot remain an unexamined universal mandate. It must be reinterpreted within a broader ethic—one that honors life not merely through expansion, but through responsibility, equity, and conscious stewardship of a shared planet.

Pedophilia within the Catholic Church: *The Sin They Tried to Bury*

For decades, the Catholic Church has been engulfed in a scandal of staggering proportions: the systemic sexual abuse of minors by members of its clergy. This crisis is not the sum of isolated tragedies but the revelation of a persistent institutional pattern—silencing victims, relocating offenders, and refusing to confront the magnitude of the crimes committed. An institution that long claimed moral authority over the world has instead exposed its own hypocrisy, enacting a moral collapse in full view of history.

This abuse has not been confined to one diocese, culture, or continent. It is global. Reports from Ireland, the United States, Australia, Germany, France, Chile, and many other nations reveal horrifying levels of abuse and systematic concealment. Survivors were silenced, sometimes threatened with spiritual damnation or social ostracization. Priests credibly accused of abusing children were rarely removed from ministry or handed over to civil authorities; instead, they were quietly reassigned and relocated, thus enabling further abuse.

The landmark study conducted by the John Jay College of Criminal Justice—commissioned by the U.S. Conference of Catholic Bishops—found that between 1950 and 2002, 4,392 priests in the United States alone were credibly accused of sexually abusing minors, accounting for approximately 4% of all priests active during that period. As Karen Terry[94] *et al.* observe, "The problem was not just the sexual abuse of children; it was the conscious and systemic cover-up by Church officials that allowed the abuse to continue unchecked" (**Terry *et al.*, 2011**). The scale and duration of the abuse reveal not an ethical lapse, but a deeply embedded institutional pathology.

At the heart of this crisis lies a culture of secrecy, fortified by clerical hierarchy and a theology that elevates priests as spiritual intermediaries between God and the faithful. This imbalance of power rendered children uniquely vulnerable, while shame-based teachings on sexuality and obedience discouraged disclosure. Even when survivors bravely came forward, Church authorities often prioritized institutional reputation over human protection. The Vatican's 1962 directive *Crimen sollicitationis* (**Allen Jr.[95], 2003**) instructed bishops to handle accusations of clerical sexual misconduct in strict secrecy, thereby reinforcing silence and preventing accountability. As Thomas Doyle *et al.*[96] argue, "This veil of secrecy served only one purpose: to preserve the institution, even at the cost of sacrificing children to predators in collars" (**Doyle *et al.*, 2006**). Public scrutiny eventually forced greater transparency, but only after decades of immeasurable harm.

The damage was not only physical and psychological, but also deeply spiritual. Survivors experienced betrayal not merely by abusers but by the symbolic representatives of God. Families, parishes, and entire societies were shaken. Many victims suffered lifelong trauma such as depression, addiction, PTSD, and suicide. As Marie Keenan[97] writes, "What we are dealing with is a betrayal of the most sacred kind—an emotional and spiritual violation that cannot be simply fixed with apologies or financial settlements. These victims were not just abused physically; they were spiritually dismantled" (**Keenan, 2011**).

It is also necessary to confront how the Church's repressive sexual theology, particularly compulsory clerical celibacy and the demonization of carnal desire, may have created a climate of secrecy and denial rather than transparency and care. By refusing to allow healthy discussions of sexuality, the Church fostered an environment where pathology could remain hidden. This contradiction—moral condemnation outwardly, concealment inwardly—raises two urgent questions: how can an institution so incapable of addressing its own sexual crimes claim authority over anyone else's sexual morality? How can it condemn LGBTQ+ individuals, sex workers, or those who promote comprehensive sexuality education while its own leaders perpetrate or conceal sexual abuse?

Celibacy, far from being a noble renunciation, has often masked a dangerous repression. Christopher Hitchens drew a direct line between the institutional demand for clerical celibacy and the epidemic of sexual abuse within the Church, denouncing it as "a vain attempt to negate human nature." When sexuality is demonized, and natural desires are forced underground, they do not disappear—they fester. The scandal of clerical abuse is not an anomaly but a symptom of deeper doctrinal dysfunction. Hitchens' analysis suggests that it is not a few bad actors but the ideology itself—rooted in denial and domination—that breeds such moral collapse. The Church's efforts to bury these sins are not only a betrayal of justice but a consequence of its centuries-long war on the erotic self.

Although reforms have been announced and some clergy laicized, accountability remains incomplete. Survivors continue to seek justice. Many governments have launched inquiries and compensation programs, often in the face of Church resistance and appeals to institutional privilege.

True healing requires more than apology; it requires structural change, transparency, survivor-centered justice, and the relinquishing of moral dominance over sexual ethics. As this book argues throughout, and as mentioned before, the separation of church and sex is not only a political or legal necessity but a moral imperative.

Conversion Therapy: *The Persistence of Harm in the Name of Faith*

In the twenty-first century, few practices reveal the enduring entanglement of religion, morality, and sexuality as starkly as so-called "conversion therapy." Framed by its proponents as guidance or healing, it is, in fact, rooted in a theological premise: that non-heteronormative identities are deviations to be corrected rather than expressions to be understood.

Major medical and psychological institutions have reached a clear and consistent conclusion. The American Psychological Association states unequivocally that such practices are based on "the false and harmful idea that sexual orientation or gender identity can be changed," and further emphasizes that they are "unlikely to be successful" and carry "a risk of harm" (**APA, 2021**). This is not a matter of ideological disagreement but of scientific consensus.

Empirical research reinforces this position. In their analysis of conversion efforts, Jessica N. Fish and Stephen T. Russell[98]—who used the term SOGICE (Sexual Orientation and Gender Identity Change Efforts), concluded that exposure to such practices is "associated with adverse mental health outcomes," including depression and suicide (**Fish & Russell, 2020**). Similarly, in their cross-sectional study of 27,715 US transgender adults, Jack L. Turban *et al.*[99] found that "for transgender adults who recalled gender identity conversion efforts before age 10 years, exposure to gender identity conversion efforts was significantly associated with an increase in lifetime suicide attempts compared with transgender adults who had discussed gender identity with a professional but who were not exposed to conversion efforts" (**Turban *et al.*, 2020**). These findings do not merely question the effectiveness of conversion therapy—they expose its capacity for serious harm.

Yet the persistence of conversion therapy cannot be understood through science alone. Its endurance is deeply tied to religious narratives that frame sexuality as morally contingent. Within such frameworks, same-sex desire or gender variance is interpreted not as diversity, but as deviation. Conversion therapy, then, becomes not simply a therapeutic intervention, but a moral imperative—an attempt to reconcile the individual with doctrine.

This is where SOCAS offers a necessary reframing. The question is not only whether conversion therapy works—scientific evidence overwhelmingly indicates that it does not—but whether the very premise of "conversion" is ethically coherent. When identity is treated as a problem to be solved, therapy risks becoming an instrument of normalization rather than a space of exploration.

Defenders of conversion therapy often invoke the language of freedom—particularly freedom of speech and religious liberty. Recent legal developments, including a landmark U.S. Supreme Court decision, have reinforced this framing by characterizing such therapeutic conversations as protected speech. Yet this perspective obscures a critical reality: speech does not occur in a vacuum. It is embedded within systems of authority, trust, and power.

A licensed therapist occupies a position of influence, particularly when working with minors. When that authority is used to direct individuals toward a predetermined moral outcome, the boundary between guidance and coercion becomes increasingly blurred. What is presented as "choice" may in fact be shaped by internalized shame, familial expectations, or fear of rejection.

SOCAS challenges this framing by asking a deeper question: when speech is embedded within systems of authority and moral conditioning, can it ever be truly neutral? Or does it become a subtle yet powerful instrument of control—one that perpetuates shame while presenting itself as care? At its core, the issue is one of dignity. To affirm human dignity is to recognize that identity is not a defect to be corrected, nor a deviation to be disciplined. When therapeutic practices seek to override this principle, they risk perpetuating the very harm they claim to alleviate.

Ultimately, the persistence of conversion therapy cannot be understood merely as a therapeutic controversy—it must be recognized as a profound ethical failure with clear human rights implications. As numerous international human rights bodies have affirmed, practices that seek to suppress or alter an individual's sexual orientation or gender identity violate dignity, autonomy, and psychological integrity. When individuals—particularly minors—are subjected to interventions rooted in the premise that their identity is disordered, they are not being guided; they are being denied the right to exist authentically.

In this light, conversion therapy is not simply ineffective or outdated—it is fundamentally incompatible with any framework that claims to uphold human rights. SOCAS therefore calls for a necessary ethical shift: from attempting to "correct" identity to affirming it, from enforcing conformity to honoring authenticity, and from perpetuating inherited shame to cultivating a culture grounded in freedom, dignity, and conscious self-acceptance.

The Legislative Branch: *Disguising Religious Dogma as Public Policy*

In many modern democracies, elected lawmakers exert enormous influence over public policy—an influence that, too often, is used to smuggle religious dogma into secular legislation. When theological values infiltrate the legislative process, laws that outwardly appear neutral may, in fact, encode the moral frameworks of specific faith traditions. This insidious symbiosis, some might say subversion, of democratic governance undermines the separation of Church and State and erodes the foundations of a pluralistic society.

Indeed, too often, what masquerades as neutral legislation is, in fact, theocratic residue—public policy shaped by religious morality rather than reason or human rights. Maitreya Rael fiercely opposes this entanglement of dogma and governance, insisting that religion poisons everything—including the law. From abortion restrictions to anti-LGBTQ+ bills, we witness theocratic influence persist under the guise of protecting morality. Democracy demands more than freedom of belief; it requires freedom from belief systems that infringe upon bodily autonomy and equal protection. His critique strengthens the argument for rigorous secularism as the only viable safeguard for pluralism and justice.

Nowhere is this breach more consequential than in matters of sexuality and education. When the State aligns with religious ideology, it becomes an instrument of moral policing, regulating who may love, marry, reproduce, or learn about their own bodies. Abstinence-only education, anti-LGBTQ+ laws, restrictions on abortion and contraception, and bans on comprehensive sexuality education are not isolated policies but are symptoms of a broader systemic infection. As long as the Church continues to shape State lawmaking, there can be no true separation between Church and Sex, for sexuality, so intimately tied to personal identity, remains hostage to religious oversight rather than informed by science, ethics, and lived experience.

Religiously motivated legislators often mask their bills in the language of neutrality—invoking terms like "academic freedom," "parental rights," or "critical thinking." A case in point is the Louisiana Science Education Act **(LSEA)**, passed in 2008. Marketed as a tool to foster critical inquiry, it allows teachers to introduce supplementary materials challenging scientific theories, such as evolution, and to open the door to divine creationist perspectives. Critics rightly view this as a Trojan horse—a strategy that conceals harmful intent behind apparent benevolence—for injecting religious doctrine into public education. As Ian Binns[100] warns, such "academic freedom" bills represent "the latest effort to undermine the integrity of science and science education," cloaking religious ideology in a façade of intellectual rigor (**Binns, 2013**).

Another telling example of religious dogma cloaked in secular policy is the Adolescent Family Life Act[101] **(AFLA)** of 1981, which channeled federal funding to organizations promoting abstinence and adoption— mostly faith-based groups—under the guise of preventing teen pregnancy. In *Bowen v. Kendrick* (1988), the U.S. Supreme Court upheld its constitutionality using the *Lemon test*[102], concluding that it served a secular purpose, did not advance religion primarily, and avoided excessive entanglement with religion. Yet as legal scholar Tracy Prewitt[103] points out, the Court essentially handed the public "a lemon"—a statute that appeared neutral but in practice institutionalized religious priorities using taxpayer money (**Prewitt, 1989**).

Recent legislative trends continue to blur the line between religious conviction and public policy. In Georgia, Republican lawmakers proposed bills that would censor school library content, mandate parental opt-ins for sexuality education, require the Ten Commandments to be displayed in classrooms, and permit religious chaplains to counsel students in public schools (**AP, 2024**). Framed as efforts to "protect public morals," these proposals threaten the secular character of public education while legitimizing religious oversight in the classroom.

Equally concerning is the rise of programs like *LifeWise Academy*[104], a Christian nonprofit advocating for "released time" Bible instruction during the public school day. Though technically off-campus and privately funded, such programs exploit public school scheduling and infrastructure to facilitate religious education (**AP, 2024**). While defenders claim these initiatives support family values and offer faith-based enrichment—particularly for underprivileged students—their deeper effect is to normalize the presence of religious doctrine in secular education, raising First Amendment[105] concerns.

As LifeWise CEO Joel Penton declared, "Values of faith and the Bible are absolutely central to many families… they want to demonstrate to their children that it is central to their lives." This framing—faith as essential rather than optional—reveals the underlying intent: not merely to offer religious choice, but to embed religious identity into public systems. This perspective illustrates why such programs are advocated for and why they resonate with participating parents, while also highlighting the tension between religious freedom and state neutrality.

At its core, the principle of Church-State separation is not an abstract ideal but a necessary safeguard to ensure that laws uphold universal human rights rather than sectarian moral codes. When theology shapes legislation, governance becomes distorted; law ceases to serve the diverse body politic and instead privileges religious orthodoxy. A secular government must protect the rights of all citizens—religious and non-religious alike—ensuring freedom of conscience, bodily autonomy, and personal dignity.

When that neutrality is breached, law becomes not a reflection of collective reason but a vessel for religious righteousness masquerading as public policy. And in such a climate, there can be no true sexual freedom.

Sacred Injustice: *Scriptural Passages That Violate Human Rights*

Religious texts have long been held as moral compasses, regarded as sacred and immutable by billions around the world. Yet within these revered scriptures lie verses that—when viewed through the lens of modern human rights—stand in stark contradiction to the values of equality, dignity, bodily autonomy, and justice. While many believers interpret these texts allegorically or within historical context, it remains true that such passages continue to influence laws, gender norms, educational policies, and cultural attitudes across the globe. The harm is not merely theoretical—it is measurable, enduring, and often violently enacted.

This section does not aim to vilify any particular religion, but rather to bring critical awareness to the institutionalization of doctrines that, when left unexamined, perpetuate discrimination, gender-based violence, and the erosion of fundamental freedoms. If humanity is to evolve into a more just and compassionate civilization, we must confront the darker legacies embedded in our sacred texts. The following examples, drawn from the **Hebrew Bible**, the **Christian New Testament**, and the **Qur'an**, are not exhaustive—but they are illustrative of the urgent need for outright expurgation[106], censorship, scriptural reform, critical reinterpretation, responsible spiritual leadership, United Nations' involvement, and more importantly, a universal commitment to human rights above dogma.

Hebrew Bible / Old Testament

• Leviticus 20:13

"If a man lies with a male as with a woman, both of them have committed an abomination; they shall surely be put to death."

Used historically and currently to justify anti-LGBTQ+ violence and legal discrimination.

• Deuteronomy 22:20–21

"If … the evidence of virginity was not found for the young woman, then they shall bring out the young woman … and the men of her city shall stone her to death."

Codifies lethal punishment for perceived sexual impurity in women.

• Numbers 31:17–18

"Now therefore kill every male among the little ones and kill every woman who has known man intimately. But all the young girls who have not known man intimately, keep alive for yourselves."

Ethnic cleansing and sexual enslavement sanctioned as divine instruction.

• Exodus 21:20–21

"When a man strikes his slave, male or female, with a rod … if the slave survives a day or two, he is not to be punished, for the slave is his money."

Endorses the beating of enslaved people and defines them as property.

• Genesis 19:8

"Behold, I have two daughters who have not known any man. Let me bring them out to you and do to them as you please."

Women offered as objects to appease a violent mob—depicts women's bodies as bargaining tools.

• **Deuteronomy 25:11–12**

"If two men are fighting and the wife of one of them comes to rescue her husband from his assailant, and she reaches out and seizes him by his private parts, you shall cut off her hand. Show her no pity."

Dictates a strict penalty for a woman intervening in a fight between men by grabbing the assailant's genitals to protect her husband.

• **Deuteronomy 22:28–29**

"If a man meets a virgin who is not betrothed, and seizes her and lies with her, and they are found, then the man … shall give the father of the young woman fifty shekels of silver, and she shall be his wife."

Treats rape as a property violation against the father, effectively forcing victims to marry their rapists.

• **Leviticus 12:2–5**

"If a woman conceives and bears a male child, she shall be unclean seven days … But if she bears a female child, then she shall be unclean two weeks."

Codifies gender-based impurity, reinforcing misogynistic views of female birth.

Christian New Testament

• **Ephesians 5:22–24**

"Wives, submit to your own husbands as to the Lord … as the church submits to Christ, so also wives should submit in everything to their husbands."

Promotes patriarchal submission and gender hierarchy in marriage.

• **1 Timothy 2:11–12**

"Let a woman learn in silence with all submission. I do not permit a woman to teach or to have authority over a man."

Used to deny women access to leadership roles in religious and educational spaces.

• 1 Corinthians 14:34–35

"Let your women keep silent in the churches … for it is shameful for a woman to speak in church."

Reinforces female subjugation and exclusion from public discourse.

• Romans 1:26–27

"God gave them up to shameful lusts … men committed indecent acts with other men and received in themselves the due penalty for their perversion."

Cited to condemn homosexuality and justify conversion therapy, persecution, and shame.

Qur'an

• Surah An-Nisa (4:34)

"Men are in charge of women … As for those [wives] from whom you fear arrogance, advise them; then forsake them in bed; and [finally], strike them."

Enables domestic violence under divine sanction.

• Surah An-Nur (24:2)

"The woman and the man guilty of fornication, flog each one of them with a hundred stripes."

Legal basis for corporal punishment in cases of consensual sex outside marriage.

• Surah Al-Baqarah (2:223)

"Your wives are a place of sowing of seed for you, so come to your place of cultivation however you wish."

Objectifies women's bodies in reproductive terms, ignoring agency and mutual consent.

• Surah Al-Talaq (65:4)

"And those who no longer expect menstruation among your women—if you doubt, then their period is three months, and [also for] those who have not menstruated."

Interpreted by some scholars to suggest allowance for child marriage and divorce before puberty.

Erasing Harm & Honoring Human Rights: *A Global Call for Scriptural Responsibility*

The verses above—however ancient—are not inert relics of a bygone world. They continue to inform sermons, laws, school curricula, gender roles, marital expectations, and national policies across the globe. Sacred texts, revered for millennia, still carry tremendous weight in shaping what is deemed "moral," "natural," or "divinely sanctioned." But when such texts are used to justify violence, preserve inequality, or deny human rights, they are no longer spiritual anchors—they become weapons of oppression cloaked in sanctity.

In an age where international human rights frameworks have been painstakingly developed to protect all people—regardless of gender, orientation, belief, or background—it is no longer acceptable to allow religious exemptions to override basic dignity. The task before us is not to erase scripture, but to courageously interpret it anew, through the lens of compassion, reason, and universal justice. This does not mean discarding faith. It means refining it. It does not mean silencing tradition. It means transforming it. It means acknowledging that parts of our sacred texts were born in deeply patriarchal, tribal, and theocratic contexts—worlds where slavery, child marriage, gender apartheid[107], and sexual violence were normalized. Those historical contexts must be confronted—not revered.

Faith traditions can evolve. They have evolved. And they must continue to evolve if they are to remain relevant in a world that no longer accepts the normalization of subjugation. The reinterpretation or expurgation of human rights-violating passages is not sacrilegious—it is sacred work. It is an act of love, of accountability, and of ethical integrity. To do this, we need more than theologians. We need survivors. We need artists. We need youth. We need women. We need queers. We need people of all faiths—and of no faith—committed to rewriting what it means to be holy, not in allegiance to dogma, but in alignment with dignity.

We must also hold institutions accountable. Religious leaders must stop invoking verses that condone child marriage, marital rape, or the demonization of LGBTQ+ people. Governments must stop legislating religious morality in secular law. Schools must stop teaching abstinence-only education, based on religious ideals rather than evidence-based health science. And communities must stop protecting abusers behind the veil of sacred authority. At the same time, we must uplift those traditions and voices within every faith that have always championed love, compassion, erotic joy, and liberation. There are mystics, rebels, prophets, and poets in every religion who have dared to envision God not as a punisher of pleasure, but as its source.

Ultimately, this is not only about scripture—it is about power. It is about who gets to define what is moral, what is normal, and what is permissible. It is about reclaiming authority over our own bodies, our own lives, and our own spiritual journeys. Let us, then, build a world where no one must choose between their humanity and their heritage, where sacredness is measured not by adherence to ancient prohibitions, but by our capacity to honor the diversity, agency, and beauty of every person. The future of faith must be one that heals, not harms. One that uplifts, not erases. And one that liberates, not controls. And that begins by confronting sacred injustice with sacred courage.

And lastly, I wish to reaffirm that more than forty years ago, Rael courageously put forth a bold and ethically grounded proposal before the United Nations: the systematic expurgation of all scriptural passages within religious texts—regardless of religious tradition—that stand in direct violation of fundamental human rights. At its core, this initiative, rooted in the principles of peace, dignity, and universal justice, seeks to eliminate verses that incite hatred, legitimize violence, promote discrimination, or perpetuate sexism, homophobia, or murder. Far from being an attack on religion, this proposal is a vital appeal for religious accountability and invites a necessary re-evaluation of religious teachings so that they may evolve in alignment with the ethical imperatives of contemporary humanity. (**See Appendix C:** *Demanding Accountability—An Appeal to the United Nations to Expurgate Human Rights Violations from All Religious Texts*).

Chapter Three:
Legal and Ethical Debates

Legislating Reproductive Rights: When Courts Control the Womb

Reproductive rights—particularly the right to abortion—have long stood at the junction of law, morality, and religious ideology in the United States. Few domains so clearly expose the tensions between personal liberty, constitutional law, and theological values as the courtroom, where a handful of judges can determine the conditions under which someone may, or may not, exercise control over their reproductive organs. When courts become custodians of the womb, the state assumes a role far beyond its mandate, legislating sexual desire, conception, motherhood, and bodily autonomy. In this process, religious morality is too often cloaked in the language of constitutional jurisprudence[1].

The U.S. Supreme Court's landmark decision in *Roe v. Wade*[2] (1973) **(see Appendix A)** marked a watershed moment in American legal history, recognizing abortion as a fundamental liberty protected by the Due Process Clause of the Fourteenth Amendment[3]. Framed as a right to privacy, the ruling set a precedent by introducing a trimester-based framework that balances a woman's autonomy with the state's interest in protecting potential life. But nearly fifty years later, *Dobbs v. Jackson Women's Health Organization* (2022) **(see Appendix A)** reversed that precedent. Writing for the majority, Justice Samuel Alito declared that *Roe* had been "egregiously[4] wrong from the start," arguing that the Constitution does not guarantee a right to abortion, nor is such a right "deeply rooted in this Nation's history and tradition" **(Dobbs, 2022)**. By this logic, rights must meet a narrow originalist standard to be considered legitimate. This ruling not only overturned Roe but effectively erased the notion of abortion as a federally protected liberty, and empowered states to impose bans or restrictions, even in cases of rape, incest, or threats to maternal health.

Within days, numerous states enacted so-called "trigger laws[5]"—prewritten bans designed to activate immediately upon the fall of *Roe*. Others passed six-week "heartbeat bills[6]" or full abortion bans, regardless of gestational viability[7] or exceptions. This resulted in a fragmented and deeply unequal legal landscape where a person's reproductive rights would depend entirely on the state in which they reside. As *The New Yorker* noted, the ruling "eliminated the constitutional right to abortion and granted states the authority to restrict the procedure as they wish." This patchwork also generated legal chaos where patients, doctors, and even Uber drivers faced criminal liability in some states for aiding in abortion access. Other states responded by becoming "sanctuary states[8]," enshrining protections and passing laws to shield providers and patients from interstate legal action. Thus, the American legal map has devolved into a constitutional civil war over reproductive sovereignty.

The consequences have been devastating. So-called *abortion deserts[9]*—entire regions with no legal access to abortion—have emerged, disproportionately affecting low-income women, women of color, minors, undocumented immigrants, and those without health insurance. Some individuals must travel hundreds of miles to obtain reproductive care, while others face criminal penalties simply for aiding in access. In some states, even rideshare drivers or friends who provide transportation risk legal repercussions. Meanwhile, several states have declared themselves "sanctuary states," passing laws to protect providers and shield patients from interstate lawsuits or extradition.

Though *Dobbs* was framed as a constitutional correction, its religious underpinnings are unmistakable. Many of the states that moved swiftly to ban abortion did so using language that mirrors Christian doctrine—particularly the belief that life begins at conception. In some legislative debates, Scripture was even cited as justification for an anti-abortion policy. This blending of theocratic belief with civil law undermines the *Establishment Clause of the First Amendment*[10] (**see Appendix A**), which prohibits the government from making laws "respecting an establishment of religion." When courts or lawmakers define life, family, or bodily purpose through a single religious lens, they suppress pluralism and compromise the neutrality that secular democracy demands.

The implications of *Dobbs* also cast a long shadow over other unenumerated rights built on similar constitutional reasoning, including the right to contraception (*Griswold v. Connecticut*, 1965), same-sex intimacy (*Lawrence v. Texas*, 2003), and same-sex marriage (*Obergefell v. Hodges*, 2015) (**see Appendix A**). In a chilling concurring opinion, Justice Clarence Thomas explicitly called for the Court to "reconsider all of this Court's substantive due process precedents" (*Dobbs*, 2022). This signals a broader judicial agenda—one that may unravel decades of civil rights protections under the guise of constitutional originalism, with clear echoes of religious ideology embedded within.

By stepping into the role of moral arbiter, the Court abandons its duty as a neutral guardian of rights and instead becomes a vehicle for cultural and religious imposition. It is no coincidence that those most affected by these rulings are individuals with wombs—bodies that have historically served as battlegrounds for moral, political, and theological control. *Dobbs* reinscribes this legacy by reducing reproductive autonomy to a matter of legislative discretion rather than individual liberty. It not only disregards legal precedent but also dismisses the lived realities of millions whose health, dignity, and future depend on access to reproductive care.

At the heart of this legal battleground lies a deeper, more urgent question: Who decides? And under what framework—constitutional, moral, or theological—are those decisions made? When courts define reproductive rights through a lens shaped by religious morality, they do more than interpret the Constitution; they transform it into a tool for enforcing doctrine. This is why the central argument of this book—the need to separate Church and Sex—is not merely philosophical but imperative to the survival of secular democracy. Without a clear boundary between religious belief and civil law, the bodies of women and gender minorities will remain collateral damage in battles they never consented to fight.

Sexuality Education on Trial: Legal Battles Over What Schools Can Teach

Sexuality education in American schools has become a legal and ideological battleground, where scientific integrity, parental rights, and religious doctrine frequently collide. With no federally standardized curriculum, authority over what students learn about sex, gender, and identity rests largely in the hands of state legislatures and local school boards. This decentralized system creates a vacuum—one that has been filled by ideological agendas with far-reaching consequences for public health, equity, and civil liberties.

The rise of abstinence-only education in the United States can be traced back to the 1996 passage of *Title V of the Welfare Reform Act*[11], later incorporated into *Section 510 of the Social Security Act*[12] (**see Appendix A**). This legislation established federal grants exclusively for programs promoting sexual abstinence outside of marriage, as defined by a rigid eight-point "A–H" framework. As the Guttmacher Institute[13] has noted, these grants "emphasized abstinence from sexual activity outside of marriage, at any age," and funneled tens of millions of dollars toward programs that excluded accurate information about contraception, STI prevention, or LGBTQ+ inclusion (**Guttmacher Institute, 2025 Fact Sheet – see Appendix A**).

The perils of such policy are well documented: abstinence-only programs consistently fail to reduce rates of sexual activity, pregnancy, or sexually transmitted infections. In contrast, comprehensive sexuality education has been shown to delay the initiation of sexual activity, increase contraceptive use, and improve overall sexual health outcomes. Yet, despite this evidence, abstinence-focused models persist, driven more by religious and political ideology than by empirical science.

Without national oversight, sexuality education remains vulnerable to ideological capture. In 2022, Florida enacted the *Parental Rights in Education Act*[14]—popularly known as the "Don't Say Gay" bill (**see Appendix A**)—which prohibits classroom discussion of sexual orientation and gender identity from kindergarten through third grade and imposes vague restrictions beyond that based on subjective judgments of "age-appropriate" content. As critics observed, these laws are not merely content regulations; they function as tools of erasure, targeting LGBTQ+ identities under the guise of protecting children.

A report by *PEN America* (**see Appendix A**) documented that 39 school districts nationwide have proposed similar "educational gag orders[15]," with 38 bills targeting classroom discussions of sexual orientation and gender identity—many modeled closely on Florida's framework. These measures are part of a broader strategy to use parental-rights rhetoric as a vehicle for imposing conservative religious values onto public education.

Legal challenges quickly followed. Plaintiffs in multiple states argued that such laws violate the First and Fourteenth Amendments by discriminating against LGBTQ+ students and suppressing free expression. In one high-profile case, the ACLU[16] filed suit against a Texas law that banned diversity, equity, and inclusion (DEI[17]) initiatives and restricted classroom discussions on gender identity. The lawsuit contended that the law infringed upon students' constitutional rights and undermined inclusive education.

These legal disputes are not merely about curriculum—they are about power: who decides what knowledge is valid, and whose values define the public good. At their core, these battles over sexuality education mirror the same fundamental tension seen in abortion law: can religious or ideological objections override the principles of educational equity and pluralism?

This section underscores a critical truth: sexuality education is never neutral. When religious morality is repackaged as policy, the result is not only pedagogical bias but an institutional denial of pluralism. Such denial erodes the very democratic foundation this book defends—namely, the necessary separation of Church and Sex. Without this separation, the classroom becomes another battleground for control over bodies, identities, and the futures of young people.

SCOTUS: When Religious Beliefs Impair Legal Judgment

When Supreme Court decisions pivot on religious conviction, the boundary between faith and governance shifts—often quietly, yet profoundly. These rulings do not merely define the scope of legal rights; they determine whose moral framework governs civic life. A closer look at *Masterpiece Cakeshop*, *Fulton*, and *303 Creative* reveals a troubling trajectory: as religious priority increasingly eclipses equality, civil liberties—particularly those of LGBTQ+ individuals—are weakened under the guise of constitutional protection.

In *Masterpiece Cakeshop v. Colorado Civil Rights Commission* (2018) (**see Appendix A**), the Court addressed whether a baker could refuse to create a wedding cake for a same-sex couple on religious grounds. Rather than ruling squarely on the legality of such refusals, the Court focused on the Colorado Civil Rights Commission's alleged hostility toward the baker's religious beliefs. Justice Kennedy's opinion emphasized the need for "neutral and respectful consideration" of religion, signaling that perceived bias in enforcement could invalidate otherwise valid anti-discrimination protections. Though narrow in scope, the ruling effectively elevated religious belief to a special category of legal protection.

As Michael K. Steenson[18] observes in his analysis of *Masterpiece Cakeshop* in the *Mitchell Hamline Law Review*, for Phillips, "creating a wedding cake for a same-sex couple would be the same as participating in a celebration that conflicts with those deeply held religious beliefs" (**Steenson, 2019**). What emerges here is the transformation of personal religious conviction into a constitutional shield against public-accommodation law.

The Court deepened this trend in *Fulton v. City of Philadelphia* (2021) (**see Appendix A**), ruling that a Catholic foster-care agency could not be excluded from city contracts despite refusing to certify same-sex couples as foster parents. Chief Justice Roberts reasoned that because Philadelphia's nondiscrimination policy allowed for individualized exemptions, denying a religious exemption triggered strict judicial scrutiny. As legal scholars Thomas Berg and Douglas Laycock[19] explain, "*Fulton* clarifies *Smith* in ways that strengthen protection" for religious claimants because even theoretically available exceptions "enable discrimination against religion" (**Berg & Laycock, 2021**). This logic quietly undermines *Employment Division v. Smith* (1990) (**see Appendix A**), which held that neutral, generally applicable laws need not accommodate religious objections. By seizing upon hypothetical exemptions, the Court signaled a willingness to bend doctrine in favor of religious claims—allowing faith-based objections to override inclusive civil rights protections. When religious belief is given greater legal weight than civil rights protections, the Court ceases to function as a neutral arbiter and becomes an instrument of moral theology, thereby weakening the line between Church and State. And if that line is weakened, it becomes nearly impossible to separate Church and Sex.

That trajectory culminated in *303 Creative LLC v. Elenis* (2023) (**see Appendix A**), where the Court's ruling marked a profound turning point in how First Amendment rights are leveraged to override anti-discrimination protections, particularly those safeguarding LGBTQ+ individuals in the marketplace. It ruled that a Colorado web designer had a First Amendment right to refuse services for same-sex weddings. The majority framed the case as a free-speech dispute, and Justice Neil Gorsuch asserted that the state could not compel an artist to produce expressive content contrary to personal beliefs. Critics warned that this reasoning dangerously conflates personal beliefs with public-service obligations. As Mark Satta[20] argues, the Court "misapplied precedent while failing to even acknowledge that 303 Creative's refusal… constituted a limited form of sexual-orientation discrimination" (**Satta, 2024**). This decision built upon a larger judicial trend, one that used originalist interpretations of the Constitution[21] to elevate religious liberty claims while minimizing the lived experiences of those impacted by discrimination. Satta rightly critiqued the Court's embrace of what he called "faulty arguments," pointing out that refusing services for same-sex weddings could not be separated from the broader matrix of sexual orientation bias, even if the business claimed to serve LGBTQ+ clients in other contexts. As he explains, "Such refusals should be viewed as a type of sexual-orientation discrimination," regardless of how narrowly tailored the denial was (**Satta, 2024**).

Collectively, *Masterpiece Cakeshop*, *Fulton*, and *303 Creative* illustrate a judicial movement toward privileging religious exercise over equal access protections. This shift is reinforced by the Court's growing embrace of originalism—the doctrine that constitutional interpretation must adhere to the framers' supposed historical intent. But as Wisconsin Supreme Court Justice Rebecca Dallet cautions, taken to its logical conclusion, originalism risks "the radical rejection of long-settled constitutional principles," especially those protecting women, LGBTQ+ people, and racial minorities. By anchoring constitutional meaning strictly in the 18th or 19th century, originalist judges often overlook the fact that the framers lived in a society that normalized gender inequality and systematically excluded or condemned non-traditional relationships.

Meanwhile, religious liberty arguments are increasingly framed as constitutional shields against civil rights enforcement. When courts interpret the First Amendment in ways that prioritize doctrinal belief over equal protection, equality under the law becomes conditional. Women's autonomy, LGBTQ+ rights, and protections for religious minorities all become more vulnerable. Legal analysis that privileges historical prejudice over evolving human rights effectively embeds sectarian moral judgments into public law.

Once again, the lesson is clear: The Supreme Court is not simply interpreting legal principles— it is reshaping the ethical framework governing bodies, identity, and intimacy. Without strong secular legal protections, deeply contested theological beliefs risk becoming public policy. The project of neutrality collapses, and the state becomes a vehicle for religious moral policing. Only through secular jurisprudence can bodily autonomy, identity, and intimate freedom be preserved as rights, rather than privileges granted—or denied—by religious ideology.

The Establishment Clause Under Siege: Blurring Church and State

The Establishment Clause of the First Amendment of the U.S. Constitution **(see Appendix A)** was designed as a safeguard against theocratic influence in government, preventing the establishment of an official religion and prohibiting state favoritism toward any faith. Rooted in Enlightenment principles and forged in the crucible of early American religious pluralism, its purpose is twofold: to protect religious liberty by keeping the state out of religious affairs, and to safeguard secular governance by keeping religion out of policymaking. At its heart lies a commitment to neutrality—a state that neither advances nor inhibits religious belief, thus allowing individuals to believe or not believe free from coercion or state endorsement.

Yet in recent years, this constitutional barrier has shown signs of deep fracture. A new wave of judicial interpretations and legislative maneuvers has begun to erode the once-clear line between Church and State. What was once a shield for liberty is now being repurposed into a conduit for sectarian influence in public life, especially in education and civil governance. The result is an alarming shift: religious ideology, once confined to the private sphere, is now seeping into publicly funded institutions under the guise of constitutional freedom.

One of the most consequential decisions in this trend came in *Carson v. Makin* (2022) **(see Appendix A)**, in which the Supreme Court held that while states are not obligated to fund private education, once they choose to offer tuition assistance, they cannot exclude religious schools from such programs. Writing for the majority, Chief Justice John Roberts stated, "A State need not subsidize private education. But once a State decides to do so, it cannot disqualify some private schools solely because they are religious." This decision overturned long-standing precedents that aimed to preserve public funds for secular use, and it dramatically altered the landscape of taxpayer-funded education.

In practice, *Carson* opens the door for public dollars to flow directly into schools that may promote sectarian doctrines, discriminate on the basis of sexual orientation or gender identity, or exclude students and staff based on religious criteria. The ruling effectively transforms religious identity into a legal entitlement to public subsidy, weakening the Establishment Clause by framing it not as a limit on government entanglement with religion, but as a prohibition on excluding religion from government benefits. As a result, religious education—once clearly private—is now eligible for state support, blurring the lines between public interest and theological education.

In *Kennedy v. Bremerton School District* (2022) **(see Appendix A)**, the Court sided with a high school coach who knelt in prayer at the 50-yard line after games. Justice Neil Gorsuch, in the majority opinion, emphasized: "The Constitution and the best of our traditions counsel mutual respect and tolerance, not censorship and suppression, for religious and nonreligious views alike." This ruling overturned decades of precedent limiting religious expression in public schools, signaling a major shift in how the Establishment Clause is understood. It suggests that personal religious observance, even in public institutions and visible contexts, may no longer be seen as government endorsement, further eroding the principle of neutrality and weakening the wall separating State and Church.

The erosion continued in *Kennedy v. Bremerton School District* (2022) **(see Appendix A)**, where the Court ruled in favor of a high school football coach who prayed at the 50-yard line after games. Justice Neil Gorsuch, writing for the majority, framed the issue as a matter of individual expression: "The Constitution and the best of our traditions counsel mutual respect and tolerance, not censorship and suppression, for religious and nonreligious views alike." While framed as a defense of personal liberty, the decision undermined decades of precedent, including *Engel v. Vitale* (1962) and *Lee v. Weisman* (1992) **(see Appendix A)**, which had carefully drawn boundaries around religious activity in public schools to avoid the appearance of state endorsement.

The *Kennedy* ruling marks a pivotal shift. It implies that religious activity conducted by public officials—even in visibly public settings—no longer necessarily constitutes government endorsement. The Court's redefinition of "coercion" and its narrow reading of endorsement theory weaken the principle of neutrality in public education. For students, especially those from minority faiths or nonreligious backgrounds, this blurring sends a chilling message: religious expression is now protected even when it occurs within the framework of state authority, further eroding the secular integrity of public institutions.

Beyond the courtroom, legislative efforts have similarly targeted the Establishment Clause. One of the most significant is the rise of *Project Blitz*[22]—a coordinated campaign to promote Christian nationalism through model legislation across state governments (**see Appendix A**). As detailed by Americans United for Separation of Church and State, Project Blitz is "a coordinated national effort working to codify the U.S. as a Christian nation." Bills introduced under its influence include requirements for public schools to post the Ten Commandments, offer Bible literacy courses, and promote prayer events—all designed to reframe the role of religion in American civic life.

Under the pretense of cultural heritage or moral education, these initiatives attempt to normalize sectarian messaging in public classrooms. While often framed as voluntary or educational, they subtly reintroduce religious authority into state-funded institutions, risking the coercion of students and teachers alike. The effort to redefine religious freedom as a "sword"—one that permits faith-based intrusion into civil life—rather than as a "shield" to protect personal belief from government overreach, represents a dangerous inversion of the First Amendment's original intent.

When judicial and legislative actions converge to weaken the Establishment Clause, the consequences are profound. Public money, civic authority, and educational content become vehicles for sectarian ideology. The secular space—where law, education, and governance are meant to serve all citizens equally—is increasingly compromised by religious preference and theological moralism. This creeping entanglement of Church and State has direct implications for sexuality, identity, and bodily autonomy. Religious institutions receiving state funding can and often do promote restrictive teachings on gender roles, sexual orientation, and reproductive rights. Schools emboldened by legal protection may use religious doctrine to deny LGBTQ+ visibility, censor sexuality education, or stigmatize nontraditional families—all with public money and government sanction.

Thus, the weakening of the Establishment Clause does not just endanger pluralism—it undermines personal freedom. It makes possible the very moral policing this book seeks to expose, where sex, sexuality, and identity are no longer governed by secular principles of equality and liberty, but by the dogmas of a resurgent religious right. To reclaim the Establishment Clause is to restore the legal firewall that protects not just belief, but the freedom to live outside the confines of belief. It is to affirm that religious freedom cannot be used to impose religion on others.

Religious Exemptions: The Trojan Horse of Discrimination

The rise of religious exemptions as a legal strategy marks one of the most consequential battlegrounds in the ongoing erosion of the separation between Church and State. Originally intended to safeguard the rights of individuals to practice their religion freely, religious exemptions have increasingly been repurposed as tools to subvert civil rights protections—particularly those that safeguard bodily autonomy, gender equality, and LGBTQ+ dignity. The shift is not merely semantic or theoretical; it represents a form of structural moralism—institutional enforcement of sexual codes through law and policy—in how religious liberty is interpreted, codified, and weaponized.

This transformation traces back to the pivotal 1990 Supreme Court ruling in *Employment Division v. Smith*. In his majority opinion, Justice Antonin Scalia cautioned that, "To permit this would be to make the professed doctrines of religious belief superior to the law of the land, and in effect to permit every citizen to become a law unto himself" (**U.S. Supreme Court, 1990**). While this decision reaffirmed the supremacy of secular law, it also limited the judiciary's ability to grant religious exemptions, prompting religious groups to turn to the legislature for relief.

The legislative response came swiftly in the form of the *Religious Freedom Restoration Act*[23] (RFRA) of 1993, which reinstated the "strict scrutiny[24]" standard requiring that any law that substantially burdens religious practice must serve a compelling governmental interest and be the least restrictive means of doing so. Initially passed with broad bipartisan support—framed as a corrective measure to protect religious minorities—RFRA was later curtailed by *City of Boerne v. Flores* (1997) (**see Appendix A**), which ruled that the federal RFRA could not be applied to state laws. In response, over 20 states passed their own RFRA-style laws, often with broader language and fewer constraints, creating a decentralized legal architecture[25] ripe for exploitation.

While RFRA was originally a shield for religious conscience, it has since evolved into a sword for circumventing anti-discrimination laws. Religious conservatives have increasingly used RFRA claims to challenge mandates for contraceptive coverage, to deny services to same-sex couples, and to opt out of LGBTQ+ non-discrimination ordinances. What was once a protective measure has become a strategic loophole for ideological refusal.

Legal scholars have raised urgent alarms about this shift. Marci Hamilton (**2014**), Douglas NeJaime and Reva Siegel (**2018**), and Micah Schwartzman *et al.* (**2012**) have all documented how religious exemption frameworks increasingly function as mechanisms for undermining civil rights. These scholars argue that religious liberty, once envisioned as a space for personal conscience, is now being invoked to justify institutional discrimination—transforming liberty into privilege, and conscience into control. This reframing of religious freedom distorts its constitutional foundations and violates principles of equal treatment under the law.

The consequences are not limited to legal abstractions—they manifest in real human suffering. Public health research shows a disturbing correlation between RFRA-style legislation and deteriorating mental health outcomes among vulnerable populations. In a landmark study, John R. Blosnich[26] *et al.* (**2019**) found that after Indiana enacted its state-level RFRA in 2015, sexual minority adults experienced a statistically significant increase in poor mental health. As the researchers noted: "These laws may function as structural stigma," reinforcing exclusion not just symbolically, but materially and psychologically. Importantly, these effects were not observed among heterosexual adults, underscoring the disproportionate burden borne by LGBTQ+ individuals.

These findings confirm what critics have long feared: religious exemptions, when unchecked, become codified forms of discrimination.

They allow individuals, institutions, and corporations to deny services, benefits, and recognition to others—often in the name of a narrowly defined theological morality. Under the guise of "religious freedom," such exemptions grant license to opt out of civil rights compliance, effectively transforming public space into a contested zone of private ideology. Moreover, these exemptions have increasingly been embedded into debates around reproductive justice. Employers have cited religious grounds to deny contraceptive coverage, hospitals have refused to provide abortion care, and pharmacists have declined to fill prescriptions for emergency contraception. In each of these cases, religious exemption is not a private spiritual act—it becomes a public policy with tangible consequences, particularly for women, LGBTQ+ individuals, and religious minorities.

This strategic deployment of religious liberty undermines both legal pluralism and democratic equality. It replaces a vision of shared rights with a system of fragmented access—where what one is entitled to depends not on constitutional protections but on someone else's beliefs. Far from protecting conscience, these exemptions elevate some consciences over others, often at the expense of those already marginalized. What emerges, then, is a troubling legal paradox: a framework originally designed to defend minority rights has been co-opted to entrench majority dominance. In the name of protecting faith, the state is now complicit in extending faith-based discrimination. And in the name of religious freedom, we are witnessing the rollback of sexual, reproductive, and identity-based freedoms across the country.

This section of the book, therefore, closes with a warning and a call. If we fail to challenge the growing misuse of religious exemptions, we will continue to see the very idea of equality hollowed out from within. A secular legal order cannot survive if its core principles are routinely subordinated to theological vetoes. To reclaim religious liberty as a shared civic good, we must ensure that it cannot be used as a Trojan horse for inequality.

Chapter Four:
Emerging Perspective

Efforts to Reconcile Religious Beliefs with Evolving Societal Norms

Historically, religious institutions have often positioned themselves in opposition to social progress—particularly in matters of gender equality, sexuality, bodily autonomy, and scientific inquiry. Theological rigidity, often shaped by patriarchal interpretations and moral absolutism, has excluded women, LGBTQ+ individuals, and people with diverse identities from full spiritual recognition and civil rights. Yet this resistance, while formidable, is not absolute. Across a wide range of faith traditions, voices within are rising to challenge dogma and reimagine doctrine in light of evolving values—especially those rooted in human dignity, equality, and pluralism.

This internal reckoning has given rise to a growing body of progressive theology, which seeks to reinterpret sacred texts, doctrines, and traditions through the lens of human rights, gender justice, LGBTQ+ inclusion, moral insight, and scientific understanding. While not yet dominant in most religious institutions, progressive theological thought has become increasingly influential, particularly in the West, as it redefines what it means to live faithfully in a diverse, modern world. Rather than treating scripture as static and immutable, progressive theologians engage in dynamic re-readings—often through frameworks such as feminist theology, queer theology, and liberation theology—to challenge traditional hierarchies and construct more inclusive visions of spiritual life.

Feminist theology, for example, situates itself within a global context. As Anne M. Grey[1] (1999) observes, feminist theology is not a monolith, but rather "a family of contextual theologies committed to the struggle for justice for women and the transformation of society" (**Grey, 1999**). Its many forms—Asian, African, Latin American, Womanist, Mujerista—share a common purpose: "the liberation of humankind together with all sentient life." In this framework, spiritual awakening is inseparable from justice, and faith is no longer defined by rigid gender roles, but by a commitment to human and planetary blossoming.

Queer theology, meanwhile, goes beyond the call for LGBTQ+ inclusion. It reimagines the very concept of divinity through the lived experiences of queer individuals. Reverend Patrick Cheng[2], a leading voice in the field, argues that "Queer theology insists that God is not merely tolerant of LGBTQ people, but is revealed through queer love, relationships, and bodies" (**Cheng, 2011**). This perspective positions queerness not as an exception to religious life, but as a profound expression of it—disrupting heteronormative frameworks and inviting faith communities to recognize divinity in the full spectrum of human identity.

These shifts are not confined to academic circles but are reshaping institutional practice. In Judaism, the Reform and Reconstructionist movements[3] have long been at the forefront of inclusive theology. Both have ordained women and LGBTQ+ individuals as rabbis and cantors, officiated same-sex marriages, and incorporated inclusive interpretations of Torah and Talmud into daily spiritual practice. Reform Judaism affirms that LGBTQ+ individuals are fully welcome in positions of leadership and love, stating: "Most Reform rabbis and cantors gladly officiate at same-sex and LGBTQ+ ceremonies" (**ReformJudaism.org**). Reconstructionist Judaism similarly adopted one of the earliest non-discrimination policies based on sexual orientation, recognizing that exclusion is fundamentally incompatible with its core belief in the dignity of every human being.

In Islam, the pioneering work of Imam Daayiee Abdullah[4] (1954–2025) stands as a powerful testament to the possibility of reform from within. As one of the few openly gay imams in the U.S., he officiated same-sex weddings and offered progressive interpretations of the Qur'an grounded in mercy and justice. "We are not rewriting the Qur'an," he affirmed. "We are rereading it through the lens of compassion, justice, and equality." His work has inspired a new generation of Muslims seeking to reconcile their faith with their authentic selves.

Among Christian denominations, the Metropolitan Community Church[5] (MCC) and the United Church of Christ (UCC) have emerged as leading voices for LGBTQ+ inclusion. Founded in 1968, MCC was established specifically to serve LGBTQ+ Christians, blending Christian theology with the lived experiences of gender and sexual minorities. Now active in more than 20 countries, it affirms that faith should be a source of healing, not harm. The UCC made history in 2005 by becoming the first major Christian denomination in the U.S. to endorse same-sex marriage. This stance was not just a matter of social justice, but a theological conviction: that covenantal love, regardless of orientation, reflects divine intention. In the UCC's view, affirming LGBTQ+ rights is not a departure from faith but rather its highest fulfillment.

Outside of traditional religious institutions, new spiritual movements are also challenging the conflation of dogma with exclusion. Among them, the International Raelian Movement[6] stands out for its unapologetic embrace of sexual diversity, bodily autonomy, and gender fluidity—positions it has championed since its founding in 1974. Grounded in a secular yet spiritual worldview, Raelian teachings affirm sexuality as a joyful, intelligent expression of being human. The movement has consistently supported LGBTQ+ rights, transgender recognition, and non-binary identities—not as exceptions, but as essential aspects of the human mosaic. In the words of Rael, the movement's founder: "The more we judge, the less we love. It is better to understand others than to judge them… Love being the ultimate and only solution to save the planet, giving love to everybody is the reason why we are on the Earth."

Raelism rejects all forms of sexual guilt imposed by religious orthodoxy and instead promotes pleasure, consent, and self-discovery as pathways to personal and collective enlightenment. Through initiatives like Clitoraid—which supports victims of female genital mutilation—and International SexEd Day, which promotes pleasure-positive, comprehensive sexuality education, the Raelian Movement exemplifies how secular spirituality can advance human rights and gender justice on a global scale.

Taken together, these examples—whether arising from within ancient traditions or from new spiritual paradigms—demonstrate that faith and freedom are not inherently at odds. They model how doctrine can evolve, how texts can be reinterpreted, and how religious commitment can deepen rather than diminish in the presence of diversity. They challenge the narrative that inclusion requires compromise and instead offer a powerful counter-narrative: that the most vibrant expressions of faith are those that grow in compassion, affirm complexity, and embrace change. In doing so, these communities reclaim religion not as a tool of control, but as a vehicle for liberation. For many believers and seekers alike, this marks not an abandonment of tradition—but a return to its deepest truths, rooted in love, justice, and the sanctity of every human life.

The Case for Sexual Freedom, Pluralism, and Secularism

In today's unfolding human rights landscape, the case for sexual freedom, pluralism, and secularism must be made not as lofty abstractions but as indispensable pillars of a just and democratic society. These three values, when upheld in harmony, protect individual autonomy, guard against religious overreach, and create space for diversity of thought, identity, and belief. Far from being mutually exclusive or ideologically opposed, they offer a blueprint for social coexistence rooted in human dignity, equality, and freedom.

Sexual freedom is a cornerstone of human dignity. It is far more than the right to engage in consensual acts. It is the bedrock of bodily autonomy, gender identity expression, and intimate self-determination—a human right that cannot be sidelined without corroding the very foundations of democracy. To suppress sexuality in the name of religious doctrine or moral conformity is to deny a person the right to define themselves. Such suppression fosters shame, stigma, and structural discrimination—systemic inequality embedded in institutions and social norms—disproportionately targeting women, LGBTQ+ individuals, and those whose sexual desires fall outside heteronormative frameworks. As legal philosopher Ronald Dworkin[7] asserts, "The right to be treated with dignity includes the freedom to define one's own values and way of life, so long as it does not harm others" (**Dworkin, 2011**). Denying people the right to love whom they choose, to access reproductive healthcare, or to express their gender identity is not only a violation of rights—it is a form of state-sanctioned spiritual and psychological harm.

Sexual freedom is also inseparable from gender justice. So long as laws that are animated by religious ideologies continue to police sexuality through abortion bans, the erasure of transgender rights, or the imposition of abstinence-only curricula, the deep roots of gender oppression will remain intact. Reproductive autonomy and sexual agency are not optional liberties; they are non-negotiable components of human rights and central to achieving genuine equality.

Pluralism is the ethical architecture of coexistence. It recognizes that in a diverse society, no single worldview—religious or secular—should dominate public policy or moral norms. It requires the active coexistence of multiple beliefs, cultures, and identities, all held together by a commitment to fairness and equal protection under the law. As philosopher Amartya Sen[8] writes, "Pluralism is not an optional extra; it is a condition of freedom itself. If public reason is not plural, it cannot be free" (**Sen, 2008**). Without pluralism, freedom becomes hollow, reduced to the license of the majority to impose its will on others.

In a truly pluralistic society, religious groups are free to express their values within their communities, but they may not codify those values into a law that binds everyone. This distinction is critical, especially on matters of sexuality, reproduction, and gender expression. The right to disagree must never be confused with the right to discriminate. Religious liberty ends where civil harm begins. Tolerance cannot be a shield for hegemony[9].

Secularism is the guardian of freedom and equality. It is frequently caricatured as hostile to religion. In truth, it is the very condition that makes both religious freedom and freedom from religion possible. It shields religious institutions from government interference and ensures that the state remains neutral in matters of belief. A secular government does not silence religious voices but simply refuses to privilege them.

As philosopher Martha Nussbaum[10] explains, "The idea of liberty of conscience... requires that we respect people's religious views by not imposing a particular view of the good on all citizens" (**Nussbaum, 2008**). As such, secularism is not a rejection of belief, but an affirmation of equality. It insists that public policy be shaped by reason, scientific evidence, and universal ethics, rather than sectarian dogma.

The First Amendment to the U.S. Constitution enshrines this principle: *"Congress shall make no law respecting an establishment of religion or prohibiting the free exercise thereof."* This dual commitment—to non-establishment and to free exercise—protects the spiritual freedom of all by refusing to allow any one religious view to serve as the basis for civil law. Around the world, countries like Sweden, Canada, and France offer compelling examples of secular governance. While not without their challenges, these nations uphold religious freedom while ensuring that sexual and reproductive rights are not subject to theological veto. In these contexts, the right to believe is held in equal regard with the right not to believe.

Taken together, sexual freedom, pluralism, and secularism are the ethical triad of modern liberty, the lifeblood of a healthy, inclusive democracy. When any of these values is compromised—when religion dictates public sexuality education, when LGBTQ+ people are denied equal rights, when reproductive choices are constrained by theological edict—then liberty itself is diminished. In a global age marked by cultural complexity and ideological diversity, these principles offer a common language of respect and shared humanity. They do not seek to erase religious tradition, but to liberate conscience and ensure that no one is forced to live by someone else's faith.

The Positive Influences of Progressive Spiritual and Sex-Positive Movements

While much of this book critiques the entanglement of institutional religion and sexual repression, this section turns toward liberation, innovation, and healing. Across the globe, a growing number of progressive spiritual and sex-positive movements are reimagining the relationship between body, spirit, and sexuality—not as forces in conflict, but as sacred allies in the journey toward personal freedom and collective blossoming. These movements reject shame-based moral frameworks and instead champion pleasure, consent, inclusivity, and diversity as essential pathways to wholeness and justice.

Far from being fringe or indulgent, these communities are grounded in ethical clarity, reverence for life and the pleasures that come with it, and a bold commitment to dismantling systems of oppression. They challenge dominant narratives that view eroticism as inherently sinful, proposing instead a spirituality that honors the body as a site of wisdom, joy, and divine expression.

In contrast to religious traditions that confine sexuality to narrow marital contexts or define it solely through procreation, progressive and sex-positive communities celebrate erotic expression as a vital and dignified part of human and spiritual life. Drawing inspiration from ancient traditions like Tantra, and from modern philosophies such as neo-Paganism, feminist spirituality—a non-patriarchal approach to the sacred centering embodied wisdom and liberation—and the Raelian Movement, they seek to restore pleasure to its rightful place as sacred, embodied knowledge and reframe it as a source of insight, empowerment, and cosmic connection rather than guilt or danger.

The Raelian Movement has long been a pioneering voice in advocating for sexual freedom, gender equality, and LGBTQ+ rights. Uniquely blending science-based spirituality with hedonistic ethics, the Raelian teachings affirm that sexuality, when expressed consensually and joyfully, is not only natural but an art form and a path to enlightenment. It encourages individuals to awaken their capacity for sensuality and loving connection, free from religious dogma and shame. From advocating guilt-free masturbation to launching provocative campaigns like GoTopless Day, which promotes gender equality and body positivity, the Raelian Movement consistently challenges patriarchal double standards. As Rael eloquently writes, "The gift of Sensual Meditation from the Elohim to humanity allows us to achieve a harmony with the infinite nature of all things, the ecstasy of *being* and the cosmic orgasm of consciousness" (**Rael, 1987**). This is not a call to indulgence without ethics; it is a call to transcend repression through mindful pleasure, and to honor eroticism as part of the cosmic dance of life.

The sex-positive feminist movement has also been instrumental in transforming cultural narratives around desire, consent, and freedom of relationship structure. Works like *The Ethical Slut* by Dossie Easton and Janet Hardy[11] have become foundational texts for communities embracing monogamous, polyamorous, queer, and fluid relationships. These movements emphasize agency, transparency, and mutual respect over rigid codes or binary moral judgments. As Easton and Hardy remind us: "Sexual expression is a choice, a gift, and a responsibility—not a source of guilt or hierarchy" (**Easton & Hardy, 2009**). They tell us that ethical pleasure is not only possible but profoundly healing.

Progressive spiritual communities are not only embracing inclusive theologies—they are shaping the next generation through comprehensive, age-appropriate, and spiritually grounded sexuality education. A powerful example is Our Whole Lives (OWL)[12], the sexuality education curriculum co-developed by the Unitarian Universalist Association[13] and the United Church of Christ. OWL integrates spiritual values, social justice, and science-based information, empowering youth with tools to navigate relationships, identity, and bodily autonomy with clarity and confidence.

Elsewhere, neo-Pagan and Wiccan[14] traditions celebrate sexuality through rituals that honor fertility, embodiment, and the cycles of life. From Beltane festivals[15] that celebrate fertility and sensuality, to goddess circles that explore menstruation, menopause, and queer embodiment, these communities recognize sexuality as not only natural but divine. They offer models of ritual, reverence, and inclusion, where no one is shamed for who they are or how they love.

The emergence of progressive spiritual and sex-positive movements signals a moral and spiritual renaissance—one that transcends fear-based control and reclaims the body as a site of reverence, sovereignty, and connection. These movements do not abandon religion; they liberate it. They do not reject ethics; they reconstruct them on the foundation of consent, empathy, and shared humanity. In a world still wounded by purity culture, religious condemnation, and heteronormative dominance, these communities extend a radical invitation to reclaim sexuality as a birthright, not a burden, and to affirm that freedom, not shame, is the holiest law of all.

The Role of Science and Ethics in Shaping Post-Religious Sexual Morality

In an era increasingly defined by pluralism, diversity, and scientific advancement, the traditional model of sexual morality—one grounded exclusively in religious doctrine—is proving both insufficient and out of step with contemporary understandings of human identity. This section explores how evidence-based ethics, public health research, and evolving moral reasoning converge to offer a more enlightened and inclusive vision of sexual morality—one grounded not in divine command, but in reason, empathy, and the blossoming of human beings.

Disciplines such as neuroscience, psychology, sociology, and medicine now provide a far more nuanced portrait of sexuality and gender than what was offered by centuries of traditional moral systems. In this context, ethics grounded in empirical knowledge becomes essential. They provide a framework through which we can assess behavior and policy not based on rigid orthodoxy, but on autonomy, consent, and well-being. This approach recognizes that in the absence of a universal divine authority, moral reasoning must be rooted in lived human experience, evidence, and compassion.

By "traditional moral systems," we refer to enduring religious and cultural codes—such as those found in conservative interpretations of Judeo-Christianity, Islam, Confucianism, and Victorian-era colonial law—that have long enforced rigid sexual norms. These systems often restrict sex to heterosexual marriage, marginalize same-sex relationships, and reject the broad spectrum of gender identities, equating virtue with abstinence and purity with repression. But the past century of scientific discovery challenges these inherited scripts.

For instance, neuroscience and developmental psychology have shown that sexual orientation and gender identity are not choices or moral failings, but complex, biologically influenced aspects of human identity. As neurobiologist Charles Roselli[16] explains, "Existing empirical evidence makes it clear that there is a significant biological contribution to the development of an individual's sexual identity and sexual orientation" (**Roselli, 2018**). Supporting this view, Frigerio, Ballerini, and Valdés

Hernández[17], in a systematic review of neuroimaging studies, concluded that both gender identity and sexual orientation emerge from "a combination of biological factors (genes, hormones, and gene expression) and environmental influences (including parents, peers, partners, and social models)" (**Frigerio *et al.*, 2021**). These findings dismantle reductionist narratives that treat sexuality as mere behavior or moral choice. Rather, they affirm that identity is a multifaceted, deeply human phenomenon.

The psychological and public health fields further reinforce this reframing. The American Psychological Association[18] (2021) clearly states that "diversity in gender identity and sexual orientation is a normal and positive variation of human experience—not a deviation to be corrected" (**APA, 2021**). Research confirms that when LGBTQ+ individuals—especially youth—are supported in affirming, sex-positive environments, they report higher self-esteem, reduced rates of depression and anxiety, and better long-term mental and emotional health (**Russell & Fish[19], 2016**). Conversely, when these identities are pathologized or repressed, the consequences include increased risks of suicide, substance abuse, and long-term psychological harm.

What this scientific evidence makes clear is that a just sexual morality cannot be based on stigma, shame, or fear. It must instead be based on understanding. Ethics, then, become less about enforcing conformity and more about nurturing dignity and safeguarding autonomy. Rather than moral codes rooted in fear or dogma, an evidence-based approach emphasizes relational ethics[20]—centered on mutual respect, informed consent, emotional safety, and non-harm. It is a shift from prohibition to care, from moralism to humanism.

We also see this evolution reflected in national policy models. Countries like the Netherlands and Sweden offer compelling examples of how sexual morality rooted in public health and individual rights leads to better social outcomes. These nations prioritize comprehensive sexuality education, early and universal access to contraception, inclusion of LGBTQ+ rights in public policy, and the decriminalization of consensual sexual behavior. Not coincidentally, they also report lower rates of teenage pregnancy, sexual violence, and sexually transmitted infections. In contrast to abstinence-based or punitive religious models, these societies demonstrate that an ethical framework built on well-being, evidence, and inclusion fosters healthier, happier, and more equitable communities.

Ultimately, the transition from religious to post-religious sexual ethics is not a rejection of morality, but a refinement of it. It asks not, "What is sinful?" but "What helps people blossom?" This reframing invites us to reimagine morality itself—not as a tool of control, but as a compass for compassion. Science, when paired with empathy and a commitment to justice, offers a moral foundation that honors the complexity of human desire, the sanctity of consent, and the dignity of all identities. In doing so, it moves us closer to a world where sexuality is not feared or punished but celebrated as an integral dimension of our shared humanity, marking a significant step in the human project of sexual liberation.

Toward a Future of Erotic Justice and Global Sexual Liberation

As we look toward a future unbound from the moral constraints of antiquated religious doctrines, a bold and inclusive vision of sexual freedom is taking shape—one that challenges not only theological belief but also the sociocultural and political systems that have long sought to regulate pleasure, police sexuality, and pathologize identity. This emerging vision does not merely tolerate erotic expression; it celebrates it. It calls for a sexual ethics rooted not in fear, guilt, or shame, but in empathy, autonomy, and human blossoming. At its heart is the radical affirmation that sexual freedom is not a luxury, nor a peripheral right, but an inalienable dimension of human dignity.

Central to this emerging vision is the concept of erotic justice[21]—a framework that insists that liberation must be both sexual and structural, intrinsically woven into broader struggles against racism, misogyny, homophobia, transphobia[22], and economic injustice. Legal scholar Ratna Kapur[23] introduced the term to critique how mainstream legal and human rights frameworks often sanitize or erase sexual difference, particularly within postcolonial contexts. As Kapur explains, "Erotic justice seeks to shift the discussion of sexuality beyond liberal legality and moral judgment, toward recognition of difference and the pleasures of the body" (**Kapur, 2013**).

In a parallel and complementary view, queer feminist writer and activist Amber Hollibaugh[24] reclaims erotic justice as a deeply embodied and intersectional call to embrace all that we are—especially for those historically denied the right to desire. "I want an erotic justice," she declares, "a politics of desire that refuses shame and embraces all the messy, contradictory parts of who we are" (**Hollibaugh, 2000**). Together, these visions call for more than rights; they demand transformation. They insist that erotic freedom cannot be detached from the social, legal, and economic structures that sustain inequality—and that true justice must ensure that pleasure, safety, and dignity are not the privilege of the few, but the birthright of all.

This powerful framework finds voice in a growing constellation of transnational movements[25] advocating for sexual and bodily liberation. In Latin America, feminist coalitions have ignited historic revolutions around abortion rights, reproductive justice, and the decriminalization of desire[26]. Across Africa and Asia, LGBTQ+ activists are courageously challenging colonial-era laws and reclaiming ancestral forms of gender and erotic plurality. Pride marches, queer festivals, and grassroots alliances now span the globe—offering not just visibility, but resilience, defiance, and joy. These movements are increasingly intersectional and intergenerational[27], led by youth, transgender and nonbinary leaders, people with disabilities, Indigenous voices, and sex workers—each bringing vital insight and energy to the broader project of erotic emancipation.

Importantly, these movements are neither monolithic nor bound by Western frameworks. As legal scholar Carl Stychin[28] cautions, sexual rights claims "have the potential to conflict with, rather than complement, each other" when universalized in ways that ignore local culture, history, and resistance (**Stychin, 2003**). True erotic justice, therefore, demands a decolonial, pluralistic approach—one that respects cultural specificity, lived experience, and avoids replicating the very hierarchies it seeks to dismantle. Only then can global liberation be truly inclusive, equitable, and sustainable.

Among the most visionary and consistent champions of global sexual freedom is the Raelian Movement. Since its founding in 1974, Raelian philosophy has boldly affirmed the sacredness of pleasure, the beauty of diversity, and the fundamental right to bodily autonomy. Through pioneering initiatives such as Go Topless Day, Clitoraid, and Sensual Meditation, the movement places erotic liberation at the heart of human evolution. As Maitreya Rael teaches: "Sensuality along with sexuality, which are part of the pleasure generating system, have been repressed for a long time, especially in our Western culture. Yet pleasure is such a natural and positive reaction" (**Rael, 2002**). According to Raelian teachings, the liberation of our bodies and the celebration of our sensuality are essential to achieving both inner happiness and planetary peace. This pleasure-affirming, science-inspired spirituality seamlessly aligns with the values of intersectional justice, insisting that the path to global harmony runs through the awakening of erotic intelligence[29].

Ultimately, this new sexual revolution is not merely a fight for tolerance—it is a call for transformation. It demands a fundamental reimagining of law, education, ethics, and spirituality—so that no one is punished, pathologized, or persecuted for who they are, whom they love, or how they express their joy. It calls for more than the separation of church and state—it calls for the separation of church and sex. And in its place, it imagines a fusion: a deep alliance between science, compassion, and erotic autonomy. This vision does not seek to erase belief systems but to elevate human conscience beyond fear. It does not ask us to abandon ethics, but to root them in consent, empathy, and evidence. It envisions a world where sexual freedom and social justice are not adversaries—but soulmates, dancing together at the heart of a new, liberated humanity.

Chapter Five:
The Raelian Re*LOV*ution

"

The role of a Prophet on Earth today does not only include divulging the secrets of our origins as explained in the Elohim's Messages, or revealing the promise of a wonderful future, thanks to science, it also implies acting within today's political arena so as to improve the lives of people, especially those living in countries who suffered the most from the selfishness and brutality of those who, for a short moment in time, were lucky enough to have had a slight advance. The only way to achieve world peace is to unite. That is why my role as a Prophet is not only spiritual and religious, but also political. And even if this brings me many enemies who one day might assassinate me, I will still say what I have to say.

"

Maitreya Rael

International SexEd Day

Annual International Awareness Campaign for
Comprehensive Sexuality Education

"To say nothing to your children about their sexual organs is wrong. And although it is better to explain what they are for, this is still not enough. You must explain how they can gain pleasure from them."—**Rael**

Launched in 2015 by Maitreya Rael, International SexEd Day is a bold humanitarian initiative of the International Raelian Movement (IRM), created to draw global attention to the urgent need for Comprehensive Sexuality Education (CSE) beginning in early childhood. Held each year on November 20th, in alignment with the International Day for Children's Rights, this day is far more than symbolic. It is an urgent appeal to governments, educators, and parents to uphold the recommendations of UNESCO's 2009 International Technical Guidance on Sexuality Education, which explicitly supports the introduction of age-appropriate sexuality education from age five, including discussions about masturbation as a natural aspect of self-discovery.

This position deeply resonates with the Raelian philosophy, which, for more than fifty years, has championed comprehensive, guilt-free, and pleasure-affirming sexuality education as a foundation for human fulfillment and dignity. Rooted in science and compassion, Raelian teachings affirm every human being's right to understand and explore their body without shame or repression. This perspective is strongly supported by leading international health institutions such as UNESCO, the World Health Organization (WHO), and the United Nations Population Fund (UNFPA), all of which advocate for sexuality education that is scientifically accurate, rights-based, age-appropriate, and centered on well-being.

It is revealing that, even months before the 2009 UNESCO Guidance was officially published, conservative and religious groups, particularly in the United States, mounted strong opposition. As Renate Dixon-Mueller[1] notes, "Critics who had read (or not read) the draft guidance posted on the UNESCO website objected that the report promoted masturbation, homosexuality, and abortion and charged it with being culturally insensitive and removing the responsibility for sexuality education from parents, where (they said) it belongs" (**Dixon-Mueller, 2010**). The pressure was so intense that when UNESCO revised its Guidance in 2018, the word *masturbation* was quietly removed (**UNESCO, 2018**).

While UNESCO may have sought broader political acceptance and considered cultural sensitivity through this omission, the decision remains deeply troubling. To remove such an innocuous, scientifically valid term from a technical framework written by global experts is to capitulate to ideological fearmongering[2]. The true threat to children does not come from age-appropriate mention of masturbation in educational materials—but from sexual ignorance, silencing, and institutional abuse, including the well-documented crisis of pedophilia within the Catholic Church.

Sexuality education is indeed culturally sensitive terrain. UNESCO undoubtedly revised its language to keep the guidance globally usable. Yet it remains equally true that children aged five to eight can safely and calmly learn about body awareness[3], self-touch, boundaries, emotions, and pleasure in language suited to their development. If sexuality education at this stage focuses on understanding the body, recognizing feelings, and promoting safety, how can masturbation—one of the most natural expressions of bodily curiosity—not be acknowledged as part of that reality?

As SexEd Day spokesperson and sexologist Clémence Linard, M.A., powerfully states: "The code of silence, the taboos, and the stigmatization surrounding sexuality education have significantly contributed to the global AIDS epidemic and continue to inflict immense emotional suffering on both adolescents and adults. These groups are unable to live their sexuality in a fulfilling way because the underlying politico-religious structure—persisting regardless of shifts in power—ensnares our children in a framework of outdated and destructive prohibitions. Disregarding scientific data, our educators have been disseminating outdated and inaccurate ideas for far too long. They are responsible for the needless suffering of millions of people. The guiding principles of scientific reports, validated through peer review, must be applied without censorship so that young girls and boys can be informed and protected from early childhood through an educational approach tailored to each age."

The goal of CSE is simple and profoundly humane: to provide children and adolescents with education that supports pleasure, well-being, bodily autonomy, respect, and safety, in line with the World Health Organization's definition of sexual health[4]. Comprehensive Sexuality Education is grounded in international human rights law— including the Convention on the Rights of the Child[5]—and empowers young people to develop autonomy, protect themselves from violence and exploitation, and resist religious or cultural oppression.

International SexEd Day, therefore, calls on UNESCO to restore scientific accuracy and integrity by reinstating the term masturbation in its guidance, and urges governments worldwide to implement fully comprehensive, pleasure-affirming CSE programs free from religious interference. Scientific expertise—not dogma—must guide education policy. Children deserve to grow up unburdened by guilt, safely informed, and happily connected to their bodies and emotions. As researchers Raisa Cacciatore[6] *et al.* observe, "Ignorance, misconceptions and fear hinder the implementation of young children's age-appropriate sexuality education globally. Methods to promote the sexuality education of young children are needed" (**Cacciatore *et al.*, 2020**).

Finally, it is essential to recognize the profound disconnect between how adults—especially politicians, religious leaders, and parents— perceive sexuality education and the lived experiences of children. When adults deny the importance of pleasure-affirming, scientifically grounded sexuality education, children pay the price—through stigma, discrimination, vulnerability to abuse, and psychological harm. International SexEd Day exists to end that silence. It reminds us that sexuality education is not merely an academic subject—it is a fundamental human right and a cornerstone of emotional, relational, and spiritual well-being.

Condom Distribution Campaign in Schools

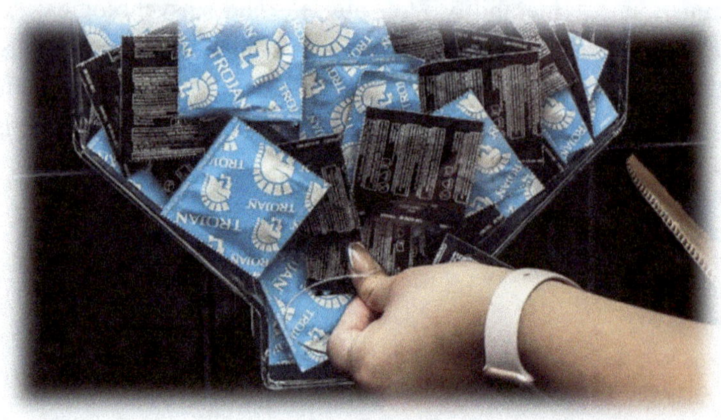

For the sake of promoting safe sexual health and comprehensive sexuality education in schools

*"Of course! This type of curriculum should be in school programs as well as distributing free condoms in schools like we did in schools 15 years ago [1993]. Even though many were against it at the time, this has helped in the long run. Who knows how many unwanted pregnancies and STI's have been avoided thanks to that small act of love? It's largely thanks to our doing this that there are even condom vending machines in some schools and this is wonderful. But it begins with accurate information and education. We can't ever hope that adults, no matter their age, will make the wise decision to use a condom if we don't educate them on the dangers of not using them."—***Rael***

Initiated in 1993 by Maitreya Rael, the Condom Distribution Campaign in Schools was a bold and urgent response to the Vatican's deeply troubling stance on contraception—particularly following a controversial declaration by Pope John Paul II in Tanzania that condom use was "sinful under any circumstance." At the height of the AIDS crisis in Africa, this pronouncement was not simply misguided; it was morally and medically reckless.

Rael condemned the Vatican's position as criminal in its consequences. He recognized that the Church's anti-condom doctrine represented a direct threat to public health and human life, especially for youth. His campaign promoted condom use as an essential, life-saving tool for preventing sexually transmitted infections (STIs) and unintended pregnancies. It deliberately challenged the substitution of religious ideology for medical science, advocating instead for rational, compassionate, evidence-based policy grounded in human rights and respect for life.

The campaign aimed not only to protect lives but also to challenge the false morality embedded in religious doctrine that stigmatizes safe sex. Its core message was simple and powerful: access to condoms saves lives, and young people deserve that protection. In particular, the initiative called for free distribution of condoms in schools, paired with comprehensive sexuality education to empower students with knowledge, the practical means to protect themselves, and the means to make responsible choices.

As Anita Brakman[7] and colleagues note, "Providing adolescents and young adults with access to free condoms in schools may increase the use of condoms by improving condom availability, eliminating cost, and decreasing embarrassment associated with purchasing condoms. Studies demonstrate that condom availability in schools is associated with the increased use of condoms and improved overall sexual health" (**Brakman et al., 2017**).

Research further shows that by the end of high school, nearly two-thirds of American youth are sexually active, and roughly one in five has had four or more sexual partners (**Starkman[8], 2002**). In this context, withholding access to condoms is not protective; it is negligent. The Raelian campaign underscored the need for public health policies that meet adolescents where they are, rather than punishing them for their natural development.

The campaign therefore advanced multiple public health goals: reducing teenage pregnancies, lowering HIV and STI transmission, and promoting responsible sexual decision-making. When condoms are accessible without stigma and paired with accurate education, students are better equipped to make informed choices regarding their sexual health.

As Jack Andrzejewski[9] *et al.* conclude, "Condom Availability Programs (CAP) are accepted by students and can be an appropriate and relevant school-based intervention... increasing condom use" (**Andrzejewski *et al.*, 2019**).

Pope John Paul II's opposition to condoms—voiced at a time when HIV/AIDS was ravaging entire communities in sub-Saharan Africa—stands not only as a tragic failure of moral leadership but also as an example of how religious doctrine, when left unchallenged, can undermine public health and cost human lives. His insistence that condom use was sinful, even in the context of epidemic-level health emergencies, had far-reaching consequences. More than a decade later, in 2009, Pope Benedict XVI reiterated this regressive stance, claiming that condoms were "not the answer" to Africa's AIDS crisis and might even worsen the problem—a statement that drew sharp condemnation from global health agencies and scientists alike. Even Pope Francis, despite a more progressive tone on some issues, avoided endorsing condom use during a 2015 visit to Africa, maintaining a silence that carried real-world consequences.

This pattern demonstrates how doctrinal absolutism can sabotage life-saving public health policy. In communities where religious authority shapes social norms, opposition from religious leaders does not remain theoretical—it affects behavior, health outcomes, and mortality. When religious figures with global influence advocate against condoms, they amplify stigma and fear and discourage life-saving prevention efforts among the very populations most at risk.

The Raelian campaign confronts this danger directly. It insists on a clear separation between church and sex, and by extension, between church and public health policy. This separation is not about undermining faith; it is pro-life in the truest sense. No religious doctrine should prevent individuals—especially adolescents—from receiving accurate information or accessing effective protection against disease.

The campaign also frames condom access as a matter of equity and justice. In many underserved communities, school-based programs may represent the only reliable means of obtaining protection. Denying this access exacerbates inequality and vulnerability. Equally important, the campaign encourages open, stigma-free dialogue among parents, educators, and students. By normalizing conversations about safe sex, schools help dissolve taboos, replace fear with understanding, and foster relationships grounded in honesty and respect.

Ultimately, the Condom Distribution Campaign in Schools is far more than a public health measure. It is part of a broader revolution in consciousness—one that challenges oppressive moral systems, reclaims bodily autonomy, and affirms sexual health as a fundamental human right. In doing so, it advances the ethical foundation of a world where compassion, science, and dignity prevail over guilt and repression.

International GoTopless Day

Free your Breasts! Free your Mind!

"As long as men are allowed to be topless in public, women should have the same constitutional right. Or else, men should have to wear something to hide their chests."—**Rael**

The mission of GoTopless is to promote gender equality by challenging both laws and social norms that permit men—but not women—to be topless in public. At its core, this campaign denounces the double standard that has led to countless women being fined, arrested, and publicly humiliated for exposing their chests in the same way that men do freely. GoTopless defends the principle that women deserve the same constitutional rights as men when it comes to bodily autonomy and public expression, and that gender should never be a barrier to freedom.

Founded by Rael in 2007, GoTopless was launched as a direct challenge to this unconstitutional discrimination and as a celebration of both gender equality and sexual freedom. Each year, on August 26—the anniversary of women's suffrage in the United States—GoTopless Day is held across the world to raise awareness, spark public dialogue, and demand legal and cultural shifts regarding topless rights.

The date is deeply symbolic: on August 26, 1920, the U.S. Constitution was amended to grant women the right to vote. Fifty years later, Congress officially recognized this milestone as Women's Equality Day. Yet more than a century later, full equality remains elusive, particularly in the intimate and visible realm of bodily freedom. Women today must still fight for the right to exist publicly on equal terms—unencumbered by shame, censorship, or coercion.

GoTopless works to reclaim the perception of women's breasts as natural, dignified, and worthy of neither concealment nor sexualized stigma—regardless of whether they are nursing or not. There is no more reason to mandate the covering of breasts than of arms or ankles. Moreover, the movement affirms that it is not the presence of a woman's chest that incites objectification or arousal, but the conditioned impulse in the observer. Just as men are expected to regulate their behavior when confronted with revealing clothing, so too can they learn to appreciate without projecting, admire without harassing, and respond with consciousness rather than compulsion. Elevating awareness above impulse lays the foundation for a more respectful, peaceful, and equitable society.

According to GoTopless President Nadine Gary, "Across Europe and elsewhere, the past twenty years have brought a growing wave of repression, with many young women unconsciously imitating the puritanical attitudes toward the female body promoted by American media and social networks. GoTopless is committed to reminding women that equality includes the right to be topless." She added, "Topless equality is profoundly empowering because it helps liberate women—and ultimately everyone—from centuries of Judeo-Christian guilt and shame surrounding the human body."

As Nassim Alisobhani[10] argues, "Laws discriminating on the basis of a woman's anatomy bear no relationship to a woman's capabilities or role in society; they merely subjugate her to a second-class citizenship solely because of the way society sexualizes her body... Female topless prohibitions are the embodiment of gender discrimination. It is one of the remaining laws that blatantly treat men and women differently on the basis of how society views their bodies and the biological differences between the sexes... The common justifications for these laws are based on antiquated Victorian and Judeo-Christian values that have no place in our modern society" (**Alisobhani, 2018**).

Indeed, opposition to topless equality—by both men and women—is often rooted in religious traditions that conflate modesty with virtue. Many conservative faiths uphold strict dress codes that demand women's bodies be hidden in order to be respected. These moral codes, often enforced without question, perpetuate patriarchal assumptions that reduce female visibility to sinfulness. Under such systems, exposure of the female chest becomes not just taboo, but morally condemned. But this association is not universal—it is learned. And it can be unlearned.

Religious teachings do not operate in isolation; they intersect with social norms that hypersexualize the female body and reinforce the belief that women's chests are inherently provocative. Some critics even claim that topless women threaten family values or public morality. But such arguments are based not in evidence, but in inherited discomfort and control. As Colleen Marron[11] observes, "Males may exhibit their bare chests on outdoor public property their entire lives. In many locations, this fundamental right to bodily autonomy afforded to men is denied to women… The assumption that female breasts require coverage due to their provocative nature normalizes and entrenches problematic issues, particularly the objectification of women, into law. The fundamental right to bodily autonomy requires protection over arbitrary and capricious social norms" (**Marron, 2022**).

A particularly misguided objection to topless equality is the idea that the sight of a topless woman could psychologically harm children. This claim is not supported by empirical research. Children are inherently curious, adaptive, and unburdened by adult shame—until that shame is taught to them. When adults respond to the human body with shame, fear, or taboo, children absorb and internalize those attitudes. Conversely, when they are raised in environments where bodies are seen as natural, children grow up with healthier self-images and fewer hang-ups about nudity and sexuality. In many cultures where toplessness is normalized, children experience no adverse effects—on the contrary, they tend to show greater ease and body confidence. The real threats to children's well-being lie in abuse, violence, and neglect—not in the harmless sight of a human torso.

The continued use of the "protect the children" argument reveals more about adult discomfort than it does about any measurable harm. It reflects cultural taboos that treat the female body as inherently shameful or dangerous. In truth, fostering openness, education, and acceptance is far more protective than any law mandating nipple concealment. A culture that embraces body positivity—rather than repression—creates safer, healthier, and more honest human beings.

Religious leaders often play a powerful role in shaping these cultural norms. When they condemn female toplessness, their followers often adopt these views without question, reinforcing outdated restrictions masquerading as divine guidance. But when progressive spiritual leaders champion body freedom as a sacred human right, they give others permission to question inherited dogmas, confront their biases, and step into greater personal and collective liberation. Through his vocal support of GoTopless Day, Rael affirms the Raelian Movement's enduring commitment to gender equality, erotic dignity, and freedom of expression.

Those who interpret religious texts literally tend to view toplessness as rebellion, not liberation. But resistance to outdated norms is the very engine of progress. The fight against topless discrimination is about more than dress—it is about autonomy, respect, and full citizenship. It is about dismantling systems of control disguised as morality. So long as women are forbidden to do what men do freely, the promise of equality remains unfulfilled.

GoTopless Day is more than a protest—it is a celebration, an act of courage, and a radical affirmation of human dignity. This is why it will continue its fight to ensure that women around the world enjoy the same rights as men to reclaim, reveal, and celebrate their bodies without fear or shame. It is a fight for equality, for justice, and for a world in which nudity is no longer confused with obscenity, and in which freedom of expression extends fully to all human beings regardless of gender.

Clitoraid: Clitoris Awareness Month

Restoring a Sense of Dignity and Pleasure in Women

"Instead of using the money raised by Clitoraid to treat just a few women, we should create the first Raelian 'Pleasure Hospital' and perform surgeries on all African women for free, with the help of volunteer Raelian and non-Raelian doctors."—**Rael**

Clitoraid, a nonprofit humanitarian initiative founded by Rael in 2006, stands as a bold and compassionate response to the global atrocity of female genital mutilation (FGM). Rooted in the Raelian philosophy that sexual pleasure is a basic human right, Clitoraid's mission is threefold: to offer clitoral reconstructive surgery to survivors of FGM, to raise international awareness about the practice, and to help restore what was violently stolen—their bodily integrity, human dignity, and right to sexual pleasure.

Far from viewing sexual pleasure as a taboo, the Raelian Movement affirms that it is a fundamental human right and reclaiming one's ability to feel and express that pleasure is a vital aspect of healing, liberation, self-love, and empowerment. This conviction forms the backbone of Clitoraid's work, as it offers survivors a chance to experience wholeness, sensuality, and bodily sovereignty again through surgery and psychological care.

As Amr Seifeldin[12] notes, "Clitoral reconstructive surgery after female genital mutilation provides an improvement in patients' psychology, noted by an increase in confidence, self-esteem, and feminine body image. It has also improved sexual desire, arousal, and satisfaction, with minimal improvement in orgasm, lubrication, and pain. We suggest it be offered to FGM victims who consult gynecology clinics, in other hospitals, and training doctors in genital reconstructive techniques" **(Seifeldin, 2016)**.

Since its inception, Clitoraid has trained a growing number of physicians in this specialized form of genital restorative surgery, enabling it to deliver high-quality, compassionate care to FGM survivors worldwide. To date, dozens of women have undergone clitoral reconstruction through Clitoraid-affiliated programs in the United States, France, and beyond. Remarkably, all patients have reported improvements, and approximately 60% have experienced orgasm for the first time in their lives—a profound and life-altering milestone for women once told that such pleasure was forever out of reach.

One of Clitoraid's most ambitious undertakings has been the creation of the *Pleasure Hospital* in Burkina Faso, a facility envisioned as a permanent center offering free surgery and psychological care to FGM survivors. Contrary to widespread assumptions, opposition to the hospital did not primarily stem from local cultural or religious norms. In fact, the hospital enjoyed widespread public and governmental support, including from First Lady Chantal Compaoré[13], who was scheduled to inaugurate the center. Rather, the resistance came from financial and political interests threatened by Clitoraid's non-profit model. Local surgeons such as Dr. Charlemagne Ouedraogo, who charged high fees for similar procedures, saw the hospital's free services as a competitive threat. Rather than collaborate, they launched efforts to block its opening—motivated not by medical concern but by monopolistic protectionism.

Compounding the situation was the prejudice against Clitoraid's Raelian affiliation, which opponents weaponized to discredit the organization as a "sect" rather than recognizing its legitimate humanitarian contribution. Dr. Ouedraogo, a prominent Catholic figure and member of the Sovereign Military Order of Malta, led a defamation campaign against Clitoraid, falsely alleging that the hospital was a front for nefarious activity. His influence, bolstered by ties to then-President Blaise Compaoré and powerful religious-political networks, temporarily succeeded in halting the hospital's operations. Yet justice prevailed: in 2014, Burkina Faso's Supreme Court ruled in favor of the Raelian

Movement, ordering Dr. Ouedraogo to pay damages for defamation. Ironically, months later, Compaoré himself was ousted in a popular uprising, a symbolic reminder of the impermanence of power rooted in corruption, collusion, and religious bias.

The struggle surrounding the Pleasure Hospital underscores how humanitarian progress is often obstructed not by cultural resistance but by a toxic blend of economic self-interest, institutional religion, and political manipulation. These forces, acting in concert, work to block access to healing—not because the need is in question, but because profit and orthodoxy take precedence over justice. Even now, Clitoraid must navigate legal hurdles, institutional resistance, and cultural taboos as it works to expand access to surgery, secure partnerships with hospitals and universities, and raise funds for continued operations. Religious and medical gatekeeping remain entrenched, yet the organization presses forward with conviction and creativity.

Despite the obstacles, Clitoraid's mission remains unwavering. Through global awareness campaigns, educational outreach, and strategic advocacy, it continues to challenge the stigma surrounding FGM and promote female sexual autonomy as a cornerstone of human dignity. Its work is not only about restoring physical sensation but also about healing psychological trauma and dismantling the deeply embedded systems that normalize gender-based violence. By helping survivors reclaim their right to pleasure, Clitoraid offers a radical and restorative model of post-trauma empowerment that resonates far beyond the surgical room.

As Nadine Gary, Clitoraid's Director of Operations, explains, "Since 2009, Clitoraid has provided clitoral restorative surgery (CRS) to over 550 genitally mutilated women—most of them living in the United States." She underscores a staggering reality often overlooked: "Very few people realize that more than half a million FGM survivors currently reside in the U.S. as a result of immigration." Clitoraid has also offered surgeries in Burkina Faso and other parts of West Africa, extending its reach to communities most affected by this practice. For Gary, the deeper struggle is not only medical but moral and cultural: "Society must rid itself of the sexual shame and guilt disseminated by archaic patriarchal religions—both tribal and mainstream—that have historically demeaned and subjugated women. Repressing female sexuality has long been a strategy to dominate and control." But today, she adds, the tides are shifting: "Thanks to increased access to education, more and more women are awakening to the fact that traditions and cultures which violate their sexual integrity are not worthy of preservation. When they violate our sexual freedom, they violate our dignity."

Looking ahead, Clitoraid is focused on expanding its reach. The organization aims to train more surgeons in reconstructive techniques, forge new partnerships with medical institutions, and increase access to restorative surgery for women across continents. It also seeks to deepen its educational efforts, challenging cultural assumptions and elevating public discourse around female sexuality and bodily integrity. By aligning with global human rights organizations and medical ethicists, Clitoraid continues to press for the worldwide abolition of FGM and for the recognition of pleasure as an essential facet of female identity—not something shameful or secondary, but sacred and central.

In a world that still punishes women's bodies and silences their pleasure, helping an FGM survivor experience her first orgasm is not just medical—it is revolutionary. It is an act of loving rebellion, a sacred reclaiming of what should never have been stolen. And it is a testament to the power of a movement that sees erotic dignity not as a threat to morality, but as its highest expression.

Clonaid: Yes, to Human Reproductive Cloning!

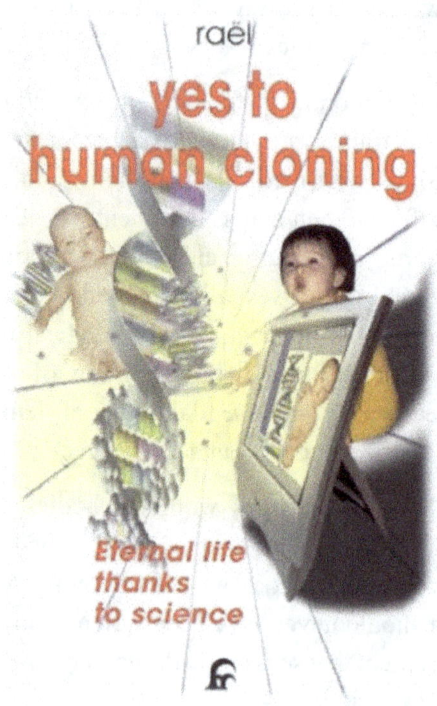

The Pro-Life Technology of the Future

"People who wish to benefit from the fruits of scientific progress should have the right to do so. We, Raelians, believe that science should be our religion, since science saves lives, while religion and superstition kill. Individuals must have the freedom to decide whether or not they want to benefit from scientific advancements."—**Rael**

In 1997, shortly after the groundbreaking cloning of Dolly the Sheep, Rael founded Clonaid, a pioneering company dedicated to developing human cloning technologies. While the idea originated with Rael, he has had no operational involvement in the company. Dr. Brigitte Boisselier, head of Clonaid and spokesperson for the Raelian Movement, clarifies, "Clonaid is a private company, and the Raelian Movement has no involvement in its business operations." The connection between Clonaid and the Raelian Movement is philosophical rather than institutional anchored in the shared belief that human cloning represents not only a leap in reproductive science but also a gateway to humanity's future, including the eventual possibility of immortality.

In 2002, Clonaid made global headlines when it announced the birth of Eve, reportedly the world's first human clone. Though this claim was met with widespread skepticism and has yet to be scientifically verified, the Raelian Movement remains unwavering in its support for human cloning. For Raelians, cloning is not a dystopian threat—it is a promising frontier, a technology that can advance human understanding and unlock the scientific potential for eternal life. In their view, it represents not only a reproductive tool but a transformative vision of humanity's future, rooted in freedom, science, and consciousness.

Clonaid captured global attention in 2002 with its announcement of the birth of Eve, claimed to be the world's first human clone. Though this claim remains unverified by the scientific community and was met with intense skepticism, the Raelian Movement has remained a steadfast advocate for the potential of human cloning. Raelians do not view cloning as a dystopian[14] threat, but as a pro-life technology and transformative innovation—one that opens unprecedented avenues for understanding life, extending it, and ultimately transcending the limits of mortality. In their view, cloning is more than a reproductive technique; it is a bold affirmation of humanity's future, rooted in freedom, science, and consciousness.

Boisselier argues, "In his book, *Yes to Human Cloning* and in numerous conferences, Rael emphasized that human cloning is the only path to overcoming death—the ultimate disease. Today, science is increasingly validating what Rael predicted: cloning offers the most promising route to immortality," she continued. "Scientists in Russia and elsewhere are already exploring the transfer of human consciousness into computers. The next phase will involve uploading that digital identity into a cloned body. What Rael envisioned in 1974 is no longer science fiction—it is a rapidly approaching reality. But to realize it, we must overcome fear and religious dogma."

Resistance to human cloning is not new in the broader context of medical history. Society has repeatedly reacted with fear to groundbreaking innovations. Anesthesia was once condemned as unnatural and immoral. Organ transplants were considered grotesque violations of bodily sanctity. In vitro fertilization (IVF), now mainstream, was once vilified for producing "test-tube babies" and accused of dehumanizing reproduction. Yet over time, each of these technologies became normalized, even celebrated. Anesthesia is now routine, heart transplants save thousands of lives annually, and IVF is embraced by over 90% of the public—a staggering rise from only 15% support in the early 1980s.

These historical examples are a stark reminder that humanity's initial resistance to scientific breakthroughs is often rooted not in reason but in fear, religious dogma, or cultural inertia[15]. Innovations that were once feared eventually became indispensable. Today's emerging technologies—whether cloning, genetically modified organisms (GMOs), artificial intelligence (AI), or nanotechnology—are no different. They challenge us to rise above fear and imagine new possibilities. Science must not be stifled by superstition or paralyzed by moral panic, especially when it can alleviate suffering, restore hope, save lives, enhance the quality of life, and expand human potential. Today's innovations have the potential to define tomorrow's reality.

So why does human cloning continue to provoke such visceral fear? That fear stems from a volatile mix of unfamiliarity, sensationalist media, and entrenched religious opposition. Yet, at its core, cloning is simply another form of assisted reproductive technology—a deeply pro-life intervention that can bring joy to those otherwise denied the experience of parenthood. Under the Americans with Disabilities Act[16] (ADA), infertility is considered a disability, meaning that access to reproductive technologies—including cloning—should be protected as a fundamental right. To ban cloning is not just regressive; it may, in fact, be unconstitutional, as it infringes on personal autonomy and reproductive freedom. In the words of Brigitte Boisselier, "The ban on human cloning is not only outdated—it denies people access to existing technologies and, more profoundly, prevents us from curing death itself." Furthermore, Rael adds, "Removing legal and moral bans on cloning is not just about scientific freedom, but also about preparing for a new chapter in human destiny."

Legalizing reproductive cloning would open inclusive paths for a diverse range of families. Same-sex couples, individuals with fertility challenges, and parents mourning the loss of a child could all find hope through cloning. The technology offers a new way to conceive, build families, and reclaim futures once considered lost. In this light, cloning becomes a tool of compassion—an expansion of procreative freedom grounded in dignity, autonomy, and love. As ethicist Carson Strong[17] argues, "It is argued that freedom to use cloning is a form of procreative freedom and, as such, deserves respect... It is concluded that human reproductive cloning would be ethically justifiable in at least some cases involving infertile couples, provided that it could be performed without an elevated risk of anomalies" (**Strong, 2005**).

For Raelians, cloning is more than reproductive assistance—it is a profound expression of their vision for immortality. Rael envisions a future in which cloning, combined with digital identity and consciousness preservation and transfer, enables individuals to achieve a form of scientific reincarnation. In this scenario, the mind can be uploaded into a computer and later "reborn" into a cloned body. What once seemed like science fiction is fast becoming a serious field of exploration. This vision invites us to confront our assumptions about death, identity, and the body—and to evolve our ethical frameworks to match the new horizons of possibility.

Predictably, major religions fiercely oppose cloning, interpreting it as a trespass against divine authority. Christianity, Islam, and Judaism, among others, view life as a sacred gift that must not be replicated through human technology. Cloning is denounced as "playing God," a profanation of natural order. While Raelians envision immortality as a scientific achievement, traditional faiths frame it as a metaphysical reward—a spiritual ascension reserved for the soul, not the body. This conflict is not merely philosophical; it exposes a deeper rift between science and religion, between progress and preservation.

The Raelian Movement, however, offers a clear counterpoint: this opposition is rooted not in ethics but in outdated dogmas. To deny individuals the right to clone themselves is to deny them reproductive liberty. Just as couples have the right to reproduce through sex or IVF, they should also have the right to reproduce through reproductive cloning—without interference from religious institutions or government bodies. In this sense, cloning is not just a scientific pursuit but a moral revolution: it expands our understanding of rights, of freedom, and of what it means to be human.

By championing cloning, Raelians seek to give voice to the voiceless: the infertile, the grieving, the marginalized. They aim to redefine reproductive justice and reclaim the future from fear. In doing so, they dare to ask the ultimate question: What if death is no longer our final destiny? What if we can live again—not in heaven, but here, in renewed physical form, with continuity of consciousness? That is the promise of human cloning. And that is why Raelians proudly declare: Yes, to human reproductive cloning.

Rael Rainbow Team: Fatwa of Love

Spreading LOVE does save lives

"Sexual orientation is genetic and not influenced by the environment. Understanding that sexual orientation is as natural for a homosexual as it is for a heterosexual is the key to eradicating discrimination against sexual minorities."—**Rael**

The Rael Rainbow Team, formerly known as Aramis International, is a global organization devoted to the advancement of LGBTQ+ rights and the celebration of sexual diversity. Founded by Rael in 2004, the group emerged as a direct response to the injustices endured by sexual minorities—particularly in regions where laws and cultural norms continue to suppress and criminalize non-heteronormative identities. Through advocacy, education, and global visibility campaigns, the Rael Rainbow Team provides a critical platform to confront legal repression, social stigma, and systemic discrimination, while promoting sexual freedom as a universal human right. Its mission reflects the core values of the Raelian Movement: that sexuality is not a moral dilemma to be judged, but a natural expression of human uniqueness to be honored and celebrated.

In one of the most striking acts of spiritual resistance in modern history, Rael became the first religious leader in the world to issue a "Fatwa of Love," a bold response to a deadly religious decree. In 2005, Iranian Ayatollah Ali al-Sistani issued a fatwa calling for the execution of LGBTQ+ individuals, further inciting an already brutal climate of hate and persecution in Iran. Rael's response was immediate and profound. His "Fatwa of Love" denounced the call to violence and instead elevated the principles of compassion, empathy, and the inviolable right to sexual diversity. Thousands of Raelians worldwide joined the movement, sending postcards and messages—each a "Fatwa of Love"—directly to the Ayatollah. These cards affirmed the humanity of LGBTQ+ people and urged an end to violence and state-sponsored hatred. In a quiet yet monumental shift, the Ayatollah's office eventually removed the original "Fatwa of Killing" from its website. This outcome stands as a testament to the transformative power of love over cruelty, and to Rael's unwavering belief that true spiritual leadership is defined not by obedience, but by the courageous defense of the oppressed.

This struggle remains urgent. LGBTQ+ individuals in Iran continue to suffer among the harshest legal and social conditions in the world. Under Iran's Penal Code, same-sex relationships are criminalized with punishments ranging from flogging to execution. Those suspected of homosexuality face arrest, torture, and public humiliation. Outside the legal system, LGBTQ+ Iranians endure systemic harassment, surveillance, and violence—often at the hands of the morality police. The threat of being outed can result in job loss, family rejection, or exile. Mental health challenges are widespread, yet support is virtually nonexistent. Suicide rates remain disproportionately high due to the crushing weight of fear, secrecy, and alienation.

Even transgender individuals—while legally recognized in Iran—face coercive practices. Many are pressured into undergoing sex reassignment surgery simply to be granted basic recognition. These procedures, though sometimes state-funded, are less about empowerment and more about enforcing rigid gender binaries. What should be a personal, sovereign decision becomes an imposed path of conformity. Meanwhile, anti-discrimination protections in employment, education, housing, or healthcare are entirely absent. In this climate, survival itself is a daily act of resistance; to dream of dignity or thriving is revolutionary.

And yet, amid this darkness, the Rael Rainbow Team continues to shine a bright and unwavering light. Through international outreach campaigns, solidarity events, media advocacy, and humanitarian support, the team brings much-needed visibility to the plight of LGBTQ+ individuals across the globe—and especially in countries like Iran. Their message is unmistakably clear: no human being should be persecuted for who they love or how they express their identity. They affirm that love is sacred, diversity is beautiful, and sexuality is not a sin, but a celebration. In a world still gripped by fear and hatred, the Rael Rainbow Team lives out the Raelian principle that true spirituality is rooted in liberation rather than condemnation.

As Aisya Aymanee Zaharin and Maria Pallotta-Chiarolli[18] note, "Due to the strong majority of Islamic conservatives who continue to be prevalent in Iran and other Muslim countries, Muslim transgender women are still suffering from heightened stigma and transphobia, discrimination and injustice, violence and persecution" (**Zaharin & Pallotta-Chiarolli, 2020**). These realities are why the work of the Rael Rainbow Team is so vital—not just in raising awareness, but in offering solidarity and hope to those enduring unspeakable repression.

Perhaps the most profound gift offered by the Rael Rainbow Team is its deeply liberating philosophy, one that radically affirms the worth of LGBTQ+ individuals without hesitation or exception. As François-Yves Roussel, Raelian Bishop and Global Leader of the Rael Rainbow Team, explains: "One of the greatest gifts for an LGBTQ+ person who joins the Rael Rainbow Team is the profound relief from society's imposed stress—a rare liberation unique to our philosophy. From the moment one discovers the Raelian Messages, the complete absence of guilt is striking. There is no God to judge, sexual orientation is genetic—therefore natural—and a legitimate expression of oneself. Then, little by little, one realizes that this freedom is truly lived within the community, which reinforces the teachings and brings immense well-being, simply by being able to be oneself, without fear or constraint."

This rare blend of radical love, science-based affirmation, and unapologetic defense of queer lives is what sets the Rael Rainbow Team apart. More than an advocacy group, it is a spiritual sanctuary and a revolutionary force. Its work reminds us that transformation begins not with laws alone, but with courage, compassion, and the refusal to accept hate as destiny. The "Fatwa of Love" remains both a historic act and a living promise—a radiant declaration that love will always be louder than fear, and that no force is more enduring than the freedom to be fully, joyfully, unapologetically oneself.

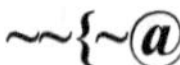

Apostatize Now!

Renouncing anti-Human Rights Religions

"Send your apostasy form to your parish so you can freely live your life far away from this dictatorially induced guilt and the spreading of Catholic Talibanization. And then freely enjoy a beautiful and free sexual life, which can include homosexuality, birth control, abortion and sexual equality – among other things condemned by the Catholic mullahs."—**Rael**

To *renounce anti–Human Rights religions* is to affirm one's right to reject any faith system—especially one entered through baptism or ritual initiation—that violates the dignity of the individual. It means publicly breaking ties with religious doctrines, teachings, or institutions that promote intolerance, deny equality, and perpetuate discrimination and injustice under the guise of moral or spiritual authority.

The "Apostatize Now!" campaign, launched by Rael in the late 1990s, was created to empower individuals—particularly those baptized as infants—to formally declare their departure from such religions. More than symbolic, apostasy is a radical act of personal sovereignty: a declaration of freedom of conscience, sexual and reproductive autonomy, and the right to dissent from institutions that enforce obedience at the cost of liberty. This campaign specifically challenges religious doctrines that are anti-LGBTQ+, anti–sexuality education, anti–reproductive rights, and anti–gender equality. In doing so, it invites individuals to take a principled stand against theocratic control, patriarchal domination, and systemic oppression.

Launched at a time when religious extremism was gaining ground across the world, the campaign also challenges the abuse of religious authority to justify violence, exclusion, and moral policing. Rael envisions a world where everyone is free to choose their beliefs without fear of persecution, familial coercion, or the threat of death. Encouraging people to apostatize officially, especially when done publicly, is a way to challenge the political and psychological grip of religious institutions that still shape public morality and inhibit human progress. The campaign aspires to usher in a more rational, inclusive, and spiritually emancipated society—one rooted in compassion rather than control.

As Mirjam van Schaik[19] notes, "The freedom of religion or belief is internationally recognized. However, studies demonstrate that the implementation of the right to apostasy, an essential aspect of this freedom, encounters difficulties in state practices" (**van Schaik, 2023**). Indeed, apostasy remains criminalized in several countries and deeply stigmatized in many more. The "Apostatize Now!" movement highlights the urgent need for global secularism and the separation of church and sex. It defends the individual's right to break away from oppressive religious frameworks—especially when those frameworks attack sexual, reproductive, and educational freedoms.

A vital aspect of the campaign addresses the indoctrination of children through rituals imposed before they are capable of consent: infant baptism, male circumcision, and female genital mutilation (FGM). The Raelian philosophy asserts that every human being should be free to choose their beliefs upon reaching maturity. Rituals imposed in childhood violate this principle by embedding identity and worldview before understanding can form. Rael argues that spirituality should not be inherited—it should be consciously chosen. When children are baptized or subjected to other religious rites, they are often denied the opportunity to explore diverse spiritual or philosophical paths. Instead, the Raelian approach promotes an educational model grounded in openness and curiosity, where children learn about multiple worldviews without indoctrination. This fosters the development of intellectual autonomy, critical thinking, and spiritual self-determination.

The campaign also invites a broader global reflection on religion's role in society. It challenges doctrines rooted in fear, guilt, and blind obedience, advocating instead for a spirituality based on tolerance, compassion, and reason. "Apostatize Now!" is an invitation to join a movement grounded in love, respect, and freedom—a movement striving for a more enlightened and harmonious humanity. One of the most profound dimensions of the campaign is its call for spiritual decolonization.

Rael explicitly extends this invitation to Indigenous peoples around the world—to apostatize from the religions imposed upon them by colonizers, particularly Christianity. For countless Native and First Nations communities, conversion was not a free choice but the result of conquest, forced assimilation, and cultural erasure. Missionaries and colonial empires imposed Christianity as a tool of domination, displacing sacred traditions and identities. For these communities, apostatizing means returning to pre-colonial spiritual traditions, which is not merely an act of cultural revival but a sacred responsibility. It is a way to reclaim ancestral dignity and reestablish spiritual sovereignty.

Importantly, apostasy from Christianity does not mean rejecting Jesus. On the contrary, Raelians honor Jesus as a prophet and messenger of the Elohim. What is rejected is the institution that has distorted his message for power and control. As Rael declares, "The need for spiritual decolonization is really urgent. The people of Kama—the ancient name of the African continent before colonization—and all Indigenous Peoples around the world must apostatize from Christianity, a religion that insults the memory of their ancestors. Those ancestors cannot rest in peace while their descendants continue to practice the religion of their colonizers, those who conquered them in bloodshed and forced them to convert to Christianity through violence. The spiritual decolonization of Kama is an indispensable condition for the future development of this continent."

In this spirit, *Apostatize Now!* is more than a campaign. It is a call to consciousness, a movement of liberation, and a declaration of spiritual sovereignty. It invites all people—regardless of background—to reclaim their inner freedom, reject fear-based obedience, and embrace a new paradigm rooted in reason, love, and peace. In a world still struggling to separate power from dogma, and conscience from coercion, apostasy becomes not only a right but a revolutionary act of love.

Rael's Girls and the Decriminalization of Prostitution

Supporting those who choose to work in the sex industry

"Selling your sex for money is not worse than selling any other part of your body, including your brain. Some societies criminalize the sexual part because they were shaped by Judeo, Islamic, Christian values, which describe sex as bad. I prefer to see a girl selling her body for sex than a scientist selling his brain to the weapons industry which will use his knowledge to kill millions of people."—**Rael**

In a world where money governs nearly every facet of human life, prostitution—like any form of labor—reflects the reality of people exchanging parts of themselves for survival, pleasure, or fulfillment. As Rael provocatively asserts, "Some people 'prostitute their brains' as intellectual workers, others their hands as factory workers, and still others their bodies as sex workers. If all are exchanging parts of themselves for money, then morally speaking, why should sexual labor be uniquely stigmatized?" This incisive question lies at the heart of Rael's vision for sexual freedom and dignity.

In 2005, Rael's Girls was founded in direct response to JC's Girls, a Christian evangelical group led by a former sex worker who sought to "save" others through repentance and religious reformation. While JC's

Girls used guilt and forgiveness to promote Christian doctrine, Rael's Girls emerged as a bold and unapologetic affirmation of sexual autonomy and the legitimacy of sex work. The initiative also challenged the growing alliance between the Christian right, radical feminists, and the Catholic Church in their collective moral crusade against prostitution—an alliance that frames sex work as inherently degrading, exploitative, or sinful.

For the Church, prostitution is condemned as a vice that violates human dignity by reducing people to mere instruments of pleasure. But this condemnation rests on a narrow view of sexuality rooted in religious dogma that deems pleasure outside procreation as inherently sinful. In many religious institutions, discussions of pleasure are shrouded in shame and control, leaving no space for consent-based, self-affirming erotic expression. From the Christian right's perspective, opposition to sex work aligns with their ideal of sexual purity and traditional family values. For many radical feminists, prostitution is viewed as an inevitable form of male dominance and patriarchal exploitation, irrespective of consent or agency. Together, these groups—though ideologically opposed on many other issues—form a potent coalition that reinforces conservative sexual norms and often weaponizes feminist discourse to justify the repression of sex workers.

Across all three Abrahamic religions—Christianity, Judaism, and Islam—prostitution is typically vilified as immoral, a symptom of sexual permissiveness and cultural decay, and the erosion of traditional values. These views have resulted in moral crusades against prostitution and underpinned a resurgence of legislative crackdowns on sex work, frequently justified by exaggerated or poorly evidenced claims designed to spark public fear and moral outrage. Yet as sociologist Ronald Weitzer[20] notes, "Claims that all prostitution involves exploitation, that violence is always present, or that no woman could freely choose sex work, are ideologically driven and unsupported by rigorous social science research" (**Weitzer, 2006**). He and others advocate for decriminalization as a means of harm reduction and empowerment. Notably, Scott Cunningham & Manisha Shah[21] found that when indoor prostitution was decriminalized, reported rape offenses dropped by 30% and female gonorrhea cases declined by over 40%—clear evidence that evidence-based policy can vastly improve public health and safety (**Cunningham & Shah, 2018**).

Rael's Girls are women—some actively engaged in sex work, others simply advocates of erotic freedom—who are conscious, empowered, and unashamed. Unlike those who proselytize through guilt or shame, Rael's Girls offer non-judgmental support, practical resources, and compassionate companionship. Their goal is not to convert, but to affirm the right of every individual to choose their own path—professionally, sexually, and spiritually. Their message is clear and powerful: *No God, No Guilt*. People should not feel shame for how they express themselves, how they earn a living, or how they embody pleasure. Life is not meant to be defined by repression, but by exploration, joy, peace, and sensual fulfillment. Rael's Girls also recognize sensuality, charisma, eroticism, seduction, and personal entertainment as legitimate avenues of income— pathways that can bring empowerment, beauty, and connection to both clients and providers.

Rael emphasizes that rather than judging or marginalizing sex workers, society must respect and support them as it would any other profession. He argues that much of the emotional instability and violence associated with sex work is rooted not in the work itself, but in the societal repression and moral hypocrisy that surrounds it. By legitimizing sex work and decriminalizing the profession, society can begin to dismantle the toxic layers of shame, fear, and hostility that create unsafe conditions and perpetuate harm.

At its core, this is about freedom. When people are trafficked, abused, or coerced into sex work, society must intervene to protect them. But when adults engage in sex work by choice, their autonomy must be honored. Criminalizing consensual sex work not only violates human rights—it drives the industry underground, where exploitation thrives, and protection is scarce. To move forward, we must discard outdated dogmas that sanction sex only within marriage or under divine approval. Such beliefs continue to stifle growth, demonize the body, and undermine human blossoming. Sensuality and erotic labor are not aberrations; they are part of the natural spectrum of human behavior and are encoded in our genetic makeup.

True forgiveness and compassion should not be extended to those who express sexual freedom, but rather to those who—out of ignorance or fear—continue to uphold oppressive moral codes that harm others. The work of Rael's Girls invites us to reframe sex work not as sin, but as sacred self-expression, and to view sex work not as a social ill, but as a valid, conscious, empowering, and even beautiful profession—worthy of dignity, protection, and pride.

NoPedo: Don't Touch My Children!

Deliver us from EVIL!

"If nobody educates children about their sexual and sensual life, they are much more at risk of being victims of pedophiles. A child not having any knowledge about sexuality and especially the pleasure it creates, is the perfect victim for these criminals. Education is the best prevention."—
Rael

Over the past two decades, mounting evidence has confirmed what many survivors had long known, but few institutions dared to acknowledge: a staggering number of Catholic priests across the globe have been accused—and in many cases convicted—of sexually abusing minors. These crimes were not committed in isolation, nor were they the result of a few "bad apples." Rather, they unfolded under a deeply entrenched system of silence, protection, and complicity, often with bishops and senior church officials actively concealing the abuse. For every case that has come to light, countless others remain buried in shame, trauma, or institutional cover-up. The lack of widespread media reporting before 2002, when *The Boston Globe* published its groundbreaking investigation, should not be mistaken for an absence of abuse. On the contrary, patterns of predation had been festering within the Church for decades, protected by layers of denial and legal obstruction.

As researcher Karen Terry[22] notes, "Though the peak of abuse incidents occurred in the 1970s and early 1980s, there was a substantial delay in the reporting of incidents…This delay in reporting led to an unfortunate reality: few cases of child sexual abuse by priests were processed through the criminal justice system. This is because in most states the statutes of limitations—which varied by state and over time—had expired by the time most victims reported their abuse" (**Terry, 2018**). The long lag in justice has only deepened the wounds inflicted by the Church's betrayal of its most vulnerable followers.

In response to this institutional horror, Rael founded the *NoPedo* association over twenty years ago as a direct challenge to the culture of impunity that allowed such crimes to persist. NoPedo was created not just to condemn pedophilia, but to expose the systemic mechanisms—particularly within religious institutions—that enabled and concealed it. The Catholic Church, despite repeated claims that these were isolated incidents, has been shown through numerous investigations to have facilitated the quiet relocation of known abusers from one parish to another rather than reporting them to civil authorities. This pattern of protection allowed predators continued access to children while shielding the Church from public scrutiny and legal consequences.

The resulting fallout has been enormous. In the United States alone, dioceses have paid billions of dollars in settlements, with many forced into bankruptcy, selling off properties and other assets to compensate victims and silence lawsuits. But no amount of financial restitution can erase the trauma endured. For Rael and the Raelian Movement, these crimes—and the systemic complicity that enabled them—represent not only a spiritual failure but a criminal enterprise. As Rael states unambiguously, "The Catholic Church should be denied sovereign state status and be recognized as a dangerous, criminal organization."

The Raelian Movement goes beyond moral outrage—it acts. Through public awareness campaigns, legal advocacy, and international collaboration, it has worked to bring perpetrators and complicit institutions to justice. NoPedo was launched years before mainstream outlets began reporting systematically on the Catholic Church's abuses. It was among the first international voices to break the conspiracy of silence and offer victims a platform to speak, heal, and seek justice. In doing so, the Raelian Movement contributed to growing global pressure on religious institutions to confront their abuse histories and enact meaningful reforms.

Essentially, the Raelian Movement maintains an unambiguous and uncompromising stance: pedophilia is not only a severe psychological disorder—it is a profound violation of bodily autonomy, innocence, and human dignity. The Movement operates under a zero-tolerance policy. Any member, regardless of position or tenure, found to have engaged in or condoned such abuse is to be immediately expelled and reported to the relevant legal authorities. This position is non-negotiable. It stems from the Raelian belief that love, sexuality, and spiritual freedom must always be consensual, joyful, and adult in nature—never coerced, never abused, and never inflicted and exploited upon the vulnerable.

NB: The word "pedophilia" is used in SOCAS in accordance with its widely accepted clinical and legal definitions, namely: an adult's sexual attraction to prepubescent children, and any sexual activity involving individuals below the age of consent. The Raelian Movement—including its founder and all its members—rejects and condemns any harmful, coercive, or non-consensual acts, especially those involving children. This "NoPedo" section does not seek to blur that boundary but rather to challenge the hypocrisy and inaction of religious institutions (particularly the Catholic Church), which have historically condemned sexuality in public while covering up or excusing abusive and unlawful behavior in private.

Sensuality Education

Becoming a sensual human being at any age

"When all of humanity will enjoy its sensuality to the fullest, the risk of a world conflict will have disappeared completely."—**Rael**

Sensuality lies at the heart of Rael's teachings—an essential dimension of what it means to be fully human and an untapped source of awakening, healing, and happiness. To understand its role within Sensuality Education, one must first grasp the practice of *Sensual Meditation*[23]—a foundational pillar of the Raelian philosophy.

Sensual Meditation is a technique designed to sharpen our sensory awareness and optimize our ability to experience both internal and external pleasures more deeply, consciously, and harmoniously. Guided by the principle *"Awakening the mind by awakening the body,"* it teaches us to fully engage with life's pleasures—not in haste or superficially, but with consciousness and deliberate joy. For Rael, true enlightenment is not reached by denying the body, but by awakening it in order to awaken the mind.

Contrary to many religious traditions that promote detachment from the physical as a path to spiritual purity, Raelian philosophy affirms the sacred unity of body and mind. This synergy, not duality, is key to personal growth. Through this integration, we awaken to our fullest potential, experiencing life not as something to be endured or transcended—but as something to be felt, loved, and celebrated.

This path of awakening begins with the embrace of three liberating values: nonconformism, the celebration of our differences, and freedom from the oppressive, repressive, and suppressive forces that seek to confine us. Every human being deserves the right to express themselves authentically, sensually, and unapologetically. This journey of becoming is not a metaphor; it's a lived, embodied state of liberation. In this light, *Sensuality Education*[24] must be introduced around the world—both in schools and in adult programs—as a revolutionary tool for human development. It teaches people to welcome the sensations of pleasure they naturally experience, rather than deny or repress them. Importantly, it must be free from the guilt-inducing moral frameworks inherited from conservative, anti-Epicurean, and religious ideologies that distort pleasure into sin.

At its core, Sensuality Education nurtures a deeper embrace of Femininity, which, when fully honored, holds the transformative power to heal and even save humanity. As we refine our sensual and sensory awareness, we expand our consciousness and from that expansion arises what Rael calls supraconsciousness—a heightened state of awareness marked by universal love and cosmic interconnectedness that transcends the ordinary limits of the human mind. It represents the most evolved level of consciousness in which an individual becomes deeply attuned to the infinite nature of the universe. This expansion of consciousness profoundly elevates our Emotional Intelligence (EQ), fostering a world where empathy, presence, and love replace domination and fear. Imagine a planet led by emotionally awakened individuals, where policies and relationships are shaped not by trauma or repression, but by kindness, sensitivity, and mutual respect. In such a world, peace would no longer be a utopian ideal, but an achievable way of life.

This is the transformative power and radical promise of Sensuality Education. By reconnecting us with the sacred unity of body and mind, it unlocks our emotional potential, nurtures emotional development, and paves the way for global harmony. As an indispensable component in our quest for a better world, it empowers us to create a society rooted in compassion, acceptance, empathy, and the fearless celebration of pleasure, that is to say, a society where pleasure is not taboo, where love in all its forms is abundant, and where every human being can blossom without fear, shame, or guilt. Let us then shape a world where empathy and sensuality reign, where people are taught not to fear their bodies but to honor them, not to suppress their desires but to explore them with respect and joy. In doing so, we lay the foundation for a humanity that is not only awakened but fully alive.

This is the radical promise of Sensuality Education: a sacred return to ourselves. By reconnecting us to the body and reclaiming pleasure as a source of wisdom, it nurtures not only our individual happiness but also our collective development. It invites us to build a world where love is abundant, where pleasure is not taboo, and where no one must live in fear, shame, or guilt simply for being who they are. Let us then shape a humanity where sensuality and empathy are taught, lived, and honored. Where people are encouraged not to fear their desires, but to explore them with dignity and pleasure. In doing so, we lay the groundwork for a future that is not only awakened—but fully alive.

Femininity can Save Humanity

Femininity is a solution to world conflicts

"If femininity is a remedy for mankind and is the way to prevent its destruction, then to develop it becomes a necessity and the responsibility of each human being, regardless of his or her gender."—**Rael**

As previously explored, femininity holds a profound transformative potential to help humanity evolve beyond violence, domination, and inequality. Rooted in empathy, nurturance, cooperation, and emotional intelligence, femininity offers a pathway to a more compassionate and sustainable world. These qualities, while traditionally associated with women, are not confined to any gender—they are essential human attributes that all individuals can cultivate to meet the urgent challenges of our global age.

One of the foundational tenets of Raelian philosophy is the elevation of emotional intelligence (EQ). In this light, femininity, with its emphasis on refinement, compassion, empathy, gracefulness, and kindness, emerges as a powerful force for expanding EQ at both the individual and societal levels. Imagine a world in which both leaders and citizens embody high emotional intelligence: conflicts would be resolved peacefully, policies would be drafted with inclusivity and care, and societies would be governed with wisdom that flows from the heart as much as from the mind.

A foundational tenet of Raelian philosophy is the cultivation of emotional intelligence (EQ) as a central dimension of spiritual evolution. In this light, femininity—expressed through compassion, refinement, grace, kindness, and empathy—emerges as a powerful catalyst for expanding EQ at both the personal and collective levels. Imagine a society where leaders, teachers, parents, and citizens embody high emotional intelligence: where diplomacy prevails over conflict, where laws are shaped by inclusivity and care, and where governance flows as much from the heart as from the intellect.

At its core, femininity embodies the nurturing and caregiving aspect of human nature—qualities essential for building communities grounded in justice, support, and sustainability. When societies elevate nurturance as a cultural ideal, their priorities naturally shift toward healthcare, education, environmental preservation, and social equity. In such cultures, science and technology are placed at the service of well-being, ensuring that every individual's basic needs are met and that everyone is empowered to reach their fullest potential.

Femininity carries within it a rich, intuitive wisdom that transcends linear thought, offering a deeper lens through which to perceive the world. It cultivates an expanded awareness that considers not only the immediate impact of our actions but also their long-term effects. This innate feeling inspires choices anchored in ethics, sustainability, and a profound sense of care for both current and future generations. Guided by empathy and discernment, feminine consciousness shapes a path toward decisions that uplift, protect, and serve the collective well-being.

Historically, feminine leadership has played a key role in peacebuilding, nonviolent resistance, and reconciliation. Across spiritual movements, social justice campaigns, and diplomatic efforts, feminine energy has consistently championed healing over harm, dialogue over destruction. In an age marked by division, war, and escalating violence, femininity offers a blueprint for coexistence based on empathy, understanding, and nonviolence.

Importantly, the Raelian vision does not advocate for the dominance of femininity over masculinity, but for their harmonious integration. True human blossoming requires both energies—assertiveness tempered by empathy, strength guided by grace, logic balanced by intuition. When these forces are in harmony, we move beyond rigid gender binaries and access a more holistic, conscious, and peaceful way of living. Femininity also naturally gives rise to a concern for social justice and equality. Its emphasis on care and fairness challenges systems of oppression and exclusion, encouraging societies to dismantle discrimination and embrace diversity as a strength. In this sense, to embrace femininity is to advocate for the rights of all—regardless of gender, race, sexuality, or economic status—and to create a culture in which all people are free to thrive.

As Shizue Kaneko, Raelian Bishop and international coordinator of International Femininity Day, eloquently states: "Femininity is a powerful force for individuals and humanity at large, paving the way to peace and survival. The refinement of our thoughts and bodies is interconnected, serving as a deterrent to violence and a step towards global harmony. Holding delicate and refined thoughts is incompatible with harboring a brutal and violent attitude simultaneously. Embracing femininity is, therefore, not just a choice but a responsibility for everyone."

Indeed, embracing femininity is not a retreat from power, but a redefinition of it. It is the choice to evolve—not through force, but through love, not through fear, but through understanding. By integrating feminine values into our institutions, relationships, and worldviews, we can meet our most pressing challenges with wisdom, kindness, and strength.

In the words of Rael, "Developing our femininity not only allows us to develop our consciousness and to be happier, but it also makes our world more peaceful, because it's extremely difficult for a refined and gentle person to handle a gun."

Conclusion

Redefining the Role of the Church: *The Future Role of Faith Institutions in a Sexually Liberated World*

For much of recorded history, organized religion—especially within the monotheistic traditions—has played a dominant role in shaping sexual norms, gender roles, and moral codes. From prescribing rigid expectations of femininity and masculinity to condemning same-sex love, from banning pleasure to glorifying chastity, many religious institutions built their authority on the surveillance and control of bodies. In doing so, they caused generations to internalize shame, repress their identities, and fear divine punishment for natural expressions of affection, love, and erotic joy.

But today, we are witnessing a profound cultural, scientific, and ethical awakening. Thanks to advances in neuroscience, psychology, human rights, and sexuality education, we now understand that sexual diversity is not deviance, that pleasure is not sin, and that autonomy over one's body is not rebellion—it is the very foundation of dignity, freedom, and well-being. In this new context, the Church's traditional role as the enforcer of purity codes and moral absolutes is not only obsolete—it is actively harmful.

As we step into a sexually liberated future, one of the most urgent and transformative questions we must ask is: "What becomes of the Church in a world where hedonism—the doctrine that pleasure and the avoidance of pain are life's highest goods—bodily autonomy, and sexual expression are no longer taboo but celebrated? The answer lies not in irrelevance, but in radical reinvention. If faith institutions, particularly monotheistic ones, are to remain vital in this new era, they must undergo a courageous reimagining of their purpose. This does not require the abandonment of religion—on the contrary, it calls for a return to its most sacred roots: love, compassion, wonder, humility, connection, and care for the vulnerable. The churches, mosques, synagogues, temples, and spiritual communities of the future must no longer be temples of guilt and conformity. They must become sanctuaries of healing rather than shame, of inclusion rather than exclusion, and of dialogue rather than dogma.

Theologian Mary E. Hunt[1] has long called for a "transformative theology[2]" that challenges patriarchy, uplifts marginalized voices, and centers justice, embodiment, and ethical sexuality. "If theology is to remain a vital resource in people's lives," she writes, "it must engage with sexuality not as threat, but as grace—as a gift to be understood, not a danger to be condemned" (**Hunt, 2009**). In her writings and public talks, she consistently draws on the concept of transformative theology to critique traditional structures and to call for liberation-focused spiritual frameworks. This shift invites faith leaders to evolve from moral gatekeepers into facilitators of erotic dignity, spiritual healing, and communal joyfulness.

To take on this new role, faith institutions must relinquish their historical obsession with control and purity. They must reject their legacy as arbiters of what constitutes a "holy" or "acceptable" form of love. Instead, they are called to listen deeply, affirm difference, and celebrate the sacredness of each person's lived experience. Rather than vilifying pleasure, they can reclaim it as divine—a gateway to joy, intimacy, and spiritual connection.

Some communities are already leading the way. The Metropolitan Community Churches (MCC), for example, have centered LGBTQ+ rights and sex-positive theology since their inception. Their liturgies[3] celebrate erotic love, and their teachings affirm that the divine resides in every body. Their example is not fringe—it is prophetic.

Public theology, too, offers a broader lens through which spiritual communities can evolve. It invites faith institutions to see themselves as part of civil society, responsible not for imposing belief, but for engaging with ethical questions of justice, compassion, and embodiment. As theologian Katie G. Cannon[4] reminds us, "Moral wisdom must emerge from the underside of history, from the cries of the excluded, including those who have been shamed for their sexual expression" (**Gushee, 2020**). Faith institutions that truly listen to these cries—without rushing to fix, convert, or judge—can become powerful spaces for trauma healing, honest conversation, and the joyful integration of spirit and flesh.

This transformation demands more than symbolic gestures or inclusive language. It requires structural and doctrinal change, including:

- **Removing or reframing** sacred texts and teachings that promote violence, misogyny, homophobia, or sexual repression.

- **Affirming LGBTQ+ identities**, not as tolerated deviations, but as radiant expressions of the divine spectrum of life.

- **Celebrating sexual pleasure and bodily autonomy**, especially for women and gender-diverse individuals who have long been denied both.

- **Supporting comprehensive sexuality education**, grounded in science, mutual respect, and empathy.

One of the greatest obstacles to this evolution is fear—fear of losing institutional power, of unraveling centuries-old hierarchies, of relinquishing gendered dominance and fear-based obedience. But control is not the same as spiritual leadership, and relevance does not come from authority—it comes from authenticity.

If churches and other spiritual communities are willing to embrace humility, acknowledge past harms, and open themselves to pluralism, science, and freedom, they can become co-creators of humanity's next spiritual renaissance. The future does not ask them to disappear, but to re-emerge as ethical fellowships, planetary councils, meditation circles, or justice-centered communities where bodies are honored, identities are celebrated, and love is never restricted by doctrine. As Reverend Nadia Bolz-Weber[5] so powerfully declares: "If the Church has any future, it is as a place where the sexually shamed are restored, the judged are embraced, and the sacredness of our bodies is proclaimed without apology" (**Bolz-Weber, 2019**). That is the spiritual reformation our time demands.

At the heart of this book lies a call for spiritual maturity—a departure from inherited dogma and toward a conscious, compassionate, and body-affirming ethics. Spirituality can once again help us explore the great mysteries of life, the depths of our consciousness, and the infinite beauty of our interconnectedness—without ever limiting how we love, touch, or express joy. The sexually liberated world of tomorrow extends an open invitation to all faith institutions: reclaim your sacred purpose—not by policing bodies, but by nurturing hearts, not by enforcing moral conformity, but by inspiring ethical living grounded in love and freedom. Those institutions bold enough to walk this path—not as rulers, but as companions—will not merely survive. They will be transformed. And they will be welcomed with open arms.

Respecting Freedom of Expression: *Why Secular Freedoms Must Lead the Way Forward*

Freedom of expression is the lifeblood of any truly democratic and enlightened society. It is the oxygen of intellectual inquiry, artistic creativity, scientific discovery, and personal growth. Without it, no meaningful movement for justice—whether for civil rights, women's liberation, LGBTQ+ dignity, or sexual freedom—could have ever taken root. And in the ongoing effort to emancipate sexuality from centuries of stigma and to restore pleasure to its rightful place in human experience, secular freedoms must lead the way.

Historically, religious institutions have often sought—and received—special protections: blasphemy laws, exemptions from anti-discrimination policies, and censorship privileges that allow them to silence dissent, vilify difference, and restrict access to comprehensive sexuality education. In many parts of the world, these protections continue to uphold systems that suppress women's rights, criminalize queer existence, and obstruct scientific truth under the guise of "respecting religious beliefs." But when religious dogma is used to deny human dignity, silence inquiry, or punish diversity, it ceases to be an expression of freedom and becomes an abuse of it.

Secularism is not the enemy of faith. On the contrary, it is the only framework in which genuine religious freedom can thrive. In a pluralistic world, secular governance ensures that all beliefs—not just dominant ones—can coexist without coercion or imposition. It guarantees that each person—regardless of creed, culture, or identity—has the right to speak, question, explore, dissent, and live authentically. And nowhere is this more essential than in the realm of sexuality, where religious interference has inflicted centuries of pain, repression, and shame.

Sexual liberation and freedom of expression are inextricably linked. You cannot have one without the other. In societies where individuals are punished for expressing their sexual orientation, exploring gender identity, or simply speaking openly about pleasure and desire, repression festers not only in public policy but in private consciousness. Shame becomes systemic. Violence becomes justified. Censorship becomes law.

To cultivate a society in which sexual and emotional freedom can flourish, we must protect the right to speak candidly about bodies, gender, intimacy, and eroticism—whether through education, art, literature, science, or activism. We must uplift and defend the voices that challenge moral orthodoxy: feminists, queer theorists, sex educators, artists, scientists, and spiritual visionaries like Maitreya Rael, who boldly advocate for sex-positive ethics in defiance of dogmatic repression. Indeed, it is often the most transformative truths—those that affirm our right to love freely, to question inherited authority, and to disobey unjust norms—that are first labeled "offensive" by those invested in maintaining control. But history reminds us that today's heresies are often tomorrow's human rights.

A secular society does not silence religion—it simply prevents any one religion from silencing others. It ensures that biology and sexuality are taught in schools based on evidence, not theology. It guarantees that no woman is forced to carry a pregnancy against her will, no child is denied accurate, age-appropriate information about sexuality, no same-sex couple is refused equal protection under the law, and no artist is punished for celebrating the erotic beauty of the human form. In this model, religion retains its place—as a source of personal meaning, ethical reflection, and cultural tradition—but it does not dominate public institutions, shape educational curricula, or dictate medical policy. Freedom of belief must coexist with freedom from imposition.

Freedom of expression is not a luxury. It is not negotiable. It is the foundation of democracy, the engine of progress, and the birthplace of cultural and spiritual renewal. It is what allows us to confront injustice, imagine alternatives, and reinvent ourselves. And it is under assault wherever authoritarianism, religious fundamentalism, or cultural censorship takes hold. Whether through the banning of books depicting queer love, the censorship of curricula on gender identity, the intimidation of journalists exposing clergy abuse, or the silencing of artists who portray unapologetic sensuality—these are not acts of protection. They are acts of erasure.

The Raelian Movement stands firmly in defense of the freedom to think, speak, feel, and love without shame or restriction. It recognizes that sexual freedom is not separate from spiritual freedom—it is an essential expression of it. To defend freedom of expression is not merely to defend a legal right; it is to safeguard happiness, preserve truth, and enable individual and collective transformation.

In the world we must now build, we cannot allow "sacred" taboos to silence the voices of liberation. Instead, we must amplify those who question, who challenge, who dream. Secular freedoms do not strip life of meaning—they make space for each of us to create our own. And in that space, a new civilization can emerge—one rooted not in obedience, but in consciousness; not in silence, but in self-expression; not in fear, but in freedom.

The Healing Process: *Embracing a Journey to True Freedom and Self-Discovery*

The journey toward sexual liberation is, at its core, a journey of healing—a reclamation of our bodies, our pleasure, and our right to define ourselves on our own terms. After centuries of moral conditioning, repression, and institutionalized guilt imposed by religious dogma, healing becomes not only necessary—it becomes revolutionary. And like all true inner revolutions, it unfolds slowly, gently, and uniquely, awakening at the pace of one's own inner readiness.

For many, this path begins in the aftermath of childhood indoctrination. Shame was planted early on, cloaked in sacred language, reinforced by cultural taboos, and disguised as love. Bodies were labeled "sinful." Curiosity was silenced. Sexual expressions were judged. Pleasure was condemned. Even the most innocent acts of self-exploration— touching one's body, asking questions about sex, or exploring gender— were burdened with secrecy, confusion, and fear. The body, instead of being experienced as a source of pleasure and connection, became a site of surveillance and moral anxiety.

The first step in healing is reconnection—a return to the body, to sensation, to emotional honesty, and to the sacredness of pleasure. This is not indulgence for its own sake; it is wholeness. It is the deep, embodied truth that pleasure is not a temptation to resist, but a gift to honor. That the body is not a vessel of sin, but a temple of love, curiosity, and delight, that sexuality, far from being something to purify, suppress, or punish, is a vital, life-affirming force within us all.

To reclaim this truth requires unlearning. It means unraveling years, sometimes decades, of inherited guilt and internalized false morality. It means naming the trauma, lifting the shame, and giving ourselves radical permission: to feel, to explore, to question, to desire, and ultimately—to blossom. Though healing is deeply personal, its power multiplies in community. When nurtured in safe, affirming, and sex-positive environments, it becomes a collective act of liberation. Vulnerability is no longer punished, and pleasure is no longer whispered. It is celebrated.

The Raelian teachings offer a shining path through this process. With its emphasis on sensual meditation, body–mind oneness, and erotic justice, Rael's message affirms that healing is not about escaping the body—it is about inhabiting it fully. It invites us to reframe desire not as something dangerous, but divine, not as weakness, but as wisdom. In this view, sexuality becomes a doorway to consciousness, a sacred engine of happiness, connection, and spiritual evolution.

In a society still haunted by puritanical residue, those who reclaim their sexual freedom are often labeled heretics, deviants, or rebels. But healing makes us more than rebels—it makes us creators. It empowers us to reshape culture, reimagine relationships, and rewrite the narratives by which we live. Survivors of religious sexual trauma, once silenced by dogma, emerge as educators, artists, lovers, and architects of liberation. They become healers who uplift rather than shame, who liberate rather than condemn. One healed life can transform families. Communities. Even entire systems.

Healing is also deeply political. It challenges the very structures that have benefited from our silence and suffering. It exposes institutions that preach abstinence while protecting abusers, that legislate morality while denying science, and that weaponize fear to police desire. At the same time, healing is profoundly spiritual. It reclaims the sanctity of the body, the holiness of authenticity, and the divinity of pleasure. Rael's revolutionary message—that humanity was created in love, by advanced scientists, and destined to evolve toward peace, sensuality, and love—offers a cosmology where body and mind are no longer at war but harmonized in pursuit of enlightenment.

The healing process is not the privilege of a chosen few. It is the birthright of all. It belongs to the priest struggling with doubt. To the queer youth seeking acceptance. To the woman denied reproductive freedom. To the man afraid to cry. To the elder rediscovering erotic pleasure. To the child who deserves a world without shame. To heal is to reclaim life on our own terms. It is to declare: "I am not broken. I am whole. I am worthy of love, pleasure, peace, and truth." In embracing this journey, we affirm not only our own humanity—but the humanity of others. We become part of a larger movement, a planetary healing, a collective rebirth, a new culture where mind and body are no longer divided, where no one is punished for who they are, and where the chains of outdated doctrines are finally broken.

This is the promise of a sex-positive, spiritually awakened future. And it begins with each of us—right here, right now.

"

It would be helpful if we started in silence and just listened to each other's voices. Whether we can muster such maturity amid toxic political attitudes remains to be seen. If we are to have a meaningful national discussion of moral issues, we will need to start with the sexual issues, not because they are the most important, but because they are the fire engulfing the tower. Let's get it all on the table… and let's do so openly and boldly, without the code language that we often use in moral debates, without our usual cherry-picking of Scriptures, without our usual blistering indignation, without the bullying that elevates one's viewpoint into divine certainty."

"

Tom Ehrich

NOTES

DEDICATION

1. Religious Dogma

A set of principles or beliefs declared by religious (or ideological) authorities as absolute and unquestionable truths. Often accepted without critical examination or empirical evidence, religious dogma tends to discourage dissent or reinterpretation and is typically used to maintain moral, spiritual, or institutional control.

2. Spiritual Colonization

The imposition of one belief system, religious framework, or spiritual worldview onto another culture or population, often through coercion, domination, or systematic erasure of indigenous beliefs.

3. Genocidal Silence

The deliberate suppression, denial, or erasure of discourse, memory, or acknowledgment surrounding an act of genocide or mass violence.

4. Sanctimonious Authority

A form of leadership or power that presents itself as morally or spiritually superior while often displaying hypocrisy or self-righteousness. Typically used to describe institutions or figures—especially religious or political—who enforce moral codes while failing to embody genuine humility, compassion, or ethical integrity.

5. Messiah

From the Hebrew *Mashiach*, meaning "anointed one." In Judaism, a future leader who will bring peace and justice. In Christianity, Jesus is considered the Messiah. In Raelian thought, the Messiah is a messenger chosen by the Elohim to guide humanity through science, peace, and awakening—not a supernatural figure.

6. Unapologetic Freedom

The full and fearless expression of one's identity, desires, or beliefs without guilt, shame, or the need to conform to societal expectations. It emphasizes self-ownership, radical honesty, and living authentically—even when that

ACKNOWLEDGMENTS

1. Academic Rigor

In scholarly practice, academic rigor denotes the systematic application of critical analysis, evidentiary standards, and methodological consistency in the production of knowledge. It involves careful evaluation of sources, precise citation, logical coherence, and engagement with existing scholarship, ensuring that claims remain verifiable, contestable, and grounded in recognized academic norms rather than ideological bias or speculation.

2. Cosmic Consciousness.

A concept originating in philosophical and mystical discourse describing a heightened form of awareness in which individuals experience a direct, intuitive perception of the unity of self, humanity, and the universe. In contemporary spiritual and humanistic frameworks—including Raelian philosophy—the term is used to denote an advanced stage of consciousness marked by the integration of scientific understanding, emotional intelligence, and a lived sense of planetary and cosmic interconnectedness, often associated with ethical responsibility, empathy, and the pursuit of global harmony.

3. Unrestrained Self-Expression

Used here to denote the ethical and political right to articulate one's identity, sexuality, beliefs, and creative voice without institutional censorship or moral sanction. The term situates expression within broader frameworks of human rights, secular governance, and bodily autonomy, emphasizing that cultural, religious, or state authority must not suppress personal or collective forms of meaning-making and self-definition.

FOREWORD

1. Maitreya Rael, Intelligent Design: Message from the Designers

Founder and spiritual guide of the International Raelian Movement, Maitreya Rael is known for his teachings on humanity's extraterrestrial origins, sensual meditation, happiness, and the demystification of traditional religions. *Intelligent Design: Message from the Designers,* proposes that life on Earth was scientifically created by an advanced extraterrestrial civilization, the Elohim, and calls for a new age rooted in science, peace, and universal love. Rael's message promotes a sex-positive philosophy, human cloning as a path to immortality, and the dismantling of dogma in favor of rational inquiry, freedom, and self-realization.

2. Abrahamic Traditions

The Abrahamic Traditions include Judaism, Christianity, and Islam, all of which consider Abraham a foundational patriarch. Despite doctrinal differences, they share a belief in one God, prophetic authority, sacred texts, and ethical mandates. These religions have significantly influenced global cultural, political, and moral systems, often shaping debates around sexuality, gender, and religious authority.

3. Catholic Church

Known as both a transmitter and enforcer of religious sexual repression across cultures and centuries, over the centuries, the Church has been a dominant moral force in the Western world, particularly in prescribing and policing sexual behavior through canon law, doctrine, and clerical teaching. Its historical promotion of celibacy, virginity, anti-masturbation and anti-contraceptive stances, along with the idealization of the Virgin Mary and the pathologization of non-heteronormative desire, have deeply shaped societal attitudes toward pleasure, gender, and erotic autonomy.

4. Heteronormative Templates

This term refers to deeply embedded societal blueprints that assume heterosexual relationships are the standard or ideal form of intimacy, reproduction, and family. These cultural assumptions inform everything from education and media to legal systems and religious doctrine, often rendering non-heterosexual or non-cisgender identities invisible, deviant, or "other." Challenging heteronormative templates is essential for affirming diverse sexual orientations, gender identities, and relational models in both public policy and personal consciousness.

5. Original Sin

Rooted in Christian theology, the doctrine of Original Sin teaches that humanity is born in a state of sin due to the transgression of Adam and Eve. This belief has deeply shaped Western attitudes toward the body, pleasure, and sexuality, casting erotic desire as a consequence of moral failing. For centuries, the concept has provided theological justification for sexual repression, celibacy, and shame-based moral teachings—many of which continue to influence contemporary sex education, gender roles, and religious doctrine. Raelian philosophy directly challenges this worldview, asserting that pleasure, not guilt, should be our ethical compass.

6. Comprehensive Sexuality Education (CSE)

CSE is an educational approach grounded in evidence-based, age-appropriate, and rights-affirming pedagogy. It extends beyond biological reproduction to include emotional intelligence, communication, respect for diversity, gender identity, consent, relationships, pleasure, and sexual rights. Programs based on CSE have been shown to delay sexual initiation, reduce rates of sexually transmitted infections (STIs), challenge harmful gender norms, and empower youth with accurate knowledge and life skills. CSE stands in direct contrast to abstinence-only or morality-based teachings, offering a holistic model that affirms sexuality as a natural and positive part of being human. It is endorsed by international organizations such as UNESCO, WHO, and UNFPA, and is central to the Raelian advocacy for sexual education free from religious bias and repression.

7. Sexually Transmitted Infections (STIs)

STIs are a diverse group of infections transmitted through sexual contact, though some can also spread through blood, childbirth, or skin-to-skin contact. Despite medical advances, STIs remain a major global public health concern, often exacerbated by stigma, lack of education, inadequate access to care, and religious taboos around sexuality. STIs such as chlamydia, gonorrhea, and syphilis are bacterial and typically curable with antibiotics, while others like HIV and herpes are viral and may be managed but not cured. Comprehensive Sexuality Education (CSE) plays a critical role in STI prevention by promoting condom use, regular testing, destigmatization, and open dialogue. In contrast to abstinence-only models, which rely on shame and fear, CSE emphasizes informed choice and responsibility rooted in respect and science. The Raelian approach to sexual education affirms sexual pleasure while also advocating for public health literacy and the de-religionization of medical discourse.

8. Contraception

Refers to methods or devices used to prevent pregnancy. These include hormonal options (e.g., pills, patches), barrier methods (e.g., condoms), IUDs, sterilization, and behavioral strategies like fertility awareness. In the context of sexual rights, access to contraception supports informed decision-making, bodily autonomy, and gender equality.

9. Sexual Revolution

Refers to the cultural and political shifts that redefined attitudes toward sex, especially during the mid-20th century. It emphasized individual sexual freedom, challenged religious and legal controls over private life, and laid the groundwork for modern movements for reproductive rights, queer visibility, and comprehensive sex education.

10. Secularism

Refers to the political and philosophical stance that government and religious institutions should remain independent of each other. In SOCAS, secularism is seen as essential for safeguarding sexual rights, bodily autonomy, and education policies from religious moralism. It does not oppose personal spirituality but resists the imposition of religious norms on public life.

11. Taboos

Deep-seated prohibitions that define what is socially or morally "untouchable." In many traditions, sexual taboos serve to control desire and reinforce hierarchies—often pathologizing pleasure, demonizing bodies, and silencing dissent. SOCAS interrogates these constraints as part of a broader push for erotic justice and intellectual liberation.

12. Gender Equality

A core principle of human rights and democratic societies, gender equality resists the hierarchical roles often dictated by religious and cultural orthodoxy. SOCAS underscores it as essential to sexual justice, body autonomy, and emotional dignity across all identities.

13. Human Rights

In the SOCAS framework, human rights serve as the ethical and legal bedrock for dismantling systems of oppression rooted in religious dogma. They include not only civil and political freedoms, but also economic, sexual, and reproductive rights. Emphasizing bodily autonomy, freedom of thought, and equality before the law, this concept is central to affirming the dignity of every human being to live and love without fear, stigma, or institutionalized shame. Adopted in the aftermath of WWII, the Universal Declaration of Human Rights (UDHR) articulates a universal vision of dignity, liberty, and equality. While not legally binding, it has profoundly shaped international law, civil rights frameworks, and global advocacy for sexual freedom and gender equality—core themes in the SOCAS paradigm.

14. Religious Authoritarianism

Refers to the consolidation of moral and political control by religious institutions or leaders who claim divine authority to dictate personal, social, and sexual norms. This form of rule is often marked by censorship, enforced obedience, and punishment of dissent—particularly around issues of gender, sexuality, reproductive freedom, and bodily autonomy. It thrives on fear, guilt, and rigid orthodoxy, often masquerading as moral guardianship. SOCAS identifies religious authoritarianism as a core driver of erotic repression and as an ideological engine behind laws, taboos, and institutions that criminalize sexual diversity and spiritual self-determination.

PREFACE

1. Deceitful Media

Refers to mass communication platforms that, rather than inform or empower, spread misinformation, amplify moral panic, and discredit dissenting voices. SOCAS calls out deceitful media for perpetuating harmful myths about sexuality, stigmatizing nontraditional identities, and vilifying movements like Raelism that challenge dogma. These media outlets often reinforce fear and shame by catering to the moral expectations of religious authoritarianism or political conformity. Combatting such distortion is essential to fostering an honest, evidence-based public discourse about sex, ethics, and liberation.

2. Social Justice

A framework for correcting structural inequalities and uplifting marginalized voices. SOCAS embraces social justice as essential to sexual liberation and human flourishing—advocating for policies and paradigms that respect bodily autonomy, challenge patriarchal and religious hierarchies, and support the full spectrum of human diversity. At its core, it is about restoring balance, repairing harm, and reimagining a world rooted in dignity and love.

3. Sexual Orientation

Sexual orientation is not a choice, sin, or disorder—but a natural expression of human diversity. SOCAS critiques how religious dogma and patriarchal norms have historically pathologized same-sex desire and romantic difference, framing such orientations as morally deviant. Instead, this work affirms that sexual orientation is part of one's human dignity and deserving of unconditional respect and freedom.

4. Gender Identity

Gender identity challenges rigid binary classifications imposed by traditional religious and social structures. SOCAS asserts that a person's felt and lived experience of gender deserves full recognition and support. In contrast to authoritarian norms that police gender expression, this book embraces gender identity as a deeply personal, evolving, and sacred facet of the self.

5. Christopher Hitchens

A fierce critic of religious authority, Christopher Hitchens (1949–2011) was a British-American intellectual and author whose works—particularly *God Is Not Great: How Religion Poisons Everything*—challenge the moral legitimacy of organized religion. In SOCAS, Hitchens is cited for his unapologetic defense of secularism, reason, and personal freedom. His polemics against religious dogma and authoritarianism help frame SOCAS's argument for disentangling sexual ethics from theological control.

6. Sam Harris

A neuroscientist and outspoken atheist, Sam Harris is best known for *Letter to a Christian Nation* and *The End of Faith*, in which he argues that religious belief—particularly in its dogmatic and moralistic forms—is incompatible with scientific inquiry and human flourishing. In SOCAS, Harris is cited for his sharp critique of the emotional and social harms caused by religious sexual repression, and for his call to ground morality not in divine command but in human well-being, reason, and evidence.

7. Blind Reverence

Refers to the uncritical submission to figures of authority—particularly religious—where questioning is discouraged, and obedience is exalted. SOCAS critiques this posture as antithetical to human freedom and sexual self-determination, framing it as a cultural habit that perpetuates shame, ignorance, and systemic control over bodies and desires.

8. Human Dignity

The foundational recognition that each person deserves respect, autonomy, and freedom from humiliation or degradation. SOCAS frames human dignity as inseparable from sexual self-determination, arguing that oppressive religious norms often violate this principle by denying individuals control over their bodies, identities, and desires.

9. Sexual Authenticity

Refers to the courageous act of living one's sexuality in alignment with inner truth, desire, and identity—without guilt, denial, or conformity to externally imposed norms. SOCAS emphasizes that reclaiming sexual authenticity is a revolutionary act, especially in societies where religious dogma and shame suppress genuine erotic expression.

10. Marty Klein

Cited for his unwavering defense of sexual freedom and rational, evidence-based sexual ethics. In *America's War on Sex*, Klein exposes how moral panic, religious ideology, and political agendas have undermined personal liberty and distorted public discourse around sexuality. SOCAS draws from his work to illustrate how sexual rights are often targeted by broader campaigns against civil liberties and human agency.

11. Destructive Ideologies

Refer to entrenched systems of thought that normalize control, fear, and moral judgment—especially around sexuality and identity. These ideologies, often cloaked in sanctimonious authority, are exposed in SOCAS for perpetuating cycles of guilt, shame, and dehumanization. The book challenges their legitimacy by advocating for critical thinking, compassion, and scientific awareness as antidotes to inherited oppression.

12. Internalized Beliefs

Refer to the invisible mental frameworks we adopt—often from childhood—based on dominant societal norms. In SOCAS, internalized beliefs are examined as silent architects of shame, repression, and self-censorship. Whether religious or cultural, these ingrained thought patterns can inhibit erotic authenticity, perpetuate guilt, and hinder self-acceptance. The book advocates for their compassionate examination and conscious reprogramming as part of sexual liberation and spiritual awakening.

13. Unapologetic Joy

More than fleeting happiness, this phrase captures a deep, fearless celebration of being—erotic, emotional, and spiritual. It is an act of resistance against puritanical doctrines and cultural scripts that treat pleasure as dangerous or shameful. In *Separation of Church and Sex*, unapologetic joy is both a right and a revolutionary stance—a form of healing and reclamation through fully embodied living.

INTRODUCTION

1. Sanctimony

Operates as a subtle yet potent form of moral coercion. In religious and ideological frameworks, it often manifests as the performance of virtue that substitutes ethical substance with pious appearance. Rather than advancing moral clarity or compassion, it shames dissent and polices the boundaries of acceptability through public displays of "purity." In SOCAS, sanctimony is critiqued as a tool of virtue signaling that reinforces conformist behavior, suppresses honest inquiry, and weaponizes morality in the service of social control.

2. Antiquated Dogma

These belief systems often survive by masquerading as eternal truths, even though they reflect the cultural anxieties and power dynamics of distant eras. In SOCAS, antiquated dogma is critically examined as a force that obstructs social evolution, particularly in areas of sexual ethics and bodily autonomy. Whether embedded in legal codes, religious teachings, or educational curricula, such dogma sustains fear, shame, and submission—undermining reason, compassion, and the liberating potential of erotic justice. Dismantling it is central to reclaiming intellectual and sensual freedom.

3. Marcella Althaus-Reid

Marcella Althaus-Reid challenged the sanitized, patriarchal, and heteronormative frameworks that dominate Christian theology by foregrounding sexuality, class, and postcolonial realities. Her *indecent theology* insists that true theological reflection must begin with the lived realities of the excluded, particularly queer and impoverished bodies. She disrupts the notion of theological "decency," exposing how claims of neutrality often mask deep-rooted power structures. In SOCAS, her work is honored as a revolutionary contribution to erotic justice and the decolonization of spiritual discourse.

4. Sexual Minorities

The term encompasses lesbian, gay, bisexual, transgender, queer, intersex, asexual, and other non-normative identities (LGBTQIA+), though it remains dynamic and context-dependent. SOCAS recognizes that sexual minorities are not "minor" in number or significance, but are rendered marginal through legal, cultural, and theological exclusion. Their systematic pathologization and criminalization are key indicators of how societies define and police "acceptable" sexual behavior. Embracing the dignity, agency, and plurality of sexual minorities is essential to building a world rooted in erotic justice and inclusive human rights.

5. Ostracism

Historically rooted in practices such as the Athenian civic banishment system, ostracism persists today in both institutional and informal ways—via cancel culture, religious excommunication, legal marginalization, or social shunning. In SOCAS, ostracism is analyzed as a regulatory mechanism that enforces conformity to dominant norms, especially regarding sexuality, gender roles, and belief systems. It is a tactic that often masquerades as moral correction but ultimately functions to maintain existing power hierarchies by silencing deviance, dissent, and sexual nonconformity.

6. Politicization

Politicization occurs when domains like sex education, gender identity, or public health are co-opted by religious or political forces to advance particular agendas. In SOCAS, it signals how institutions distort human experience—especially around sexuality—not through open inquiry, but through strategic manipulation that fuels division, cements authority, and impedes progress.

7. Limited Injunction

Injunctions are tools of judicial authority that can protect rights or, conversely, enforce control. In the context of SOCAS, injunctions have been used to block access to sexual health services, restrict freedom of expression, or criminalize bodily autonomy—especially in cases involving reproductive rights, LGBTQ+ activism, or comprehensive sex education. Their deployment reflects how the legal system can serve as both a safeguard and a weapon in cultural and moral conflicts.

8. Structures of Power

Structures of power are not limited to governments or laws; they operate through norms, ideologies, and institutions that define who is heard, protected, or punished. In SOCAS, particular attention is paid to how these structures regulate sexuality, gender roles, and moral behavior—often privileging dominant identities while marginalizing others. By mapping how power operates through schools, churches, courts, and media, SOCAS exposes the ways these structures sustain inequality under the guise of order, tradition, or morality.

9. Heteronormative Frameworks

Heteronormative frameworks structure laws, education, media, and religious teachings around the assumption that heterosexual, cisgender relationships are the standard for legitimacy and morality. In SOCAS, such frameworks are exposed as ideological tools that discipline desire, restrict bodily autonomy, and delegitimize the lived realities of LGBTQ+ individuals. These systems not only marginalize sexual and gender diversity but also uphold patriarchal, reproductive, and colonial values under the guise of "family," "tradition," or "biology." Challenging heteronormativity is thus essential to dismantling the moral hierarchies that suppress erotic justice and human flourishing.

10. Book of Leviticus

Leviticus has historically served as a cornerstone for religious doctrines on sexual morality, gender hierarchy, and bodily regulation. Verses from Leviticus—particularly 18:22 and 20:13—have been repeatedly invoked to justify the condemnation of same-sex relations and enforce heteronormative, patriarchal norms. In SOCAS, the Book of Leviticus is critically examined not as a divine decree but as a socio-political document reflecting ancient tribal anxieties about purity, order, and survival. Its ongoing use to stigmatize LGBTQ+ identities illustrates how archaic codes are weaponized in contemporary moral discourse, often stripped from historical context and wielded in the service of exclusion, control, and religious authoritarianism.

11. Pauline Epistles

The Pauline Epistles—especially Romans, Corinthians, Galatians, and Ephesians—have had enduring influence on Western moral thought, particularly concerning gender roles, sexuality, and authority. Verses commonly cited to condemn same-sex intimacy, enforce female subordination, or promote celibacy are found in this corpus. In SOCAS, these texts are critically examined not as timeless moral absolutes but as historical writings reflective of specific patriarchal, post-Temple, and Greco-Roman contexts. The use of Pauline passages to justify exclusion, shame, or legal repression—especially against sexual minorities— demonstrates how ancient theological opinions are often reframed as divine commands to sustain religious and cultural power structures.

12. Moral Codes

Moral codes serve as tools of social regulation, shaping identity, relationships, and conduct through internalized norms. In SOCAS, they are analyzed not as universal truths but as historically contingent frameworks that often reflect the interests of dominant groups. Religious moral codes—especially those concerning sexuality and gender—have long been used to legitimize oppression, stigmatize desire, and criminalize difference. By interrogating how these codes are constructed, enforced, and selectively interpreted, SOCAS reveals their role in sustaining patriarchy, heteronormativity, and colonial moral hierarchies under the guise of divine or objective authority.

13. Sexual Norms

Sexual norms operate as mechanisms of regulation, shaping desires and identities through moral codes, legal systems, religious teachings, and social conditioning. In SOCAS, these norms are interrogated as neither universal nor natural, but as historically contingent frameworks that often reinforce heteronormativity, patriarchy, and colonial ideologies. By prescribing what is "normal," "deviant," or "moral," sexual norms marginalize difference and discipline bodies—particularly those of women, queer people, and other sexual minorities. Unmasking their constructed nature is essential to advancing erotic justice and reclaiming sexual freedom as a human right.

14. Social Nonconformity

Social nonconformity challenges dominant frameworks by exposing their constructed nature. In SOCAS, it is understood not as deviance but as a form of resistance—often necessary for progress, authenticity, and liberation. Those who transgress dominant sexual, gendered, or moral expectations frequently face stigmatization, ostracism, or institutional punishment. Yet such nonconformity also creates space for cultural renewal, ethical pluralism, and new forms of relationality. Rather than pathologizing difference, SOCAS affirms nonconformity as a vital expression of freedom and human dignity.

15. Nor Faiza Mohd Tohit and Mainul Haque

Public health scholars based in Malaysia whose collaborative research explores sexual and reproductive health, including barriers to comprehensive sexuality education, menstrual equity, and the sociocultural taboos that undermine sexual health rights. Their work highlights how systemic stigma and policy gaps intersect to marginalize vulnerable populations.

16. Queer Theology

Queer theology disrupts traditional doctrines by foregrounding the embodied realities of LGBTQ+ people as sources of spiritual insight. Drawing from liberation theology, feminist theology, and queer theory, it critiques moral absolutism and reclaims spirituality as a site of affirmation, not shame. In SOCAS, queer theology is embraced as a transformative discourse that destabilizes binary thinking and offers alternative visions of divine love, relationality, and erotic truth beyond institutional control.

17. Feminist Theology

Feminist theology critiques the androcentric foundations of major religious systems by centering women's experiences, questioning male-dominated interpretations of the divine, and exposing how sacred texts have been used to justify subordination. In SOCAS, it is valued as a transformative discourse that destabilizes hierarchical power, affirms embodied spiritual wisdom, and opens space for inclusive, justice-oriented expressions of faith. Like queer theology, it seeks not only reform but reimagination of the sacred as a site of liberation rather than control.

18. Liberation Theology

Emerging primarily in Latin America in the 1960s and 1970s, liberation theology reframed salvation not as individual transcendence but as collective emancipation from social, economic, and political oppression. In SOCAS, it is honored for its radical potential to align spirituality with justice. Its method—reading scripture through the eyes of the oppressed—inspired later movements such as feminist and queer theology. Liberation theology also exposes how traditional religious institutions often align with structures of domination, and it calls for a reorientation of faith toward solidarity, equity, and transformative change.

19. Secular Humanism

Secular humanism rejects divine authority as the basis for morality, asserting instead that ethical systems should emerge from rational reflection, empathy, and shared human experience. In SOCAS, secular humanism is recognized as a vital countercurrent to religious moralism—particularly in matters of sexuality, bodily autonomy, and personal freedom. It challenges theocratic control by affirming the right to live, love, and think freely without fear of divine punishment or institutional repression. While not without its own blind spots, secular humanism remains a key ally in the pursuit of erotic justice, pluralism, and evidence-based public policy.

20. Doctrinal Rigidity

Doctrinal rigidity functions as a mechanism of control, insulating belief systems from challenge and preserving institutional authority. In SOCAS, it is examined as a major barrier to sexual liberation, gender equity, and moral pluralism. By presenting historically constructed beliefs as timeless truths, rigid doctrines suppress dissent, pathologize difference, and legitimize punitive systems. This rigidity not only impedes ethical evolution but also undermines the possibility of compassion-driven, evidence-based engagement with human sexuality and identity.

21. Genuine Emancipation

Genuine emancipation is not limited to the formal granting of rights; it demands the transformation of internalized beliefs, structural inequalities, and moral hierarchies. In SOCAS, it refers to the full release from imposed guilt, sexual repression, and doctrinal control. It affirms the right to pleasure, dignity, and self-determination—not as privileges bestowed by institutions, but as intrinsic dimensions of being human. True emancipation thus requires not only freedom from external domination but also freedom from within; shame, silence, and the inherited fear of joy.

22. Inherited Assumptions

Inherited assumptions shape how individuals interpret morality, sexuality, authority, and identity—often long before conscious belief is formed. In SOCAS, they are examined as foundational to systems of internalized oppression: unspoken codes that regulate behavior and perception through guilt, fear, or reverence. These assumptions frequently uphold patriarchal, heteronormative, and theocratic worldviews, passing down restrictive moral codes disguised as tradition or common sense. Unmasking and re-evaluating them is essential to achieving genuine emancipation and reclaiming one's ethical and erotic autonomy.

CHAPTER ONE

1. Thorkild Jacobsen

A leading scholar of ancient Mesopotamian religion and myth, Jacobsen emphasized the humanistic and symbolic dimensions of early sacred narratives. His work helps reveal how early myths encoded social hierarchies, gender roles, and divine authority—insights that support SOCAS critiques of patriarchal religious origins.

2. Holistic Cosmology

Contrary to dualistic or mechanistic models, holistic cosmology affirms that matter, consciousness, and meaning are interwoven. In SOCAS, it serves as an alternative to hierarchical, theistic frameworks that separate body from spirit and place humans above nature. This cosmology reclaims eroticism, empathy, and ecological awareness as sacred dimensions of existence—supporting a paradigm of liberation grounded in interconnectedness rather than domination.

3. Sacred Prostitution

Though debated among historians, the concept of sacred prostitution reflects how some early cultures ritualized sexuality as a sacred force rather than a moral transgression. In SOCAS, it is reexamined not as a scandalous myth but as a window into pre-patriarchal understandings of eroticism, divinity, and feminine power. The later demonization of such rites by emerging monotheistic religions marked a cultural shift—from revering sexual expression as sacred to repressing it as sinful. Whether historical or symbolic, the term invites critical inquiry into how societies construct the boundary between the holy and the erotic.

4. Stephanie Budin

A historian and specialist in the ancient Near East, Stephanie Budin is widely known for her critical work on gender, sexuality, and religion in antiquity. In particular, she has challenged the long-standing scholarly narrative surrounding "sacred prostitution," arguing that the concept lacks reliable historical evidence and reflects modern projections onto ancient societies. In SOCAS, Budin's scholarship is essential for deconstructing myths that have been used to exoticize, eroticize, or delegitimize early sexual practices—revealing how patriarchal and colonial biases have distorted our understanding of ancient erotic and spiritual life.

5. Fertility Cults

Often mischaracterized by patriarchal scholarship as primitive or licentious, fertility cults reflect early reverence for the generative forces of nature, the female body, and erotic vitality. In SOCAS, they are reexamined as expressions of embodied spirituality that honor life cycles, sensuality, and balance between the sexes. The later demonization or erasure of such traditions—especially by monotheistic religions—marks a historical shift toward moral repression and the devaluation of erotic and feminine power.

6. Samuel Noah Kramer

One of the foremost scholars of Sumerian civilization, Kramer is credited with bringing to light foundational myths, laws, and literary texts of ancient Mesopotamia. His work revealed early expressions of gender roles, divine kingship, and sacred sexuality. In SOCAS, his research is significant for tracing how early civilizations encoded moral order, erotic symbolism, and cosmological power into myth—providing a pre-biblical context for understanding later patriarchal religious systems.

7. Cylinder Seals

Beyond their bureaucratic role, cylinder seals offer vital insight into the mytho-erotic imagination of early civilizations. In SOCAS, they are examined as visual texts encoding gender hierarchies, divine authority, and fertility symbolism. Their imagery—often featuring gods, priestesses, and sexualized motifs—reflects how religious and political power were intertwined with representations of the body, desire, and cosmic order. These miniature artifacts challenge later taboos by revealing a world where sexuality and the sacred were not opposed but mutually constitutive.

8. Asceticism

Historically valorized in many religious systems, asceticism has often served to elevate suffering, celibacy, and bodily denial as paths to holiness. In SOCAS, it is critically examined as a moral ideal that contributed to the repression of sexuality and the stigmatization of pleasure—especially for women and sexual minorities. By positioning desire as sinful or distracting, asceticism reinforces dualistic thinking that separates body from spirit, and discipline from joy, legitimizing structures that control erotic and emotional expression in the name of virtue.

9. Celibacy

While sometimes chosen as a form of personal or spiritual commitment, celibacy has also been institutionalized as a moral ideal—particularly within Christian and other religious traditions—as a marker of holiness and authority. In SOCAS, celibacy is examined not simply as a lifestyle, but as a doctrine historically used to suppress erotic expression, pathologize desire, and elevate denial as virtue. It has often served to reinforce gender hierarchies, control clergy, and stigmatize non-procreative sex, positioning sexuality as a threat to spiritual purity rather than a source of joy, connection, or knowledge.

10. Continence

Often framed as a form of moral or spiritual mastery, continence has historically been elevated in religious traditions as a sign of holiness—especially in contrast to sexual indulgence. In SOCAS, it is critically examined as part of a broader tradition of bodily denial used to regulate desire and uphold patriarchal authority. By glorifying restraint and stigmatizing sensual pleasure, continence contributes to a legacy of guilt, repression, and the devaluation of erotic expression, particularly for those whose sexualities fall outside heteronormative, procreative norms.

11. Renunciation

Rooted in ascetic and religious traditions, renunciation has been idealized as a path to transcendence or holiness—especially through the rejection of sexuality, wealth, or personal ambition. In SOCAS, it is critically examined as a construct that often glorifies suffering and self-denial, while marginalizing joy, sensuality, and erotic freedom. By elevating abstention as virtue, renunciation has historically served to discipline bodies, suppress desire, and consolidate spiritual authority, particularly in patriarchal and theocratic systems.

12. Spiritual Purity

Traditionally linked to sexual restraint, obedience, and bodily denial, spiritual purity has served as a powerful tool for regulating behavior—especially in religious systems that equate the body with sin. In SOCAS, it is analyzed as a moral construct that frequently targets women, queer individuals, and sexually autonomous people, casting their desires as defilements rather than expressions of wholeness. Framed as virtue, the pursuit of purity often conceals mechanisms of control that elevate shame over joy and submission over liberation. Reclaiming spirituality without purity mandates is central to erotic justice.

13. Sexual Abstinence

While often presented as a neutral or virtuous lifestyle choice, sexual abstinence has been institutionalized in many religious and educational settings as a compulsory moral ideal. In SOCAS, it is analyzed as a mechanism that reinforces shame around desire, suppresses sexual agency, and upholds patriarchal and heteronormative control. When promoted without context or choice—as in abstinence-only education—it becomes a form of moral coercion that undermines informed consent, bodily autonomy, and erotic literacy.

14. Augustine of Hippo

A foundational figure in Christian theology, Augustine profoundly shaped Western attitudes toward sin, sexuality, and the body. His doctrine of original sin and linking of lust with moral fallenness contributed to centuries of guilt-based sexual ethics. In SOCAS, Augustine is critically examined for sacralizing bodily denial and elevating celibacy as a spiritual ideal, thereby embedding misogyny, erotic repression, and fear of pleasure into Christian moral frameworks that still influence contemporary laws and cultural norms.

15. Moral Corruption

While often invoked to justify censorship, punishment, or social control, the concept of moral corruption is itself deeply subjective and historically weaponized. In SOCAS, it is examined as a rhetorical device used by religious authorities, political regimes, and cultural institutions to pathologize sexual freedom, queer identity, and feminist dissent. Framed as a threat to family, nation, or divine order, accusations of moral corruption have been used to legitimize repression and silence nonconformity—serving more as a tool of power than a reflection of ethical reality.

16. Loss of Sexual Innocence

The concept reflects deeply entrenched beliefs that link sexuality with guilt, danger, or moral decline—particularly for women and queer individuals. In SOCAS, it is critiqued as a mythologized construct rooted in patriarchal control, where sexual initiation is cast not as growth or empowerment, but as "fall from grace." This framing perpetuates shame, reinforces virginity fetishism, and pathologizes erotic awakening. Deconstructing this notion is essential to affirming sexuality as a natural, joyful, and autonomous dimension of human experience.

17. Andrew Louth

In his critical study of *Confessions*, Andrew Louth explores Augustine's theological development, particularly his struggle with desire, guilt, and the concept of divine grace. Louth emphasizes how Augustine's inward turn—the framing of sexual experience as a fall from spiritual integrity—became foundational to Western Christian notions of sin and purity. In SOCAS, this reading is crucial for understanding how personal erotic experience was reframed as moral failure, laying ideological groundwork for centuries of sexual repression, internalized shame, and ecclesiastical control over the body.

18. Song of Songs

A poetic and sensual text within the Hebrew Bible, *Song of Songs* stands apart from other scriptural writings for its explicit celebration of erotic love, bodily beauty, and mutual desire—without moral condemnation or theological justification. In SOCAS, it is reclaimed as a rare canonical affirmation of sexual joy and relational intimacy, contrasting sharply with later doctrines that equated eroticism with sin. Its presence in scripture reveals the suppressed yet enduring thread of sacred sensuality, often obscured by patriarchal interpretations that allegorize or spiritualize its erotic content to fit moralistic frameworks.

19. Illuminated Manuscripts

Far from neutral artifacts, illuminated manuscripts were tools of theological transmission and cultural power. In SOCAS, they are examined not only for their artistic value but for the ideological content they preserved and glorified—often reinforcing Christian cosmology, moral codes, and patriarchal interpretations of scripture. Their visual beauty veiled moral rigidity, and their sacred authority helped cement doctrines that suppressed sexual freedom, gender diversity, and sensual expression. Deconstructing these texts includes analyzing what was illuminated—and what was omitted.

20. John Boswell

A historian of medieval Christianity, John Boswell is renowned for his groundbreaking work on the history of sexuality, particularly in *Christianity, Social Tolerance, and Homosexuality* (1980). He challenged the prevailing view that Christianity had always condemned homosexuality, revealing periods of tolerance and even ritualized same-sex unions in early Christian Europe. In SOCAS, Boswell's scholarship is vital for exposing how homophobia was not an inevitable feature of Christian doctrine, but a later construction influenced by shifting political, theological, and cultural forces. His work helps dismantle the myth of timeless sexual repression within religious history.

21. Dyan Elliott

A medieval historian and scholar of gender and sexuality in Christian thought, Dyan Elliott is known for her work on clerical celibacy, female sanctity, and the sexual politics of religious authority. Her research—particularly in *The Bride of Christ* and *The Corrupter of Boys*—reveals how ecclesiastical purity was constructed through anxieties about sexuality, gender roles, and power. In SOCAS, Elliott's scholarship is crucial for tracing how institutional Christianity pathologized desire, regulated bodies, and embedded sexual repression into theological and legal frameworks still echoed today.

22. Spiritual Marriage

Celebrated in hagiographies and mystical writings, spiritual marriage was idealized as the highest form of union—transcending carnal desire in favor of pure, divine intimacy. In SOCAS, it is analyzed as a theological construct that both sacralized female devotion and erased erotic agency. By offering women a path to holiness through symbolic, desexualized union with Christ, the doctrine reinforced celibacy, moral purity, and patriarchal control. It reflects how religious institutions spiritualized longing while systematically policing actual sexual expression.

23. Religious Allegory

While often celebrated for its literary richness, religious allegory also functions as a pedagogical and ideological tool. In SOCAS, it is examined for how it encodes gender roles, sexual norms, and moral hierarchies into seemingly universal truths. Allegories—especially those involving purity, sin, or divine union—frequently reinforce patriarchal values and reframe bodily desire as a metaphor for spiritual struggle. Deconstructing these layers reveals how spiritual symbolism has been used to sublimate, moralize, or suppress erotic and embodied experience.

24. François-Marie Arouet (Voltaire)

A leading voice of the Enlightenment, Voltaire was a fierce critic of religious tyranny, clerical hypocrisy, and moral absolutism. Through satire and philosophical essays, he championed reason, tolerance, and civil liberties. In SOCAS, his legacy is honored for challenging the alliance between church and state, though his critiques rarely extended to dismantling sexual repression or gendered moral codes embedded within Enlightenment rationalism.

25. Denis Diderot

Philosopher, novelist, and editor of the *Encyclopédie*, Diderot sought to liberate knowledge from ecclesiastical control and elevate empirical inquiry over dogma. His writings explored sensuality, materialism, and the complexity of human desire. In SOCAS, Diderot is recognized for subtly undermining religious moralism and opening discursive space for erotic inquiry—though his engagement with sexuality remained constrained by 18th-century norms of male privilege and rational decorum.

26. Jean-Jacques Rousseau

A foundational thinker in modern political and educational philosophy, Rousseau idealized nature, childhood innocence, and the moral simplicity of pre-civilized life. In SOCAS, he is critically examined for projecting these ideals into restrictive sexual ethics—especially through his promotion of chastity, maternal virtue, and gendered roles in *Émile* and *La Nouvelle Héloïse*. His romanticization of purity contributed to a sentimental moral framework that subtly reinforced patriarchal control under the guise of natural law.

27. Jonathan Israel

A British historian renowned for his extensive scholarship on the Enlightenment, Jonathan Israel is best known for his multi-volume work on the *Radical Enlightenment*. He distinguishes between a moderate Enlightenment—compatible with religious and social conservatism—and a radical current rooted in Spinoza's thought, which championed reason, secularism, democracy, and individual liberty in more uncompromising terms. In SOCAS, Israel's analysis is crucial for exposing how Enlightenment ideals of emancipation were unevenly applied—often excluding gender and sexuality from their vision of freedom. His work helps situate the struggle for erotic justice within a broader historical contest over who counts as fully human, rational, and free.

28. The Enlightenment

Often celebrated as the birthplace of modern liberty and rational inquiry, the Enlightenment was also marked by contradictions. In SOCAS, it is examined both for its radical potential and its limitations: while it advanced freedom of speech, religious tolerance, and political reform, it largely excluded women, sexual minorities, and colonized peoples from its vision of universal rights. Enlightenment thinkers challenged ecclesiastical dogma, but many retained deep anxieties about sexuality, embodiment, and non-normative desire. The movement's legacy is thus double-edged—crucial for dismantling theocratic power, yet complicit in constructing new hierarchies of reason, race, and sexual morality.

29. Baruch Spinoza

A 17th-century Dutch-Jewish philosopher, Spinoza laid the groundwork for radical Enlightenment thought by rejecting divine law, advocating for secular ethics, and proposing a pantheistic vision of God as synonymous with nature. His *Ethics* challenged the dualism of body and mind and denied the moral legitimacy of religious authority. In SOCAS, Spinoza is honored as a foundational thinker whose emphasis on reason, freedom, and immanence undermines the logic of moral repression and opens space for a non-theistic, body-affirming ethical framework—one in which desire is not sinful, but part of our natural striving toward joy and understanding.

30. Freedom of Thought

Celebrated during the Enlightenment and enshrined in modern human rights discourse, freedom of thought is central to challenging theocratic control and moral absolutism. In SOCAS, it is positioned as a precondition for erotic justice: the liberation of bodies begins with the liberation of minds. Without the ability to question inherited dogmas—especially those related to sex, gender, and morality—true autonomy remains impossible. The suppression of thought through religious doctrine, censorship, or ideological indoctrination is thus not merely intellectual repression, but an assault on human dignity and sexual self-determination.

31. Immanuel Kant

A central figure in modern Western philosophy, Kant's emphasis on reason, duty, and universal moral law shaped Enlightenment ethics and post-Enlightenment moral thought. In *The Groundwork of the Metaphysics of Morals* and *Critique of Practical Reason*, he posited that moral action is guided by rational autonomy and categorical imperatives. In SOCAS, Kant is examined critically for constructing a moral framework that often elevates abstraction over embodiment. While advocating for human dignity and freedom of thought, his suspicion of sensual pleasure and insistence on self-mastery contributed to the moral elevation of restraint and the devaluation of erotic life as a legitimate site of ethical meaning.

32. Moral Absolutism

While it may offer ethical certainty, moral absolutism often functions as a rigid framework that suppresses nuance, empathy, and pluralism. In SOCAS, it is critiqued for legitimizing oppressive laws, sexual repression, and doctrinal violence under the guise of eternal truth. By denying the contextual and evolving nature of moral life, absolutism reinforces hierarchical power structures that resist liberation and pathologize difference—especially in matters of sexuality, gender, and bodily autonomy.

33. Self-Determination

Traditionally invoked in political contexts such as national sovereignty or decolonization, self-determination also holds profound relevance for sexual and bodily autonomy. In SOCAS, it is a foundational principle that opposes theocratic, patriarchal, and moralistic control over personal identity and desire. True emancipation requires not only freedom of thought, but the lived ability to shape one's erotic, relational, and ethical life without fear, guilt, or institutional constraint. Self-determination affirms the dignity of choosing for oneself—even in the face of inherited dogma or cultural taboo.

34. Jeremy Bentham

An English philosopher and social reformer, Bentham is best known as the founder of utilitarianism—the ethical theory that defines morality by the greatest happiness for the greatest number. Unusually progressive for his time, Bentham also condemned laws criminalizing homosexuality and defended individual liberty in matters of sexual conduct. In SOCAS, he is recognized as a rare Enlightenment figure who viewed sexual pleasure not as a moral threat but as a legitimate good. His unpublished manuscripts on sexual liberty, though suppressed for decades, reveal an early philosophical foundation for erotic justice rooted in rational ethics and human dignity rather than religious taboo.

35. Pantheism

Associated with thinkers like Spinoza and various mystical traditions, pantheism challenges the hierarchical cosmologies of monotheistic religions by dissolving the boundary between the divine and the material world. In SOCAS, it is recognized as a life-affirming alternative to ascetic and punitive moral frameworks. By sanctifying nature, the body, and desire, pantheism subverts doctrines that vilify sensuality or elevate spiritual abstraction above lived experience—offering a vision of erotic, ecological, and existential unity instead.

36. Geeta Beeharry-Paray

In this scholarly article, Geeta Beeharry-Paray critically examines Denis Diderot's *Les Bijoux indiscrets* (1748), situating the novel within Enlightenment literary culture and questioning whether it functions as pastiche, forgery, or a satirical critique of contemporary libertine and conte moral traditions. Her work contributes to understanding how early modern erotic fiction used allegory and humor to challenge social and moral norms, revealing the deep interplay between discourse about sex, power, and cultural authority in early Enlightenment texts.

37. Isis and Osiris

Central figures in ancient Egyptian mythology, Isis and Osiris represent themes of death, rebirth, divine rulership, and sacred union. Isis, a powerful goddess of magic and fertility, resurrects Osiris after his murder and dismemberment—reclaiming his body, reassembling him, and conceiving their son Horus. In SOCAS, this myth is examined as a rare example of female divine agency within patriarchal cosmology. It reflects a pre-Abrahamic sacred narrative in which erotic devotion, grief, and creation are intertwined, and in which feminine power is portrayed not as subordinate but as central to the cosmic and moral order.

38. Lise Manniche

A Danish Egyptologist and scholar of ancient Egyptian culture, Lise Manniche authored *Sexual Life in Ancient Egypt*, a pioneering study that examines intimate practices, gender norms, and erotic representation in ancient Egyptian society. By exploring texts, sculptures, reliefs, and material culture, she challenges assumptions that sexuality in antiquity was uniformly repressive, revealing the diversity of sexual expressions across social classes and historical periods. Manniche's work provides valuable historical grounding for SOCAS's critique of inherited sexual taboos and helps situate modern sexual morality within a long continuum of cultural variation.

39. Concubines

Though sometimes framed as consensual or protected relationships, concubinage often reflected deeply patriarchal structures in which women's sexuality was commodified, controlled, or instrumentalized—especially in polygynous, imperial, or slaveholding societies. In SOCAS, concubines are examined as historical figures caught in systems that normalized unequal erotic arrangements, blurring the lines between intimacy, exploitation, and property. Their roles—both visible and erased—highlight how institutionalized inequality was encoded into sexual and domestic life, and how dominant narratives romanticized these arrangements while obscuring issues of consent and autonomy.

40. Necrophilia

Beyond its clinical and criminal framing, necrophilia holds symbolic significance in cultural and religious history. In SOCAS, it is approached not to sensationalize, but to interrogate how death, purity, and sexuality have been interwoven in myth, ritual, and law. From the embalming practices of ancient Egypt to gothic religious iconography that eroticizes martyrdom, necrophilic imagery often reflects deeper anxieties about control, desire, and the female body. Examining these motifs helps expose how domination over the passive or lifeless body has served as a metaphor for patriarchal conquest and the suppression of erotic agency.

41. Polygamy

Historically practiced in various religious, tribal, and imperial systems, polygamy reflects gendered structures of power, lineage, and property. In SOCAS, it is not judged monolithically but analyzed in terms of how it has been used to institutionalize asymmetrical sexual access, reinforce patriarchal authority, and regulate women's reproductive labor. While some traditions have framed polygamy as sacred or stabilizing, it often functioned to consolidate male privilege and control over multiple female bodies—revealing how marriage can operate as a mechanism of erotic and economic domination.

42. Pharaohs

As living gods and absolute rulers, pharaohs embodied both spiritual and sexual sovereignty in ancient Egypt. In SOCAS, they are examined as figures through whom state power, religious legitimacy, and gender hierarchy converged. While often idealized in official art and texts, their reigns relied on priestly control, divine lineage myths, and ritualized authority over both land and bodies. The sacralization of their sexuality—through practices like divine kingship, fertility symbolism, and temple rituals—illustrates how erotic power could be institutionalized to reinforce theocratic rule.

43. Gods and Goddesses of Fertility

Across ancient civilizations, fertility deities embodied the generative forces of nature, reproduction, and erotic vitality. Figures such as **Ishtar** (Mesopotamia), **Aphrodite** (Greece), **Hathor** (Egypt), **Freya** (Norse), and **Xochiquetzal** (Aztec) were venerated not only for their reproductive power but for their connection to love, pleasure, and the life cycle. In SOCAS, these deities are examined as cultural expressions of the sacred erotic, later demonized or marginalized by monotheistic religions that severed sexuality from divinity. Their enduring presence reflects a historical consciousness in which desire and fertility were not sources of sin, but dimensions of cosmic balance and creative power.

44. Hierogamic Ceremonies

Also known as "sacred marriage" rites, hierogamic ceremonies reflected ancient cosmologies in which erotic union was central to maintaining balance between heaven and earth. In SOCAS, these rituals are revisited as evidence of pre-monotheistic traditions that honored sexuality as divine. Whether enacted symbolically or physically, they reveal how eroticism was once ritualized as a source of renewal, not sin. The later suppression or moral condemnation of such rites by patriarchal religions marks a shift from embodied reverence to disembodied moralism—erasing sacred sensuality from spiritual life.

45. Julia A. Assante

In this influential 1998 study, Julia A. Assante critically reevaluates the ancient Mesopotamian terms *kar.kid* and *harimtu*—traditionally translated as "prostitute"—arguing that modern assumptions about prostitution have been inaccurately projected onto ancient texts and social categories. Her work highlights the need to understand sexual terminology in its own historical and cultural context rather than through modern biases. This analysis contributes to SOCAS's broader critique of how sexual roles and identities are constructed, labeled, and often misinterpreted across cultures and epochs.

46. Pederasty

In ancient Greece, pederasty was embedded in elite male culture and valorized as a form of educational intimacy tied to civic and moral development. In SOCAS, it is not romanticized but interrogated as a historically contingent system that normalized asymmetrical power relations under the guise of virtue. While often framed as noble or philosophical, pederasty reveals how sexual practices can be ritualized to maintain social hierarchies—particularly through age, class, and gender roles. Its reevaluation challenges the myth of universal moral progress and invites deeper reflection on how societies define consent, mentorship, and erotic legitimacy.

47. Sir Kenneth James Dover

A British classical scholar best known for his groundbreaking study, *Greek Homosexuality* (1978), Sir Kenneth James Dover offered one of the first systematic academic treatments of same-sex relations in ancient Greece. His work revealed the structured, hierarchical nature of pederastic relationships and challenged earlier romanticized or censored interpretations. In SOCAS, Dover's research is recognized as foundational in exposing how sexuality was socially constructed and ritualized within ancient power dynamics. At the same time, his clinical and at times dispassionate tone invites critical reflection on how modern scholarship engages with erotic history—balancing documentation with ethical responsibility.

48. The Kouros Statues

Arising in Archaic Greece (circa 7th–5th century BCE), kouros statues are idealized, nude male figures representing youth, athleticism, and heroic beauty. While often associated with funerary or votive contexts, these statues also functioned as cultural symbols of male virtue, civic identity, and eroticized form. In SOCAS, kouroi are examined as visual expressions of an aesthetic and moral order in which the male body was celebrated as the pinnacle of form, rationality, and self-control, while the female body remained largely excluded or controlled within visual and civic spaces. Their stylized nudity reflects a cultural erotic code deeply embedded in gendered power and pedagogical ideals.

49. Plato

A towering figure of Western philosophy, Plato profoundly shaped metaphysical, ethical, and political thought through his dialogues, many of which center on themes of love, virtue, and the soul. In SOCAS, Plato is examined both for his valorization of erotic love—as in *The Symposium* and *Phaedrus*—and for his foundational role in elevating abstract, disembodied ideals over the physical and sensual. His influence reinforced a dualism between body and spirit that would echo through Christian theology and Enlightenment moral philosophy. While his dialogues affirm homoerotic affection as a vehicle for philosophical insight, they also introduce hierarchies of love that marginalize the erotic potential of embodiment, especially feminine and non-procreative sexuality.

50. John J. Winkler

An influential classicist and scholar of ancient Greek literature and sexuality, John J. Winkler challenged conventional readings of Greek texts that sanitize or moralize erotic practices. His work, including *The Constraints of Desire*, critically examines how ancient Greek culture constructed gender, desire, and social norms—revealing the complex interplay of eroticism, power, and representation. In SOCAS, Winkler's scholarship is valued for exposing the myths and ideologies that shape historical understandings of sexuality, and for modeling an approach that treats erotic life as historically contingent rather than inherently deviant or dangerous.

51. Ecclesiastical Doctrine

Developed through councils, creeds, and clerical interpretations, ecclesiastical doctrine has served as a central mechanism for moral governance—especially in matters of sex, gender, and bodily conduct. In SOCAS, it is examined as a primary source of religious moral absolutism that framed sexuality through the lenses of sin, shame, and purity. By codifying patriarchal and heteronormative values as divine law, ecclesiastical doctrines legitimized systems of control that continue to shape laws, education, and cultural attitudes toward erotic life. Their authority has often silenced dissent, pathologized pleasure, and sanctified submission in the name of moral order.

52. Renaissance Humanists

Figures like Petrarch, Erasmus, and Pico della Mirandola helped shift European thought from medieval theocentrism toward a more anthropocentric worldview rooted in classical revival. In SOCAS, Renaissance humanists are acknowledged for advancing secular inquiry and the dignity of human reason, but also critiqued for largely preserving patriarchal and heteronormative frameworks. While celebrating the intellect and artistic potential of man, they often reinforced gendered binaries and moral restraint inherited from both Christian doctrine and classical antiquity. Their selective embrace of "the human" left erotic freedom and bodily autonomy only partially liberated.

53. Purusharthas

In Hindu philosophy, the *purusharthas* represent the four fundamental aims of human life: **dharma** (ethical duty), **artha** (material prosperity), **kama** (pleasure and desire), and **moksha** (spiritual liberation). Unlike Western moral systems that often pit pleasure against virtue, the *purusharthas* acknowledge *kama*—including erotic pleasure—as a legitimate and necessary pursuit within a balanced life. In SOCAS, this framework is highlighted as an alternative to ascetic dualism, offering a more integrated model of human flourishing. By affirming sensuality as one path toward harmony rather than moral failure, the *purusharthas* challenge the repression of desire embedded in many theocratic and colonial moral orders.

54. Ruth Vanita and Saleem Kidwai

Co-editors of the landmark anthology *Same-Sex Love in India: Readings from Literature and History* (2000), Ruth Vanita and Saleem Kidwai recovered centuries of Indian texts affirming homoerotic desire across religious, literary, and historical traditions. Their work challenges the colonial myth that same-sex love is a Western import, revealing a long indigenous presence of queer affection and eroticism in South Asian culture. In SOCAS, their research is foundational for decolonizing sexual history and reclaiming erased narratives of desire, plurality, and relational diversity.

55. Pluralism

Pluralism challenges monolithic truth claims by embracing difference not as a threat, but as a condition of ethical and social vitality. In SOCAS, it underpins the critique of moral absolutism and doctrinal rigidity— especially regarding sexuality, gender, and belief. True pluralism requires more than tolerance; it demands structural openness to voices historically excluded or pathologized. By valuing multiplicity over purity, pluralism creates space for erotic justice, spiritual diversity, and the decentralization of moral authority.

56. Kama Sutra

Often misrepresented in the West as merely a sex manual, the *Kama Sutra* is a 3rd–5th century CE Sanskrit text attributed to Vatsyayana that offers a comprehensive philosophy of love, pleasure (*kama*), and relational ethics. It addresses not only sexual technique, but also courtship, gender roles, aesthetics, and emotional refinement within the broader framework of the *purusharthas*. In SOCAS, the *Kama Sutra* is reclaimed as a sophisticated pre-colonial guide to erotic life that affirms desire, pleasure, and sexual plurality—challenging the later moral strictures imposed by colonial, Victorian, and religious systems.

57. Vatsyayana

An ancient Indian philosopher believed to have authored the *Kama Sutra* between the 3rd and 5th centuries CE, Vatsyayana framed erotic pleasure (*kama*) as an essential component of human fulfillment within a balanced ethical life. Unlike later colonial or puritanical interpretations, his approach was neither obscene nor ascetic but rooted in philosophical reflection and social realism. In SOCAS, Vatsyayana is recognized as an early advocate for a nuanced, pleasure-affirming understanding of sexuality—offering a vision where erotic knowledge was seen not as dangerous, but as integral to individual and relational well-being.

58. Wendy Doniger and Sudhir Kakar

Wendy Doniger, a scholar of Hinduism and mythology, and Sudhir Kakar, a psychoanalyst and cultural theorist, have each explored the intersections of religion, eroticism, and symbolism in South Asian contexts. Their collaborative and individual works—such as Doniger's *The Hindus: An Alternative History* and Kakar's *Intimate Relations*—critique both Western misreadings and internal cultural suppressions of sexual diversity and sacred sensuality in Indian traditions. In SOCAS, their research is recognized for exposing how myths, rituals, and psycho-social structures encode desire, repression, and identity—offering tools for decolonizing moral discourse and restoring the spiritual legitimacy of erotic experience.

59. Frivolous

The term "frivolous" has long been used to delegitimize forms of expression associated with pleasure, femininity, or emotionality. In SOCAS, it is examined as a rhetorical tool that reinforces hierarchies of value—casting erotic joy, aesthetic play, or sensual exploration as morally suspect or intellectually inferior. This framing sustains dualisms that privilege reason over feeling, restraint over pleasure, and doctrine over lived experience. Reclaiming what has been labeled frivolous becomes part of a broader strategy to restore dignity to marginalized forms of knowing and being.

60. Peter Harvey

A prominent scholar of Theravāda Buddhism and Buddhist ethics, Peter Harvey is known for his detailed analysis of early Buddhist teachings on morality, intention, and mental discipline. His work emphasizes the cultivation of ethical awareness and restraint, not through divine law but through mindfulness and compassion. In SOCAS, Harvey's contributions are valued for offering a non-theistic moral framework that neither demonizes desire nor idolizes repression but instead contextualizes it within the path to liberation. His approach provides a useful comparative lens through which to critique Western religious models that associate sexuality with guilt and impurity.

61. Ruth Vanita and Saleem Kidwai

Editors of the influential anthology *Same-Sex Love in India* (2000), Ruth Vanita and Saleem Kidwai, unearthed literary and historical texts affirming queer presence in Indian culture long before colonial criminalization. Their work challenges the notion that homosexuality is a Western import and provides vital evidence of indigenous sexual diversity. In SOCAS, their scholarship is foundational for decolonizing sexual history and restoring erased narratives of desire, love, and plurality within South Asian traditions.

62. Khajuraho and Konark

The temples of Khajuraho (Madhya Pradesh) and Konark (Odisha) are celebrated for their intricate carvings, including explicit erotic sculptures that form part of larger cosmological and philosophical narratives. Far from being gratuitous, these works reflect a worldview in which sensuality, divinity, and cosmic order were intertwined. In SOCAS, Khajuraho and Konark are reclaimed as architectural affirmations of erotic pluralism—challenging colonial and modern narratives that equate sacredness with sexual denial. Their artistry reflects a pre-colonial ethos where desire was not excluded from the sacred but sculpted into stone as part of life's spiritual and aesthetic fullness.

63. Victorian Moral Codes

Emerging in 19th-century Britain and exported globally through colonialism, Victorian moral codes emphasized sexual restraint, gender conformity, modesty, and the sanctity of the nuclear family. These codes positioned sexuality as dangerous when detached from marriage and reproduction, pathologizing pleasure, queerness, and female desire. In SOCAS, Victorian morality is examined as a cultural engine of repression—responsible for embedding shame, censorship, and punitive norms into law, education, and religious discourse across colonized and Westernized societies. Its legacy continues to shape contemporary taboos around erotic expression and bodily autonomy.

64. Section 377 of the Indian Penal Code

Originally imposed by the British Raj, Section 377 became a legal instrument of sexual repression in postcolonial India—used to target LGBTQ+ individuals through harassment, surveillance, and moral policing. In SOCAS, it is analyzed as a legacy of Victorian moral imperialism that exported Christian sexual norms into colonized societies. The 2018 Supreme Court decision (*Navtej Singh Johar v. Union of India*) that decriminalized consensual same-sex acts marked a historic reversal— but the social and institutional residues of criminalization persist. Section 377 exemplifies how colonial laws have long outlived colonial rule, embedding heteronormativity and legal violence into modern legal systems.

65. Taoist Philosophy

Rooted in ancient Chinese thought, Taoist philosophy centers on living in harmony with the *Tao*—the dynamic, unnameable force that underlies all existence. It emphasizes natural balance, non-interference (*wu wei*), and the fluid interplay of opposites (yin and yang). In SOCAS, Taoism offers a counterpoint to Western asceticism: instead of suppressing desire, it encourages the cultivation of inner alignment, including through erotic and bodily practices. By viewing sexuality as part of the natural order rather than a moral problem, Taoist philosophy opens space for a sensual, non-dualistic ethics grounded in flow, presence, and interconnectedness.

66. Yin and Yang

In Taoist and traditional Chinese thought, *yin* and *yang* are not fixed binaries but relational energies that flow into and define one another. In SOCAS, this framework offers a radically different model from Western dualisms that pit body against spirit, or desire against virtue. Rather than moralizing sexuality, *yin–yang* cosmology affirms eroticism, fluidity, and interdependence as part of the natural and sacred order. It challenges hierarchical gender constructs by revealing how so-called opposites are co-creative and equally necessary to cosmic and personal equilibrium.

67. Kristofer Marinus Schipper

A Dutch sinologist and one of the foremost scholars of Taoism in the modern academy. Schipper's contributions are significant for SOCAS because they reveal how non-dualistic, body-affirming spiritual traditions conceive of embodiment, desire, and harmony outside the ascetic and dualistic frameworks dominant in Western religious moralism. His work underscores the importance of understanding eroticism and embodiment in religious life as integrated with cosmic and social balance rather than objects of repression.

68. Cosmic Equilibrium

In many ancient and non-Western traditions, cosmic equilibrium is not imposed by divine command but arises from the dynamic tension between complementary forces—such as *yin and yang* in Taoism or *rta* in Vedic thought. In SOCAS, this concept is central to reclaiming non-dualistic understandings of eroticism, where pleasure, body, and desire are seen as integral to universal harmony, not threats to it. Unlike moral systems rooted in fear and suppression, the pursuit of equilibrium affirms interdependence, rhythm, and embodied wisdom as keys to ethical and existential balance.

69. Emotional Resonance

In SOCAS, emotional resonance is recognized as an essential dimension of embodied knowledge—often dismissed by rationalist or ascetic traditions. While moral systems rooted in fear and obedience seek to suppress affect, emotional resonance invites vulnerability, empathy, and ethical reflection rooted in lived experience. Whether triggered by erotic encounters, art, or ritual, it disrupts rigid moral codes by making space for intuition and relational truth, challenging the supremacy of detached reason and moral absolutism.

70. Catherine Despeux and Fabrizio Pregadio

Both are leading scholars of Taoist philosophy and internal alchemy. Despeux has explored Taoist views of the subtle body, breath, and sexual energy—especially as related to female practitioners—while Pregadio has translated and interpreted key Neidan (inner alchemy) texts. In SOCAS, their work offers essential insight into non-dualistic models of embodiment, where erotic and energetic flows are seen not as distractions but as integral to spiritual cultivation, balance, and liberation—contrasting sharply with ascetic models rooted in denial.

71. Lower Dantian

Often translated as the "elixir field," the lower dantian serves as a foundational site of energetic cultivation in Taoist and Neidan traditions. In SOCAS, it is recognized as a symbol of embodied wisdom—where breath, sexual energy, and vitality converge. Unlike Western religious frameworks that emphasize moral discipline through denial of the body, Taoist practice centers awareness in the lower dantian to harmonize inner and outer forces, integrating erotic energy into the path of balance and transformation.

72. Livia Kohn

A leading scholar of Daoism and East Asian religions, Livia Kohn has written extensively on Chinese spiritual practices, inner alchemy, and the embodied dimensions of religious life. Her work explores how Daoist traditions understand the body, energy (*qi*), and harmony with nature—often integrating sexuality and vitality into holistic frameworks of health and spiritual cultivation. In SOCAS, Kohn's research helps articulate non-dualistic perspectives that contrast sharply with Western ascetic models, showing how erotic and life energies can be understood as integral to balance, awareness, and ethical embodiment.

73. Attunement

In SOCAS, attunement is understood as an ethical and erotic practice—contrasting with moral systems rooted in command and control. Whether cultivated through breath, touch, ritual, or presence, attunement fosters relational sensitivity and embodied insight. It reflects a non-dominating way of being that values reciprocity over hierarchy, and connection over conquest. Against traditions that silence desire or subordinate the body, attunement affirms intimacy, vulnerability, and the subtle intelligence of shared aliveness.

74. Somatic Awareness

In SOCAS, somatic awareness is recognized as a radical site of resistance against traditions that privilege mind over body or treat the flesh as morally suspect. Cultivated through practices like breathwork, touch, and movement, it restores the body as a locus of wisdom and ethical attunement. Rather than suppressing sensation in pursuit of purity, somatic awareness invites presence, integration, and sensual literacy—reclaiming the body not as a vessel of sin, but as a dynamic interface with the world, others, and the self.

75. Integrative Medicine

Unlike reductionist models that treat the body in isolation from mind or spirit, integrative medicine honors the complex interplay between physiological and psychosocial health. In SOCAS, it is acknowledged for challenging the clinical detachment of biomedicine and reclaiming therapeutic models rooted in embodiment, energy, and patient-centered care. Its inclusive framework parallels the book's vision of erotic and ethical integration—recognizing that healing and liberation require attention to the full spectrum of human experience, not just the treatment of symptoms.

76. Isabelle Robinet

A French sinologist and major voice in Taoist studies, Isabelle Robinet explored Taoist cosmology, meditation, and internal alchemy—especially within the Mao-shan and Shangqing traditions. Her work emphasized the integration of body and spirit, challenging Western dualisms. In SOCAS, Robinet is cited for illuminating Taoist models of transformation rooted in harmony, sensual energy, and embodied practice, offering a vital contrast to moral systems based on repression.

77. Qigong

Qigong embodies a holistic approach to wellness that integrates body, breath, and mind in pursuit of inner harmony and energetic balance. In SOCAS, it is valued as a somatic discipline that honors erotic and life force energies without moralizing them. Unlike Western moral systems that regulate sexuality through denial and guilt, qigong encourages conscious cultivation of *qi* as a vital and sacred force. Its emphasis on internal awareness, fluid movement, and energetic attunement offers a liberatory model of embodiment grounded in presence rather than repression.

78. Indigenous Cultures

In SOCAS, Indigenous cultures are recognized not as static remnants of the past but as living systems of knowledge that often honor eroticism, gender diversity, and spiritual embodiment far more holistically than colonial or Abrahamic frameworks. From Two-Spirit traditions in Turtle Island to ancestral fertility rites in Africa and the Pacific, Indigenous worldviews frequently affirm sexual plurality, communal care, and the sacredness of the body. Their marginalization under colonial violence—including forced conversion, sexual repression, and cultural erasure—marks a profound loss of erotic wisdom. Reengaging with Indigenous voices is essential to decolonizing sexuality and restoring plural, life-affirming modes of being.

79. Rites of Passage

In many Indigenous, ancient, and non-Western cultures, rites of passage honor bodily change, erotic awakening, and spiritual integration as sacred thresholds. In SOCAS, these rituals are reclaimed as communal affirmations of life transitions often pathologized or privatized in modern, moralistic societies. From puberty ceremonies to sacred unions, such rites offer models of cultural support for sexuality, maturity, and embodied identity. Their erasure under colonial and religious regimes reflects a broader loss of collective erotic literacy and intergenerational wisdom. Reviving or reimagining rites of passage can play a vital role in reclaiming sexual dignity and cultural belonging.

80. Will Roscoe

An American historian and LGBTQ+ scholar, Will Roscoe has focused extensively on same-sex traditions and gender diversity in Indigenous cultures—particularly among Native North American societies. His work, including *Changing Ones: Third and Fourth Genders in Native North America,* documents rich, pre-colonial frameworks of gender pluralism and erotic expression that challenge Western binaries. In SOCAS, Roscoe's scholarship is essential for decolonizing sexual history and restoring Indigenous narratives in which non-normative desire and identity were integrated, respected, and culturally meaningful rather than suppressed by colonial moral codes.

81. Inclusive Ethos

In SOCAS, an inclusive ethos is central to dismantling systems that privilege uniformity, purity, or moral hierarchy. Rooted in compassion and pluralism, it challenges the exclusion of queer, non-binary, disabled, and non-Western bodies and perspectives from dominant moral narratives. An inclusive ethos not only tolerates difference but honors it as essential to ethical life, spiritual depth, and erotic justice. It demands structural transformation, not tokenism, and calls for a cultural reorientation toward empathy, equity, and embodied presence.

82. Vine Deloria Jr.

A Standing Rock Sioux scholar, theologian, and activist, Vine Deloria Jr. was a leading voice in the reclamation of Indigenous sovereignty, spirituality, and intellectual traditions. His influential works—such as *God Is Red* and *Custer Died for Your Sins*—critique the colonial imposition of Christian morality and Western rationalism onto Native worldviews. In SOCAS, Deloria's insights support the deconstruction of religious authority as a tool of cultural erasure and moral control. His writing reaffirms Indigenous knowledge systems where land, body, and spirit are interconnected—and where erotic and spiritual dimensions of life are honored rather than suppressed.

83. Colonial Powers

In SOCAS, colonial powers are examined as global enforcers of religious moral codes, racial hierarchies, and sexual regulation. Through missionary efforts, legal codes like Section 377, and the criminalization of Indigenous practices, colonial regimes systematically suppressed erotic diversity, gender plurality, and embodied spiritualities. They replaced complex local systems with rigid binaries of purity and deviance, reshaping sexuality to align with imperial interests. The enduring aftershocks of this violence remain embedded in postcolonial law, education, and cultural shame, making decolonization of sex, spirit, and identity a critical act of liberation.

84. Indigenous Sexual Traditions

Indigenous Sexual Traditions

Many Indigenous cultures have honored erotic diversity, gender fluidity, and sexual rites as integral to spiritual and communal life. In SOCAS, these traditions are recognized as powerful alternatives to colonial and religious repression. From Two-Spirit identities to sacred fertility practices, they reflect holistic views of the body, desire, and kinship. Their erasure under missionary rule and legal codification reveals how colonization acted as a moral conquest—silencing traditions that once affirmed the sacredness of erotic expression.

85. Epistemological Resistance

In SOCAS, epistemological resistance is central to the rejection of moral systems that exclude or erase erotic, Indigenous, queer, or embodied knowledge. It pushes back against the monopoly of Western, theistic, or rationalist worldviews by restoring plural, experiential, and non-linear understandings of sexuality, spirit, and ethics. To resist epistemologically is to reclaim not only what we know, but *how* we are allowed to know.

86. Robin Wall Kimmerer

A Potawatomi botanist, educator, and author, Robin Wall Kimmerer blends Indigenous knowledge systems with Western science to advocate for ecological and cultural reciprocity. In works like *Braiding Sweetgrass*, she emphasizes the intelligence of the living world and the ethics of relationality. In SOCAS, her voice affirms that decolonization is not just political, but also sensual and spiritual—rooted in remembering how to feel, listen, and belong to Earth and each other. Her work exemplifies epistemological resistance through reverence, story, and embodied learning.

87. Counter-Narrative

In SOCAS, counter-narratives are tools of liberation—disrupting religious, colonial, and patriarchal mythologies that have shaped moral authority and sexual repression. Whether drawn from queer lives, Indigenous memory, or erotic expression, these stories resist imposed silences and reclaim the power to define truth. Counter-narratives do not merely reject; they reimagine, offering alternative ways of knowing, being, and belonging.

88. Indigenous Wisdom

In SOCAS, Indigenous wisdom is celebrated as an embodied, land-based epistemology that honors erotic diversity, gender plurality, and sacred sensuality. It resists the colonial dissection of body, spirit, and land, offering instead relational ways of knowing rooted in story, ritual, and reverence. Far from primitive, it is a dynamic and resilient source of healing, sustainability, and erotic justice—restoring what dominant systems have sought to erase through religious, scientific, and legal domination.

89. Monotheistic Traditions

In SOCAS, monotheistic traditions are critically examined for their role in shaping restrictive moral codes, especially around sexuality, gender roles, and bodily autonomy. While spiritually meaningful to many, these traditions have historically promoted hierarchies of purity, chastity, and patriarchal control—frequently pathologizing desire, pleasure, and nonconforming identities. Their legacy includes the criminalization of queer lives, the suppression of erotic wisdom, and the erasure of plural spiritualities. Deconstructing their normative grip is essential to reclaiming erotic justice and spiritual freedom.

90. Chastity

In SOCAS, chastity is examined as a mechanism of moral control rooted in monotheistic traditions that elevate sexual restraint as a sign of virtue. While framed as a personal choice, it often operates as a gendered obligation—especially for women, queer individuals, and clergy—used to police bodies and suppress erotic autonomy. By associating purity with denial, chastity contributes to shame-based cultures of sexuality that disconnect people from pleasure, self-trust, and embodied freedom.

91. Monolithic

In SOCAS, the term "monolithic" is used to challenge portrayals of religion, culture, or morality as singular and unchanging. Monolithic frameworks often erase nuance, suppress dissent, and marginalize alternative voices—especially those related to gender, sexuality, and embodied knowledge. By framing dominant ideologies as universal or unquestionable, monolithic thinking obstructs critical reflection and perpetuates exclusionary power structures.

92. Karen Armstrong

A former Catholic nun turned religious scholar and author, Karen Armstrong is known for her accessible yet deeply researched works on comparative religion, including *A History of God* and *The Case for God*. In SOCAS, Armstrong's analysis is relevant for understanding how monotheistic traditions developed—and how they shaped restrictive moral codes around sexuality, gender roles, and bodily denial. Her call for compassion as a central religious value intersects with SOCAS's critique of rigid doctrines and offers a bridge toward more humane, pluralistic interpretations of spiritual life.

93. Polytheistic Societies

In SOCAS, polytheistic societies are highlighted for their plural spiritual frameworks that often embraced erotic expression, gender variance, and sacred embodiment. From ancient Sumer to classical India and Egypt, these cultures revered fertility, beauty, and sensuality as divine forces. Their deities frequently modeled relational diversity and fluid identities, offering alternatives to monotheistic constraints. The erasure of these traditions under colonial and religious conquest marked a profound loss of erotic and spiritual plurality.

94. Elaine Pagels

A historian of religion and professor at Princeton University, Elaine Pagels is renowned for her groundbreaking work on early Christianity and Gnostic texts, particularly in *The Gnostic Gospels*. In SOCAS, her scholarship illuminates how early Christian diversity—especially views that embraced the body, the feminine, and mystical experience—was suppressed in favor of orthodox doctrine. Pagels reveals how institutional Christianity came to equate sexuality with sin, replacing pluralism with moral control. Her work supports the reclaiming of silenced spiritualities that honored erotic wisdom and internal revelation.

95. Mircea Eliade

A Romanian historian of religion, philosopher, and novelist, Mircea Eliade is widely known for his studies on myth, ritual, and the sacred across cultures. His works, such as *The Sacred and the Profane* and *Patterns in Comparative Religion*, explore how religious symbols and rites shape human understanding of time, space, and embodiment. In SOCAS, Eliade's concept of *hierophany*—the manifestation of the sacred in the material world—offers insight into how eroticism and ritual can be reclaimed as sacred experiences, beyond the moral strictures imposed by monotheistic traditions. His comparative approach supports efforts to decenter Western religious norms in favor of plural, embodied spiritualities.

96. Adultery

In SOCAS, adultery is analyzed not merely as a personal betrayal but as a construct historically weaponized to enforce gender norms and control female sexuality. While religious texts frequently condemn it, enforcement has been selective and gendered—reflecting double standards in moral codes. Legal and religious penalties for adultery have long served to protect patriarchal lineage, property, and honor, rather than emotional or sexual integrity. The concept remains embedded in many moral discourses around fidelity, shame, and sin.

97. Neo-Pagan

In SOCAS, Neo-Paganism is explored as a modern reclamation of spiritual pluralism and erotic embodiment, offering alternatives to the asceticism and moral rigidity of monotheistic systems. By honoring the sensual, cyclical, and immanent aspects of the divine—often through rituals celebrating fertility, sexuality, and nature—Neo-Pagan traditions challenge the disembodied spirituality of dominant religions. They serve as counter-narratives that reintegrate pleasure, gender fluidity, and ecological reverence into spiritual life.

98. Torah

In SOCAS, the Torah is examined not only as a religious text but as a source of enduring moral codes that have deeply influenced Western legal and sexual norms. Particularly through Levitical laws, it has shaped prohibitions around homosexuality, gender roles, and ritual purity. While central to Jewish identity and tradition, its verses have often been selectively interpreted to justify exclusion, control, and moral judgment— especially when adopted into Christian and colonial frameworks.

99. Mark Masterson, *et al.*

Edited by Mark Masterson, Nancy Sorkin Rabinowitz, and James Robson, this comprehensive collection of scholarly essays examines gender, sexuality, and erotic practices across ancient cultures—including the Near East, Greece, and Rome. The volume brings historical and theoretical perspectives to the study of sexual norms and roles in antiquity, challenging modern assumptions about sexuality as static or universal. In SOCAS, this work is significant for revealing the diversity and complexity of ancient sexual lives and for demonstrating how later moral strictures and shame-based frameworks were historically contingent, not inevitable.

100. David Biale

A distinguished historian of Jewish culture and thought, David Biale has written extensively on Jewish identity, gender, and sexuality, including *Power and Powerlessness in Jewish History* and *Sexuality in*

Jewish History. In SOCAS, Biale's work is referenced for its nuanced analysis of how Jewish moral and legal traditions have negotiated erotic life, gender norms, and community boundaries—revealing the interplay between religious authority and lived sexuality across history. His scholarship helps trace how ancient texts and later interpretations shaped normative sexual ethics within Jewish and broader Western contexts.

101. Covenantal Commitment

In SOCAS, covenantal commitment is explored as a powerful but often restrictive framework, particularly in Judeo-Christian contexts where it has been used to sanctify heteronormative marriage and uphold patriarchal norms. While rooted in reciprocity and moral intention, such covenants have historically excluded queer, non-monogamous, or non-traditional unions. Reclaiming covenantal language through a liberatory lens allows for reimagining commitment as consensual, evolving, and rooted in authenticity rather than rigid moral codes.

102. Jesus of Nazareth

In SOCAS, Jesus is examined not just as a religious figure but as a radical moral voice whose message was often co-opted by institutional Christianity to uphold patriarchal, anti-sexual, and hierarchical norms. While he championed inclusion and dignity—often in defiance of legalistic purity codes—later interpretations distorted his legacy into one of moral surveillance and repression. Reclaiming Jesus outside of ecclesiastical dogma allows for a vision of spiritual eroticism rooted in empathy, embodiment, and love without judgment.

103. Kecia Ali

A contemporary scholar of Islamic law and ethics, Kecia Ali has written influential works on gender, sexuality, and jurisprudence in Muslim contexts, including *Sexual Ethics and Islam* and *Marriage and Slavery in Early Islam*. Her research critically examines how religious legal traditions have regulated desire, marriage, and the body. In SOCAS, Ali's scholarship is significant for exposing how doctrines often framed as divinely fixed are in fact historically contingent and deeply gendered, offering tools to challenge moral absolutism and reclaim more just, historically informed understandings of erotic life and ethical agency.

104. Pauline Christianity

In SOCAS, Pauline Christianity is analyzed as a formative source of the sexual ethics and gender roles that shaped Christian moral codes for centuries. Paul's epistles often stress chastity, obedience, and the subjugation of the body, especially for women—laying groundwork for theological justifications of celibacy, heteronormativity, and patriarchal authority. Though his writings also contain radical spiritual egalitarianism, later interpretations privileged his more ascetic and hierarchical views, reinforcing a dualism that demonized eroticism and sacralized moral control.

105. John M. G. Barclay

A prominent New Testament scholar, John M. G. Barclay, has written extensively on early Christian ethics, grace, and community life, including *Paul and the Gift*. His work emphasizes the transformative power of grace over law-based moralism. In SOCAS, Barclay's scholarship is significant for reframing Christian moral frameworks—especially those derived from Pauline texts—away from punitive legalism toward relational and embodied understandings of freedom. His emphasis on gift and reciprocity provides a counterpoint to doctrinal rigidity and supports a liberated view of ethical life that resists shame-based control.

106. Ben Witherington III

An American New Testament scholar and theologian known for his work on early Christian history, social context, and ethical instruction in the Greco-Roman world. Witherington's research—such as in *The New Testament Story* and *Women in the Earliest Churches*—explores how early Christian communities lived, debated, and negotiated norms of behavior. In SOCAS, Witherington's scholarship is referenced for its detailed contextualization of early Christian moral codes, revealing how social, cultural, and religious currents shaped attitudes toward gender, sexuality, and community life rather than these being fixed divine mandates.

107. Peter Brown

A preeminent historian of late antiquity, Peter Brown's work transformed understanding of early Christianity by situating it within broader social, cultural, and psychological contexts. His studies on asceticism, sainthood, and the transformation of Roman society show how practices like sexual renunciation and moral rigor were not inevitable Christian essentials but historically contingent responses to power, identity, and community. In SOCAS, Brown's scholarship is valuable for revealing how bodily discipline and clerical authority became intertwined with religious virtue—showing how shame-based sexual ethics developed within specific historical pressures rather than timeless spiritual imperatives.

108. Dale Martin

A leading scholar of early Christianity and the New Testament, Dale Martin's work—such as *Sex and the Single Savior* and *The Corinthian Body*—examines how ancient Christian communities understood embodiment, gender, and sexual ethics. In SOCAS, Martin's research is significant for showing that early Christian attitudes toward the body and desire were shaped by social, cultural, and rhetorical forces rather than fixed divine mandates. His analysis helps decenter doctrinal claims about sexuality by revealing the diversity and contestation within early Christian thought and practice.

109. Peggy Sanday

An American anthropologist known for her research on gender, sexuality, and social organization in cross-cultural perspective, including *Female Power and Male Dominance*. Sanday's work highlights how ideas about gender and erotic behavior are socially constructed and vary widely across cultures. In SOCAS, her scholarship is essential for deconstructing assumptions that Western norms of sexuality are universal. By documenting societies with egalitarian gender relations and fluid sexual roles, Sanday's findings support a broader understanding of human erotic diversity beyond hierarchical and moralistic frameworks.

110. Jessica Valenti

An American feminist writer and commentator, Jessica Valenti is known for her work on gender, sexuality, and reproductive rights, including books like *Full Frontal Feminism* and *Sex Object*. Her writing critiques purity culture, misogyny, and the policing of women's bodies in both secular and religious societies. In SOCAS, Valenti's voice is referenced for exposing how sexual double standards and moralizing narratives continue to shape public discourse around consent, pleasure, and female autonomy—making a case for unapologetic sexual agency as a feminist and humanist imperative.

111. Saint Thomas Aquinas

In SOCAS, Aquinas is examined as a key architect of moral theology that deeply shaped Christian sexual ethics. In *Summa Theologica*, he categorizes sexual acts—judging them according to natural law—with heterosexual procreative sex deemed morally superior. Non-procreative acts, including masturbation, homosexuality, and contraception, were condemned as "unnatural." Aquinas's legacy endures in doctrines that pathologize desire and uphold a rigid hierarchy of sexual behaviors, making him a central figure in the historical justification of erotic repression.

112. Jaroslav Pelikan

A distinguished historian of Christian thought, Jaroslav Pelikan, authored the multi-volume *The Christian Tradition: A History of the Development of Doctrine*. His work traces the evolution of theological ideas from early Christianity through the modern era. In SOCAS, Pelikan is cited to illustrate how Christian doctrines—including those related to sexuality, sin, and purity—were not static divine truths but were shaped by historical, cultural, and philosophical contexts. His scholarship helps demystify the authority of religious dogma by revealing its human and adaptive origins.

113. Cult of the Virgin

In SOCAS, the Cult of the Virgin is explored as a powerful theological and cultural force that shaped Western ideals of femininity, chastity, and motherhood. While offering a revered feminine figure in Christian tradition, Marian devotion often reinforced restrictive gender roles—idealizing female passivity, virginity, and self-sacrifice. This veneration of purity became entangled with the moral policing of women's sexuality, casting desire outside of sanctioned motherhood as sinful. The cult thus served both spiritual and patriarchal functions, cloaking control in divine reverence.

114 Melissa Wilcox

A scholar of religion known for her research on contemporary Pagan and LGBTQ+ spiritualities, especially Wicca, queer spiritual practice, and feminist religion. Her work explores how non-normative religious communities negotiate embodiment, sexuality, and ritual outside patriarchal and monotheistic frameworks. In *Our Lady of the Excluded* and related essays, Wilcox examines how queer and Pagan traditions reclaim the sacred body and erotic imagination against histories of repression. In SOCAS, her scholarship supports analyses of how alternative spiritualities unsettle moral absolutism and affirm plural, embodied expressions of the sacred.

115. John Esposito and Yvonne Haddad

Scholars of Islamic studies, John Esposito and Yvonne Haddad, have co-authored influential work on Islam and its interactions with culture, law, and modernity, including *Religion and Migration in the Mediterranean* and *Islam, Gender, and Social Change*. Their research examines how religious traditions—including interpretations of sexuality, gender roles, and moral authority—are shaped by social, political, and historical forces rather than fixed spiritual mandates. In SOCAS, their scholarship is referenced for contextualizing how religious doctrines regarding the body and desire are negotiated within communities and how reformist and traditionalist currents contest moral norms.

116. Hijab

In SOCAS, the hijab is examined not as a singular religious obligation but as a complex symbol shaped by gender norms, colonial histories, state control, and personal agency. While often framed as a spiritual or cultural expression, it has also been politicized—both by regimes enforcing it and by those banning it. Feminist scholars and activists offer diverse perspectives: some view it as empowering and freely chosen, while others critique its role in reinforcing patriarchal modesty codes. SOCAS underscores the importance of context, autonomy, and resisting both Orientalist and fundamentalist narratives.

117. Scott Siraj al-Haqq Kugle

An American scholar of Islamic thought and sexuality, Scott Siraj al-Haqq Kugle (formerly Scott Kugle) is known for his pioneering work on gender, desire, and LGBTQ identities in Muslim contexts. His book *Homosexuality in Islam* and related writings challenges traditional legalistic readings by foregrounding compassion, ethical complexity, and the diversity of interpretive voices within Islamic scripture and history. In SOCAS, Kugle's scholarship is significant for demonstrating that frameworks of sexual ethics in religion are not monolithic; they can be rearticulated in ways that affirm embodied dignity, relational justice, and spiritual pluralism rather than rigid condemnation.

118. Amina Wadud

A groundbreaking Islamic feminist scholar and Qur'anic exegete, Amina Wadud is known for her influential book *Qur'an and Woman*, which offers a gender-inclusive interpretation of Islamic scripture. As both an academic and an activist, she challenges patriarchal readings of the Qur'an and advocates for spiritual equality, including women's leadership in prayer. In SOCAS, Wadud's work is vital in showing how sacred texts can be re-read through lenses of justice and compassion, affirming that feminist and queer-inclusive interpretations are not external impositions but authentic engagements with divine revelation.

119. Kama (as Precolonial Name for Africa)

The term *Kama* is invoked in some Afrocentric and spiritual frameworks as the original name for Africa. While etymologically linked to *Kemet* ("Black Land"), no scholarly consensus confirms its historical use as a continental name. Rather, *Kama* functions as a powerful cultural symbol of identity reclamation and pre-colonial memory. In SOCAS, the use of *Kama* aligns with pan-African efforts to reclaim indigenous African identity before colonization. This terminology honors cultural continuity and resists colonial erasure of Africa's original self-definition.

120. Uriel Nawej

A Congolese writer, philosopher, and Raelian Bishop, Uriel Nawej, is known for his critical works such as *Erotic Africa* and *White Poison*, which explore the impact of colonialism and Abrahamic religions on

African sexualities and indigenous knowledge systems. In SOCAS, Nawej's contributions are central to decolonial critiques of religious morality. His work emphasizes the erotic as a source of sacred expression and joy, arguing that sexual freedom was deeply rooted in precolonial African cultures before being suppressed by Christian and Muslim conquest. His voice aligns with broader calls for erotic justice and cultural reclamation.

121. Two-Spirit

In SOCAS, Two-Spirit identities are explored as living embodiments of gender and sexual diversity within Indigenous cosmologies—often revered rather than marginalized. The term, coined in 1990, bridges ancient traditions with contemporary self-identification, resisting Western binaries imposed by colonial and religious systems. Two-Spirit presence disrupts monolithic gender ideologies and affirms spiritual, erotic, and communal roles that honor multiplicity. It is referenced as part of a broader reclamation of Indigenous epistemologies and erotic justice.

122. Moral Colonization

In SOCAS, moral colonization is analyzed as a key mechanism through which colonial empires and missionary efforts dismantled Indigenous erotic cultures and imposed restrictive religious frameworks. Christian and Muslim colonizers often redefined what was "moral" or "civilized," labeling local practices as sinful or perverse. This not only erased diverse sexual traditions but also established long-lasting hierarchies of virtue tied to Western dominance. SOCAS critiques moral colonization as a form of epistemic and erotic violence that continues to shape contemporary legal systems, education, and cultural shame.

123. Manuela Picq and Josi Tikuna

Manuela Picq, a feminist scholar, and Josi Tikuna, an Indigenous leader, both advocate for decolonial gender justice grounded in Indigenous knowledge. In SOCAS, their voices highlight how colonial moral systems have displaced relational, land-based sexual ethics. Their work affirms the right of Indigenous peoples to reclaim cultural and erotic sovereignty beyond imposed binaries.

124. Monjeríos of Spanish California

In SOCAS, monjeríos are examined as tools of moral colonization within the Spanish mission system. These spaces institutionalized the surveillance and sexual control of Indigenous girls under the guise of religious conversion and "civilization." Separated from their families and communities, they were taught Catholic domesticity and punished for expressing autonomy or sexuality. Monjeríos reflect the intersection of gendered violence, forced assimilation, and the erasure of Indigenous erotic traditions under colonial rule.

125. Valeria Rivera and Monjeríos of Spanish California

Valeria Rivera-Quiguanás is a scholar whose research on gender and sexual diversity in educational and social contexts highlights how dominant norms shape perceptions of identity and belonging. When considered alongside historical institutions such as the *monjeríos* of Spanish California—segregated mission quarters where Indigenous girls and women were confined to enforce Catholic moral discipline—Rivera's work underscores enduring patterns of moral regulation. In SOCAS, the juxtaposition reveals how colonial and religious moral codes have long policed Indigenous bodies and gender diversity, shaping both historical practices like the *monjeríos* and contemporary attitudes toward sexual difference and autonomy.

126. Circumcision Rites

In SOCAS, circumcision rites are analyzed through a critical lens that questions the ethical implications of imposing irreversible bodily changes—particularly on minors—under the authority of religious or cultural tradition. While recognized as sacred in many societies (e.g., Judaism, Islam, certain African and Indigenous communities), these rites also reflect deeper narratives of purity, gender regulation, and control over sexual anatomy. SOCAS highlights the need for consent, bodily autonomy, and cross-cultural dialogue on ritual practices that intersect with human rights.

127. Psychosexual Disarmament

In SOCAS, psychosexual disarmament refers to the internalized dismantling of erotic agency caused by centuries of moral indoctrination.

Through doctrines of guilt, shame, and control, many religious systems have weakened people's natural capacity for joyful, consensual sexuality. This disarmament manifests in fear of pleasure, repression of desire, and a fractured relationship with the body. SOCAS frames its reversal as a core step toward erotic justice and holistic liberation.

128. Sharia

In SOCAS, Sharia is examined not as a fixed legal code but as a dynamic tradition subject to diverse interpretations. While some versions uphold justice and ethical balance, others—particularly those influenced by patriarchal or authoritarian readings—impose strict controls over sexuality, gender roles, and bodily autonomy. SOCAS critiques such uses of Sharia when it reinforces moral absolutism or suppresses individual rights, emphasizing the need for interpretations rooted in compassion, plurality, and evolving human dignity.

129. Jawad Syed

Her article traces how the concept of *modesty* (*haya*) in Islamic scripture and tradition was historically situated and later transformed into restrictive norms that have been used to justify female seclusion, gender segregation, and barriers to women's economic participation in Muslim-majority societies. Syed argues that originally protective textual provisions became patriarchal institutions through successive exegesis and cultural interpretation, resulting in deeply embedded social and emotional challenges for women's autonomy.*

130. The Proto-Scripture of Erotophobia

Not an actual ancient scripture, but a critical term used in social theory to describe the foundational body of moral norms and texts in Western religious and legal traditions that produce *erotophobia*—a culturally conditioned fear or aversion to sexuality and erotic expression. *Erotophobia* itself is defined as a fear of or negative attitude toward sex and sexual intimacy, positioned on a continuum opposite *erotophilia*, or positive attitudes toward sexuality. In SOCAS, the notion of a "proto-scripture" of erotophobia highlights how certain sacred texts and moral codes have been interpreted or institutionalized to legitimate shame, denial, and regulation of sexual desire. It emphasizes not a single source, but the assemblage of normative doctrines that function as an ideological foundation for erotic repression in many societies. This concept helps frame how fear of sexuality becomes encoded in law, religion, education, and collective psychology, shaping attitudes that position erotic life as potentially dangerous, sinful, or morally inferior to spiritual or social order.

131. Sexual Silence

In SOCAS, sexual silence is treated as a strategic tool of repression—perpetuated by religious institutions, colonial legacies, and patriarchal authority—to obscure, control, and delegitimize sexual knowledge. By rendering sex unspeakable or taboo, sexual silence reinforces moral hierarchies, curtails consent education, and upholds fear-based ideologies around pleasure and identity. SOCAS challenges this silence with a call for open, scientific, and emancipatory dialogue.

132. Psychosexual Genocide

Coined as a critical term in SOCAS, psychosexual genocide refers to the destruction of erotic and sexual agency at a collective level. Through religious doctrine, colonial repression, and heteronormative moral codes, entire populations have been stripped of their sexual selfhood and indoctrinated into shame. SOCAS identifies this process as a form of cultural and existential violence—one that leaves deep wounds on the psyche, body, and spirit.

133. Erotic Consciousness

In SOCAS, erotic consciousness is seen as a radical reclamation of the self—a return to embodied wisdom long denied by religious dogma and moral authoritarianism. It draws inspiration from thinkers like Audre Lorde, who framed the erotic as a source of deep power. By cultivating erotic consciousness, individuals resist psychosexual disarmament and reconnect with joy, presence, and emotional integrity. SOCAS promotes this awareness as foundational to erotic justice and spiritual liberation.

134. Sarah Deer

A citizen of the Muscogee (Creek) Nation and a leading Indigenous scholar, lawyer, and activist, Sarah Deer's work focuses on gender violence, tribal sovereignty, and the intersections of colonialism, law, and sexual justice. She has been instrumental in crafting legal frameworks to address sexual assault and domestic violence against Native women, including advocacy around the *Violence Against Women Act* (VAWA) and Indigenous jurisdiction. In SOCAS, Deer's scholarship underscores how colonial legal systems have long marginalized Indigenous autonomy—including Indigenous sexual and relational norms—and highlights the necessity of reclaiming community-based practices of justice rooted in self-determination, healing, and embodied dignity.

135. Catherine McKinley and Hannah Knipp

Catherine E. McKinley and Hannah Knipp are scholars whose collaborative research examines sexual violence against Indigenous women as a form of ongoing historical oppression rooted in colonial, patriarchal systems. Their work documents disproportionate rates of sexual violence and explores how structural discrimination, lack of accountability for perpetrators, and intergenerational trauma shape health, wellness, and justice outcomes for Indigenous women in the United States. In SOCAS, their research highlights how moral colonization and patriarchal violence intersect to harm Indigenous erotic and bodily autonomy while underscoring the need for trauma-informed, culturally rooted responses to sexual violence.

136. Erotic Decolonization

In SOCAS, erotic decolonization is framed as a vital dimension of broader liberation struggles. It involves unlearning colonial moral codes, reviving Indigenous and ancestral sexualities, and restoring the erotic as a source of joy, identity, and resistance. This process challenges not only external systems of control but also internalized shame and psychosexual disarmament. Erotic decolonization affirms the right to pleasure, fluidity, and full erotic expression outside imposed binaries and dogmas.

137. Erotic Memory

In SOCAS, erotic memory functions as a site of resistance and healing. It recovers stories, sensations, and desires silenced by shame, trauma, and institutional control. Whether through art, ritual, or storytelling, the act of remembering one's erotic self—across lifetimes, generations, or histories—becomes a radical reclamation of pleasure, dignity, and truth. Erotic memory is integral to the process of erotic decolonization and sexual liberation.

138. Sovereign Erotic

In SOCAS, the sovereign erotic refers to the reclaiming of sexual power as a site of resistance, wholeness, and joy. Influenced by Audre Lorde and Indigenous feminist thought, it challenges external moral authorities and internalized shame. The sovereign erotic honors desire as self-determined, relationally expansive, and rooted in consent, care, and cosmic dignity. It is a key principle in the project of erotic decolonization and liberation.

139. Sarah Reardon Smith

An Indigenous scholar and activist whose work centers on gender, sexuality, and decolonial theory, Sarah Reardon Smith explores the intersections of Indigenous sovereignty, erotic autonomy, and cultural resurgence. Her research highlights how colonial moralities and patriarchal discipline have disrupted Indigenous erotic traditions and community norms. In SOCAS, her contributions are referenced for articulating how Indigenous epistemologies reclaim the body, desire, and relational ethics from the legacies of moral colonization—affirming that erotic justice is inseparable from decolonial liberation.

140. Takatāpui

In SOCAS, *takatāpui* is highlighted as a powerful example of erotic decolonization. Reclaimed by Māori scholars and activists, the term resists Western labels like "LGBTQ+" by grounding diverse identities in ancestral language, kinship, and cosmology. It represents a refusal of colonial erasure and a celebration of integrated spiritual, sexual, and cultural sovereignty. As such, *takatāpui* challenges monolithic notions of gender and sexuality imposed by Christian missionaries and colonial legal systems.

CHAPTER TWO

1. Comprehensive Sexuality Education

In SOCAS, comprehensive sexuality education (CSE) is presented as a vital alternative to abstinence-only models and religiously imposed ignorance. Rooted in UNESCO and WHO guidelines, CSE equips learners with critical knowledge and values to make informed, respectful, and autonomous decisions. It resists sexual silence and moral authoritarianism by affirming bodily integrity, sexual diversity, and emotional literacy. SOCAS defends CSE as a human right and a foundation for erotic justice and gender equality.

2. Virginity

In SOCAS, virginity is examined as a powerful moral fiction that has shaped gender roles and sexual norms across cultures. Rooted in religious doctrines and reinforced through rites, laws, and education, the concept enforces a binary of purity and corruption, particularly for women. SOCAS challenges this construct as a tool of psychosexual repression and moral colonization, calling instead for narratives that affirm sexual agency, consent, and embodied truth over inherited shame.

3. Sanctity of Marriage

In SOCAS, the sanctity of marriage is examined as a doctrinal tool that has reinforced patriarchal, heteronormative, and procreative norms. Promoted by Abrahamic religions as the only legitimate site for sexual expression, this ideal has been used to stigmatize non-marital sex, queer relationships, and alternative family structures. SOCAS challenges this moral absolutism by affirming love, consent, and erotic authenticity over religious conformity.

4. John S. Santelli

Professor of Population and Family Health at Columbia University and a leading voice in adolescent reproductive rights and public health. His work has played a pivotal role in shaping national and global policies on youth sexual health, emphasizing evidence-based, rights-affirming approaches. He has been a vocal critic of abstinence-only education ,arguing that such programs are medically inaccurate, ethically problematic, and harmful to young people's well-being. In SOCAS, Santelli is cited as a key advocate for comprehensive sexuality education rooted in science, autonomy, and social justice.

5. Sloan Caldwell

Sloan Caldwell authored a senior thesis at Claremont McKenna College titled *"Let's Talk About Sex: The Failure of Abstinence-Only Policies in America's Public Schools"* (2015), critically evaluating how abstinence-only education fails to meet its own public health goals and infringes on students' rights to accurate sexual health information. In SOCAS, Caldwell's work is referenced as an early academic critique of moralistic sexual education, highlighting the importance of evidence-based, comprehensive approaches over shame-based policies that perpetuate sexual silence and repression.

6. Sexually Transmitted Infections (STIs)

In SOCAS, STIs are analyzed not only as public health issues but as moralized conditions often weaponized to shame sexual behavior, especially outside of heterosexual monogamy. Comprehensive sexuality education—grounded in science and rights—is emphasized as essential to STI prevention, while moralistic, fear-based approaches are critiqued for perpetuating stigma, ignorance, and silence.

7. Douglas Kirby

Dr. Douglas Kirby is a public health researcher known for his work evaluating the effectiveness of sexuality education programs. His studies have shown that comprehensive, age-appropriate education reduces risky sexual behavior and leads to better health outcomes, while abstinence-only approaches are largely ineffective. In SOCAS, Kirby's evidence-based findings support the case for sexuality education grounded in science, autonomy, and human rights, countering moralistic policies that rely on fear and silence.

8. Abstinence-Only Education

In SOCAS, abstinence-only education is critiqued as a politically driven and ethically flawed model that denies young people accurate, inclusive, and life-saving information. Often funded by conservative institutions and reinforced by religious dogma, it perpetuates stigma, fear, and sexual repression. SOCAS highlights research—including that of Douglas Kirby and John S. Santelli—that exposes its ineffectiveness in preventing STIs or teen pregnancy, while underscoring the need for comprehensive, rights-based sexuality education.

9. UNESCO International Technical Guidance on Sexuality Education

Published as a revised guidance in 2018, this document provides technical advice on designing and implementing comprehensive sexuality education (CSE) programmes that are scientifically accurate, culturally relevant, and rights-based. It defines essential content areas (such as relationships, gender, health, and human rights) and recommends age-appropriate learning objectives to empower children and young people with knowledge, skills, and positive values about sexuality and relationships. The guidance underscores the role of sexuality education in promoting well-being, gender equality, and informed decision-making, contrasting with abstinence-only models driven by moral silence or fear.

10. Brené Brown

A research professor and bestselling author known for her work on vulnerability, shame, courage, and empathy, Brené Brown has brought psychological insight into how societies internalize moral norms. Her research on *shame resilience* reveals how cultural messages—especially those tied to purity, morality, and worth—lead individuals to suppress authenticity and bodily truth. In SOCAS, Brown's work helps explain how religious and cultural shame around sexuality becomes embedded in personal identity, undermining self-trust and emotional well-being. Her emphasis on vulnerability as strength offers a framework for reclaiming erotic agency and resisting internalized moral repression.

11. Moral Redemption

In SOCAS, moral redemption is critically examined as a mechanism of control embedded in many religious traditions, where shame and guilt are followed by prescribed paths to "purity." These frameworks often require submission to external judgment rather than fostering inner ethical autonomy. By tying worthiness to compliance, moral redemption reinforces cycles of repression, especially around sexuality, identity, and bodily expression.

12. Michel Foucault

A French philosopher and historian whose work profoundly reshaped understandings of power, knowledge, and the body. In *The History of Sexuality*, Foucault argues that sexuality has been shaped not by repression alone but by complex discourses that produce and regulate sexual norms. His analysis of biopower and disciplinary institutions reveals how sexuality became central to modern power structures, moral governance, and identity formation. In SOCAS, Foucault's insights help trace how religious and medical systems have inscribed sexuality with guilt, shame, and surveillance, turning pleasure into a site of social control.

13. Mary Douglas

A British anthropologist best known for her seminal work *Purity and Danger* (1966), where she explores how concepts of purity, pollution, and taboo function as boundary-maintaining mechanisms in cultures. Douglas argued that what societies define as "unclean" or "impure" often reflects anxieties about disorder and transgression. In SOCAS, her theories illuminate how sexual and bodily taboos—particularly those institutionalized by religion—serve to uphold moral hierarchies and suppress erotic freedom by framing nonconformity as contamination.

14. Sexual Transgression

In SOCAS, sexual transgression is reframed not as immorality, but as a form of resistance against rigid dogmas that regulate pleasure and desire. Whether labeled sinful, deviant, or obscene, such acts often threaten institutional power by asserting bodily autonomy and erotic freedom. The moral panic surrounding sexual transgression frequently masks deeper anxieties about control, identity, and the erosion of patriarchal or religious authority.

15. Ilan Meyer

A prominent social epidemiologist and researcher, Ilan Meyer is best known for developing the *minority stress model*, which explains how chronic social stressors—rooted in stigma, prejudice, and discrimination—adversely affect the mental and physical health of sexual and gender minorities. His work has been influential in understanding how external moral condemnation and systemic exclusion translate into internalized shame, anxiety, and health disparities. In SOCAS, Meyer's research is referenced to show how moral authoritarianism and erotophobic cultural norms inflict measurable harm on queer lives, underscoring the need to dismantle structural stigma and affirm erotic agency and dignity.

16. Reproductive Rights

In SOCAS, reproductive rights are positioned as a central battleground in the struggle against religious and political control over the body. Religious doctrines often seek to restrict these rights under the guise of moral protection, enforcing compulsory motherhood and denying individuals—especially women, trans, and queer people—the agency to choose. The denial of reproductive rights reflects broader systems of moral colonization, where sexuality, gender, and fertility are governed by authoritarian ideologies rather than individual consent and scientific ethics.

17. Faye Ginsburg and Rayna Rapp

Anthropologists are known for their groundbreaking work on reproduction, gender, and the politics of the body. Through their edited volume *Conceiving the New World Order: The Global Politics of Reproduction* (1995), they exposed how reproductive practices are shaped by intersecting forces of religion, nationalism, science, and globalization. In SOCAS, their scholarship supports the view that reproductive rights and sexual autonomy are deeply embedded in cultural narratives and power relations, and must be understood through both local and global lenses. Their work also foregrounds the lived experiences of women navigating oppressive moral and medical regimes.

18. Citizenship

In SOCAS, citizenship is explored not only as legal belonging, but as a morally policed identity often shaped by sexual, reproductive, and religious conformity. As expressed in the line, *"Control over reproduction is fundamentally a site where cultural, religious, and political forces intersect to regulate bodies and define citizenship,"* reproductive autonomy becomes a gatekeeping mechanism. Those who diverge—queer, unmarried, non-reproductive, or sexually nonconforming individuals—are frequently seen as lesser citizens, excluded from full participation in the moral or civic order.

19. Mary Ziegler

In *Abortion and the Law in America*, legal scholar Mary Ziegler traces how abortion debates in the U.S. evolved from legal arguments into moral and political battlegrounds. In SOCAS, her work is used to show how reproductive rights have become a litmus test for moral citizenship—where access to bodily autonomy is shaped by religious values, partisan agendas, and legal strategy.

20. Natural Law Theory

In SOCAS, natural law theory is examined as a framework historically used to sacralize heteronormative and patriarchal values under the guise of universal moral order. By claiming that certain sexual behaviors are "unnatural," the theory has been used to legitimize the suppression of non-reproductive, queer, and gender-diverse expressions of sexuality, reinforcing religious authority over bodily autonomy.

21. Agata Ignaciuk and Laura Kelly

Historians Agata Ignaciuk and Laura Kelly co-authored a transnational historical study on Catholicism and contraception that examines how religious norms shaped access to birth control and family planning in the twentieth century. Their work highlights the interplay between institutional Catholic teaching, reproductive technologies, activism, and everyday practices across Europe, Africa, and Latin America. In SOCAS, their research is used to show how religious moral authority has regulated bodies and reproductive choices, revealing how doctrine and medical practice have influenced both public policy and personal autonomy over sexuality and reproductive health.

22. Humanae Vitae (1968)

In SOCAS, *Humanae Vitae* is analyzed as a defining document in the Church's modern stance on sexuality and reproduction. Despite widespread expectation of reform, the encyclical reasserted a strict ban on birth control, emphasizing that every sexual act must remain open to procreation. This rejection of artificial contraception deepened the Church's moral authority over the body and became a global symbol of religious resistance to reproductive rights, influencing policy debates, public health funding, and the framing of sexual morality across continents.

23. Theological Dictates

In SOCAS, theological dictates are critiqued as rigid pronouncements that prioritize divine command over personal agency, often used to enforce sexual conformity. These dictates have historically governed everything from celibacy and chastity to the condemnation of same-sex love, framing dissent not as difference, but as sin. As instruments of institutional control, they illustrate how theology can be wielded not only to inspire but also to dominate the intimate lives of believers.

24. Catholics for Choice

In SOCAS, *Catholics for Choice* is highlighted as a progressive Catholic advocacy group that challenges official Church positions on sexuality, contraception, and abortion . Founded in 1973, the organization asserts that faithful Catholics can support reproductive rights and sexual autonomy based on conscience, social justice, and human dignity. Their work disrupts the assumption of Catholic unanimity on issues like *Humanae Vitae*, offering a counter-narrative to theological dictates and advocating for pluralism within religious ethics.

25. John Boswell and Homosexuality

In SOCAS, John Boswell 's pioneering scholarship is referenced for challenging the assumption that Christianity has always condemned homosexuality. His influential book *Christianity, Social Tolerance, and Homosexuality* (1980) argues that early Christian communities were more tolerant of same-sex relationships than later medieval and modern institutions. Boswell uncovered historical records of same-sex unions and rituals resembling marriage in Christian contexts, offering a counter-narrative to doctrinal homophobia and reclaiming queer presence within religious history.

26. Pippa Norris and Ronald Inglehart

Political scientists Pippa Norris and Ronald Inglehart are known for their work on cultural change, modernization, and value shifts, particularly through the *World Values Survey*. They demonstrated that as societies become more economically secure and secular, attitudes toward gender equality, sexual freedom, and LGBTQ+ rights tend to become more accepting. In SOCAS, their research is used to show how moral authority and sexual norms are not fixed but evolve with social development, challenging the notion that sexual repression is inevitable or universal.

27. Spiritual Dissonance

In SOCAS, spiritual dissonance refers to the emotional and existential tension felt by individuals whose authentic sexual or gender identities are invalidated by religious teachings. Rather than a lack of faith, this dissonance often signals a deep spiritual struggle for coherence, dignity, and self-trust in the face of theological condemnation. It underscores how doctrinal rigidity can fracture the sacred relationship one holds with oneself.

28. Ryan, Huebner, Diaz, and Sanchez

In SOCAS, the work of Mark Ryan, Dominic Huebner, Guillermo Diaz, and Juan Sanchez is referenced for research showing how stigma, discrimination, and lack of social support negatively affect the mental and physical health of LGBTQ+ youth. Their studies demonstrate that rejection—from families, schools, or communities correlates with higher rates of depression, substance use, and suicide risk among sexual minorities. This body of research supports SOCAS's critique of moral systems that stigmatize desire and identity, highlighting how such cultural condemnations produce tangible harm rather than moral "order."

29. United Church of Christ (UCC)

In SOCAS, the United Church of Christ is noted as one of the most progressive Christian denominations in the United States regarding LGBTQ+ inclusion and reproductive justice. As early as 2005, it formally endorsed same-sex marriage and has consistently advocated for comprehensive sexuality education, bodily autonomy, and gender justice. UCC's theological stance exemplifies how faith traditions can evolve toward affirming sexual diversity and personal conscience rather than enforcing doctrinal rigidity.

30. Muslims for Progressive Values

In SOCAS, *Muslims for Progressive Values* is referenced as a faith-based advocacy organization that champions human rights, gender equality, and LGBTQ+ inclusion within an Islamic framework. It challenges conservative interpretations of *Sharia* and moral authoritarianism by grounding ethics in compassion, pluralism, and dignity for all. The group offers a counter-narrative to doctrinal rigidity, demonstrating that religious identity and sexual justice are not mutually exclusive but can be integrated through progressive interpretation and social activism.

31. Reform Judaism

In SOCAS, Reform Judaism is recognized as a progressive movement within Jewish tradition that affirms gender equality, LGBTQ+ rights, and reproductive freedom. Unlike Orthodox or Conservative interpretations, Reform Judaism emphasizes personal autonomy in ethical decision-making and encourages evolving interpretations of Jewish law (*halakha*) in light of modern values. It stands as a powerful example of how religious frameworks can embrace pluralism and uphold sexual and spiritual dignity without doctrinal rigidity.

32. Fatwa

In SOCAS, fatwas are examined as evolving tools of religious authority used to regulate morality, including sexuality, gender expression, and bodily autonomy. While some fatwas have affirmed compassion or reform, others have served to legitimize moral control, restrict personal freedoms, and codify heteronormative or patriarchal norms. Their influence is context-dependent and shaped by cultural, political, and theological agendas.

33. Ayatollah Ali al-Sistani

A leading contemporary Shia cleric based in Najaf, Iraq, Ayatollah Ali al-Sistani is one of the most influential religious authorities (*maraji'*) in Twelver Shia Islam. His legal opinions (*fatwas*) on a range of social, political, and ethical issues shape the lives of millions of Shia Muslims globally. In SOCAS, al-Sistani is referenced as an example of how religious legal authority engages with modern governance, personal conduct, and moral regulation—including norms surrounding gender, family, and sexuality. His interpretations reflect the ongoing negotiation between tradition and contemporary ethics within Islamic jurisprudence, illustrating both the power of theological dictates and the importance of contextual interpretation in shaping lived norms.

34. Emotional Stoicism

In SOCAS, emotional stoicism is examined as a gendered ideal historically used to uphold patriarchal norms. By promoting emotional suppression—particularly among men—it contributes to a culture of emotional detachment that can hinder intimacy, empathy, and self-awareness. It intersects with religious and cultural ideologies that valorize self-denial and control, often at the expense of authentic emotional life and connection.

35. Theological Underpinnings of Patriarchal Control

In SOCAS, this term captures how religious systems—through scriptures, clerical authority, and doctrinal traditions—have institutionalized male supremacy. From the subordination of women in Abrahamic texts to the idealization of female modesty and obedience, such theologies anchor moral codes that control bodies and sexualities. These frameworks not only regulate behavior but also internalize submission as a spiritual virtue, making liberation a theological as well as social struggle.

36. Ruether: "If God is male, then the male is God."

Feminist theologian Rosemary Radford Ruether famously declared, *"If God is male, then the male is God,"* critiquing how patriarchal imagery in theology reinforces male supremacy. In SOCAS, this statement is foundational to understanding the symbolic and structural ways religion has legitimized gender hierarchy. Ruether's insight exposes how representations of the divine shape cultural norms and how gendered conceptions of God can become theological justifications for social inequality.

37. Amina Wadud

Amina Wadud is a pioneering Muslim feminist scholar and theologian known for her groundbreaking work in Islamic gender justice. Her book *Qur'an and Woman* (1992) challenges patriarchal interpretations of the Qur'an and emphasizes egalitarian readings rooted in the text itself. In SOCAS, Wadud is cited for her bold leadership—particularly her historic act of leading mixed-gender Muslim prayer in 2005—and for advancing a theology that reconciles faith with feminist ethics. Her work embodies the struggle to reclaim spiritual authority from exclusionary traditions and foregrounds women's voices in Islamic discourse.

38. Stephanie Coontz

A historian and social critic, Stephanie Coontz is renowned for her work on the history of marriage, gender roles, and family structures. Her book *Marriage, a History* (2005) deconstructs the myth of the "traditional" marriage and exposes how economic, political, and religious forces have shaped intimate relationships over time. In SOCAS, Coontz's scholarship supports the argument that many contemporary sexual and relational norms—often claimed as timeless or divinely ordained—are in fact socially constructed and historically contingent.

39. Linchpin

In SOCAS, the term "linchpin" is used metaphorically to describe foundational concepts—such as religious dogma, heteronormativity, or gender binaries—that sustain larger systems of moral or institutional control. Challenging these linchpins becomes a crucial strategy in dismantling oppressive norms and advancing erotic justice and personal autonomy.

40. Lucy Robinson

A British historian specializing in the history of sexuality, gender, and queer lives, Lucy Robinson has researched how sexual identities have been shaped by cultural, legal, and social forces—especially in modern Britain. Her work highlights how normative sexualities have been constructed and policed, and how queer communities have resisted marginalization. In SOCAS, Robinson's scholarship is cited for demonstrating that attitudes toward sexuality are historically contingent rather than natural or fixed, and for illuminating the interplay between moral authority, law, and erotic identity formation.

41. Sara Ahmed

A feminist theorist and cultural critic, Sara Ahmed's work explores how power, emotion, and normative structures shape bodies and subjects within institutions. In books like *The Cultural Politics of Emotion* and *Living a Feminist Life*, she examines how fear, shame, and disorientation are routed through social spaces to uphold established hierarchies. In SOCAS, Ahmed's insights help illuminate how moral systems—especially those policing sexuality and gender—are maintained through affective forces that shape belonging, exclusion, and the internalization of norms. Her concept of "non-performativity" in diversity work further shows how institutional language can appear inclusive while leaving structural inequalities intact.

42. Helen E. Fisher

Biological anthropologist whose research on romantic love, attachment, and mating systems provides an evolutionary context for human sexual behavior. In *The Sex Contract* (1982) and *Anatomy of Love* (1992), Fisher argues that pair bonding, attraction, and relational transitions are biologically grounded patterns rather than moral deviations. Her work supports SOCAS's critique of shame-based sexual doctrines by demonstrating that desire and attachment are adaptive human capacities, not theological defects.

43. Episcopal Church

The Episcopal Church is the U.S. member of the worldwide Anglican Communion and is known for its progressive stances on gender, sexuality, and social justice. It has authorized the ordination of women, openly LGBTQ+ clergy, and the blessing of same-sex unions, positioning itself against more conservative religious moral frameworks. In SOCAS, the Episcopal Church is referenced as an example of how religious traditions can evolve toward inclusivity, affirming sexual and gender diversity while challenging doctrinal rigidity and moral authoritarianism within institutional religion.

44. Equal Protection Under the Law

In SOCAS, this concept is central to challenging laws and doctrines that discriminate based on sexual orientation, gender identity, or religious belief. The failure of religiously influenced legislation to uphold equal protection has led to widespread legal inequalities—from the criminalization of same-sex relationships to restrictions on reproductive rights. The principle is used to advocate for secular, inclusive governance that defends individual freedoms against moral or theological bias.

45. Public Religion Research Institute (PRRI)

The Public Religion Research Institute is an American nonprofit, nonpartisan organization that conducts independent public opinion research at the intersection of religion, culture, values, and public policy. It produces large-scale surveys and analyses that illuminate changing attitudes on topics like religion, morality, and social issues—including issues related to sexual norms, gender equality, and pluralism. PRRI's work is often used by scholars, journalists, and policymakers to understand how moral and religious values shape cultural debates and public life.

46. Karel van der Toorn

A Dutch historian of religion and scholar of ancient Near Eastern and biblical texts, Karel van der Toorn, has investigated how early religious traditions were shaped by social, political, and cultural forces rather than static divine revelation. His work—including *Scribal Culture and the Making of the Hebrew Bible*—examines the production, transmission, and interpretation of sacred texts in their historical contexts. In SOCAS, van der Toorn's scholarship is valuable for demonstrating how foundational religious doctrines were constructed through human processes, challenging claims that moral and sexual norms are timeless or divinely fixed.

47. System Justification Theory

Developed by psychologist John Jost and colleagues, System Justification Theory explains why individuals—including those from marginalized groups—may support institutions or ideologies that perpetuate their own oppression. In SOCAS, this theory helps explain how religious and cultural structures that enforce sexual repression or gender inequality are often internalized and maintained by those they harm, reinforcing cycles of guilt, silence, and moral conformity.

48. Religiosity

In SOCAS, religiosity is examined not merely as personal faith, but as a social and cultural force that can shape moral attitudes toward sex, gender, and the body. While often associated with spiritual devotion, religiosity also intersects with institutional power—reinforcing norms, sanctioning behaviors, and influencing public policy. Its effects are neither neutral nor uniform; high religiosity can correlate with both compassionate ethics and rigid moral dogmas, depending on the context.

49. Censorship

In *SOCAS*, censorship is analyzed as a tool of control used to silence alternative perspectives on sexuality, identity, and bodily autonomy. From the banning of sex-positive literature to the suppression of LGBTQ+ voices in religious or educational settings, censorship reflects the fear of unregulated truth. It is not merely about silencing words but about erasing ways of knowing, loving, and being that challenge doctrinal orthodoxy or patriarchal norms.

50. Free Speech Center

The Free Speech Center at Middle Tennessee State University is a research and advocacy organization dedicated to understanding and promoting free expression within legal, educational, and cultural contexts. It conducts research, provides resources, and hosts events on issues of speech rights, censorship, and the balance between expression and other social values. In SOCAS, the Free Speech Center's work is relevant for exploring how legal protections for free expression intersect with cultural debates over sexuality, morality, and religious authority—highlighting the tensions between individual autonomy and institutional norms that seek to regulate bodies, voices, and identities.

51. Rev. Walter Rauschenbusch

An influential American Baptist theologian and leader of the early Social Gospel movement in the late 19th and early 20th centuries, Walter Rauschenbusch emphasized the application of Christian ethics to social issues such as poverty, labor injustice, and systemic inequality. In SOCAS, Rauschenbusch's work is referenced for illustrating how religious commitment can be mobilized toward collective liberation and justice rather than moral repression. While not focused narrowly on sexuality, his critique of individualistic moralism and his advocacy for social transformation provide a theological counterpoint to traditions that promote guilt and shame as central to spiritual life.

52. Misogyny

Misogyny refers to the systemic and cultural disdain for women and femininity, upheld through traditions, teachings, and institutions that relegate women to subordinate roles. In *SOCAS*, it is interrogated as a foundational structure within many religious and patriarchal systems—fueling policies that restrict bodily autonomy, sexual freedom, and gender equality.

53. Michael J. Rosenfeld

Michael J. Rosenfeld is a Professor of Sociology at Stanford University and a social demographer whose research focuses on family structures, mate selection, and changes in intimate relationships—including same-sex couples, cohabitation trends, and how people meet in the digital age. His scholarship has documented the sociological dynamics of LGBTQ+ partnering and has been influential in understanding how social attitudes and institutions transform intimate life. In SOCAS, Rosenfeld's work is referenced for grounding discussions of marriage equality and the shifting norms around sexual and relational diversity, showing that family forms and legal recognition are embedded in broader cultural and social change.

54. Endogamy

Endogamy operates as a mechanism of boundary maintenance, often tied to religious purity, caste, race, or class hierarchies. In SOCAS, it is examined as a form of social control that limits erotic freedom and reinforces inherited moral and cultural boundaries—particularly in communities where deviation from sanctioned partnerships is seen as transgressive.

55. Muluneh Animut Tilahun., *et al.*

In *Love beyond religious conviction: the challenges of interreligious marriage in South Wollo, Ethiopia*, Tilahun and colleagues examine how Muslim–Orthodox Christian couples navigate social, familial, and religious pressures in interfaith unions. The study highlights how doctrinal expectations, community norms, and moral policing shape intimate lives, forcing couples to reconcile personal desire with inherited codes of conduct. In SOCAS, this research underscores how moral frameworks rooted in religious conviction can constrain erotic autonomy and relational belonging, evidencing how lovers become sites of cultural negotiation rather than purely private subjects of affection.

56. Spiritual Excommunication

Spiritual excommunication serves as a religiously sanctioned form of ostracism, used to sever individuals from communal belonging and sacred identity. In SOCAS, it is examined as a disciplinary weapon targeting sexual, gender, or ideological nonconformity—especially those who defy moral orthodoxy or assert erotic autonomy. It reinforces fear-based obedience while masking control as divine judgment.

57. Nancy Foner and Richard Alba

Sociologists Nancy Foner and Richard Alba are leading scholars of immigration, race, and ethnic integration whose comparative research spans North America and Western Europe. Their co-authored work, *Strangers No More*, examines how immigrants and their children navigate social, cultural, and institutional barriers to belonging, including mixed unions and intergroup relationships. In SOCAS, their scholarship is used to show how norms around religion, identity, and social inclusion intersect with moral authority and cultural boundaries, revealing that integration and intimacy across differences—whether religious, racial, or ethnic—are shaped by broader social structures, not fixed moral dictates.

58. Ecumenical Movements

Emerging in the 20th century, ecumenical movements promote Christian unity by encouraging collaboration across denominational lines. In SOCAS, they are examined for both their inclusive potential and their limitations—particularly in how they may preserve patriarchal or heteronormative theological frameworks even as they call for unity. Their relevance is assessed in light of broader efforts toward sexual and spiritual liberation.

59. Jürgen Habermas

A major figure in contemporary philosophy and sociology, Jürgen Habermas is known for his theory of communicative action and the concept of the public sphere. He critiques the colonization of lifeworlds by systems of power and emphasizes rational discourse as a foundation for democratic legitimacy. In SOCAS, his framework helps analyze how religious and moral institutions shape public norms about sexuality—not through transparent communication, but through hierarchical authority that limits genuine dialogue and autonomy.

60. Tribalism

In SOCAS, tribalism is examined as a psychological and social mechanism that reinforces moral conformity, particularly in religious communities where identity is closely policed. It fosters an "us vs. them" mentality, marginalizing those who question dogma or express divergent sexual, spiritual, or ethical perspectives. This dynamic underpins moral colonization and obstructs pluralistic and inclusive frameworks.

61. Howard E. Mason

In SOCAS, Howard E. Mason is cited as editor of *Moral Dilemmas and Moral Theory* (1996), a collection that explores ethical reasoning through classic and contemporary case studies. The anthology serves as a resource for discussing moral pluralism, autonomy, and applied ethics—key concerns in this book's critique of religious moral authority and its effects on sexual agency.

62. Cecil Coady

Cecil A. J. Coady was a British philosopher best known for his work in the philosophy of language and rhetoric, especially his book Test of Time: Rhetoric in the Age of Science. He critiqued the dominance of scientific rationalism and defended the enduring value of rhetorical reasoning—arguing that human affairs cannot be reduced to purely technical or empirical logic. In SOCAS, Coady's insights help illuminate how moral and religious authorities use language, persuasion, and narrative to naturalize doctrines about sexuality and the body, demonstrating that control over discourse is also control over ethical imagination and embodied life.

63. Stephen Genuis

Stephen J. Genuis, MD, is a Canadian clinician and medical researcher at the University of Alberta whose work spans public health, environmental medicine, and clinical aspects of sexuality and reproductive health, including adolescent sexual behavior and sexually transmitted infection prevention. He has published widely in medical journals on topics linking biological, behavioral, and social health determinants. In *SOCAS*, Genuis's engagement with sexual health reflects how scientific and moral narratives intersect in public discourse on sexuality, illustrating tensions between medical evidence, cultural norms, and moralistic frameworks shaping policy and education.

64. Anti-sodomy laws

Originating in colonial legal codes and religious doctrines, anti-sodomy laws have served as instruments of systemic discrimination against queer people. In SOCAS, they exemplify how legal systems enforce theological morality under the guise of public order, legitimizing surveillance and punishment of consensual sexual expression. Their legacy continues in many regions, despite growing international recognition of sexual rights.

65. Linda Woodhead

A British sociologist of religion, Linda Woodhead, is known for her research on secularization, belief, and the changing landscape of contemporary faith. Her work examines how religious authority, individual conscience, and cultural norms interact in modern societies. In SOCAS, Woodhead's insights are used to understand how religious moral frameworks shape attitudes toward sexuality, gender, and bodily autonomy, and how shifts in belief systems influence the negotiation of moral authority in public and private life. Woodhead's analysis highlights that changes in religiosity affect not only institutional power but also the moral vocabularies that regulate desire and belonging.

66. Leila Ahmed

An Egyptian-American historian and scholar of Islam and gender, Leila Ahmed is best known for her influential book *Women and Gender in Islam.* Her work traces how attitudes toward women, sexuality, and moral authority were shaped by early Islamic texts and later cultural interpretations. In SOCAS, Ahmed's scholarship is used to show that restrictive norms around modesty, gender roles, and sexual conduct are not monolithic or timeless but historically specific and socially constructed. Her analysis supports the critique of theological dictates that regulate bodies and reinforces the need for contextual, emancipatory readings of religious tradition.

67. Progressive theologians

Progressive theologians reframe religious discourse to center compassion, autonomy, and equality. In SOCAS, they are highlighted as key allies in dismantling oppressive interpretations of scripture and doctrine—offering alternative readings that affirm bodily dignity, sexual diversity, and moral agency. Their work underpins broader movements for spiritual liberation and theological renewal.

68. Female Genital Mutilation (FGM)

FGM is addressed in SOCAS as a form of institutionalized violence against girls and women, rooted in patriarchal control over female sexuality and bodily autonomy. Despite being condemned by the WHO, UNFPA, and human rights organizations, it persists in various regions under the guise of tradition. *SOCAS* situates FGM within a broader critique of religiously or culturally sanctioned bodily harm that undermines erotic integrity, consent, and human dignity.

69. United Nations International Children's Emergency Fund (UNICEF)

The United Nations Children's Fund is a global agency dedicated to safeguarding the rights and well-being of children. Its work spans education, nutrition, health, and protection—especially in addressing child marriage, gender-based violence, and harmful practices like Female Genital Mutilation (FGM). UNICEF promotes Comprehensive Sexuality

Education (CSE) and gender equality as pillars of sustainable development.

70. Ellen Gruenbaum

A medical anthropologist renowned for her research on gender, health, and culture, especially in African contexts. In SOCAS, Gruenbaum's work is referenced for her critical analyses of Female Genital Mutilation (FGM), highlighting the complex intersections of tradition, religion, and social pressure. Her ethnographic studies expose how FGM is not merely a cultural rite but a deeply embedded system of gender control, often rationalized through patriarchal and religious ideologies.

71. Patricia Akweongo

A Ghanaian public health expert whose research focuses on reproductive rights, gendered health disparities, and harmful cultural practices such as FGM. In SOCAS, Akweongo is referenced for her studies demonstrating how social norms, gender hierarchies, and limited access to education and care compound to restrict women's bodily autonomy—especially in contexts where tradition and religion converge to define moral health behaviors.

72. World Health Organization (WHO)

A specialized agency of the United Nations, the WHO plays a central role in global health governance, particularly in setting international standards on sexual and reproductive health. In *SOCAS*, WHO guidelines are cited for supporting comprehensive sexuality education (CSE), affirming sexual rights as human rights, and opposing practices like female genital mutilation. Their evidence-based frameworks help challenge religious and cultural doctrines that restrict bodily autonomy.

73. Sacrament of Reconciliation

Also known as confession or penance, this Catholic sacrament is centered on the forgiveness of sins through priestly mediation. In SOCAS, it is examined for its role in reinforcing religious control over sexuality— often framing sexual acts outside doctrinal norms as sins requiring absolution. This sacrament exemplifies how guilt, moral surveillance, and institutional power converge to regulate intimate behavior.

74. Maimonides

Also known as Rabbi Moses ben Maimon (1138–1204), Maimonides was a medieval Sephardic Jewish philosopher, physician, and legal scholar whose writings significantly shaped Jewish law and ethics. In SOCAS, he is cited for codifying religious views on sexuality, including detailed restrictions on sexual conduct within Halakha. His influence reflects how religious legal traditions often pathologized desire, linking bodily pleasure to moral danger and reinforcing patriarchal interpretations of divine law.

75. Laws of Teshuvah

A section of Maimonides' *Mishneh Torah*, the *Laws of Teshuvah* (Repentance) outlines the process of atonement and return to divine favor through confession, remorse, and behavioral change. In SOCAS, this legal-religious framework is examined for how it ties sin—especially sexual transgression—to a moral duty of repentance, often reinforcing cycles of guilt and self-denial rooted in patriarchal and ascetic religious systems.

76. Hans Küng

Swiss Catholic priest, theologian, and prolific author who became one of the most influential and controversial reformist voices within modern Catholicism. In SOCAS, he can be referenced for his bold challenges to papal infallibility, his advocacy for interfaith dialogue, and his vision of a more humanistic, inclusive, and rational theology. Küng's work consistently argued that institutional religion must evolve to remain relevant, especially on issues of sexuality, gender equality, and human rights. His call for reform resonates with *SOCAS*' broader critique of religious dogma and its impact on personal freedom and erotic ethics.

77. Kent Greenawalt

An American legal philosopher and constitutional scholar, Kent Greenawalt examined how law and morality intersect, especially in cases involving religion, free speech, and sexual ethics. His work explores when the state may legitimately regulate private conduct and when moral judgments—particularly those rooted in religious doctrine—should yield to individual rights. In SOCAS, Greenawalt's analysis is used to critique legal justifications that cage personal autonomy within inherited moral codes, showing how secular law can both challenge and be challenged by religio-moral claims about the body and desire.

78. International Covenant on Civil and Political Rights (ICCPR)

A cornerstone of international human rights law, the ICCPR outlines essential protections for personal liberty, non-discrimination, and bodily integrity. In SOCAS, it is referenced to highlight how religiously justified laws—particularly those that regulate sexuality or gender identity—often conflict with the covenant's guarantees, such as freedom from coercion and the right to privacy. The ICCPR serves as a legal framework for challenging moral governance rooted in religious orthodoxy.

79. Human Dignity Trust

Founded in 2011, the Human Dignity Trust provides legal assistance to activists and lawyers fighting discriminatory laws—particularly anti-LGBTQ+ statutes rooted in colonial-era penal codes and religious morality. In SOCAS, it is cited as a key factor in the global movement for erotic justice, supporting strategic litigation that affirms dignity, autonomy, and equality regardless of sexual orientation or gender identity.

80. Katherine Franke

A legal scholar and civil rights advocate, Katherine M. Franke focuses on constitutional law, gender, sexuality, and social movements. Her work—especially on intersectionality and sexual citizenship—critiques how law and moral norms shape whose bodies and desires are protected or penalized. In SOCAS, Franke's scholarship is referenced for illuminating how legal systems have been complicit in enforcing moralistic sexual hierarchies and for advancing frameworks that affirm autonomy, equality, and erotic justice under law.

81. Center for Reproductive Rights

Since its founding in 1992, the Center has been instrumental in challenging laws and policies that restrict reproductive autonomy, particularly in contexts where religious doctrine influences legal systems.

In SOCAS, it is cited as a critical actor in resisting theological encroachments on bodily sovereignty, working through courts and international bodies to uphold gender equality, reproductive freedom, and health justice.

82. European Court of Human Rights (ECHR)

The ECHR has issued landmark rulings on issues ranging from freedom of expression and privacy to gender identity and reproductive rights. In SOCAS, it is referenced for its role in challenging state laws rooted in religious morality, reinforcing that rights to family life, bodily autonomy, and sexual identity must be protected from doctrinal overreach by member states.

83. Ahmed Shaheed

A Maldivian diplomat, international human rights expert, and former United Nations Special Rapporteur on freedom of religion or belief, Ahmed Shaheed, has played a key role in holding states accountable for rights violations tied to religion, expression, and identity. His reports have highlighted how laws and policies grounded in dominant religious doctrines can infringe on individual freedoms, including sexual orientation, gender identity, and bodily autonomy. In SOCAS, Shaheed's work is cited as part of the legal and ethical framework resisting moral authoritarianism, affirming that freedom of belief must encompass plural expressions of sexuality and conscience without state or doctrinal coercion.

84. Athenagoras of Athens

Early Christian apologist who sought to defend Christianity against charges of atheism and immorality in the Roman Empire. In his *Plea Regarding Christians*, Athenagoras advocated for religious tolerance, argued for the rationality of Christian monotheism, and refuted accusations that Christians engaged in immoral practices. His work offers an early example of theological engagement with sexuality and ethics, especially in contrast to pagan customs and misrepresentations. In SOCAS, he is referenced as one of the intellectual forebears in the long tradition of using religious doctrine both to defend moral behavior and to justify social control.

85. Onah

Rooted in the Talmudic tradition (e.g., *Ketubot 61b*), *onah* designates the husband's duty to meet his wife's sexual needs, with frequency determined by his occupation and physical capacity. Unlike many religious constructs that emphasize control or repression of sexuality, *onah* reflects a more affirming and reciprocal view of erotic responsibility. In SOCAS, it is noted as a rare example of pre-modern religious law that centers on female pleasure and emotional connection, contrasting with dominant patterns of patriarchal restraint and reproductive prioritization.

86. Kevin McQuillan

McQuillan is cited in SOCAS to demonstrate that religion influences fertility when religious institutions possess both normative authority and mechanisms of enforcement, thereby shaping reproductive behavior through pronatalist doctrine rather than purely private belief.

87. Will Steffen *et al.*

In SOCAS, Steffen and colleagues are cited for the "planetary boundaries" framework, which identifies measurable ecological thresholds beyond which human activity risks destabilizing Earth's life-support systems, reinforcing the ethical relevance of demographic scale within a finite biosphere.

88. Betsy Hartmann

Hartmann is referenced in SOCAS for her critique of population alarmism and her argument that demographic discourse has often obscured structural inequalities by attributing ecological and economic crises primarily to fertility rates rather than to systems of consumption, power, and distribution.

89. Demographic Alarmism

In SOCAS, this term refers to narratives that portray population growth as the primary driver of ecological or social crisis while minimizing the roles of consumption patterns, economic inequality, and power structures, often leading to reductive or coercive policy proposals rather than rights-based and justice-centered approaches.

90. Theological Pronatalism

In SOCAS, this term denotes religious frameworks that elevate reproduction as a sacred obligation or divine mandate, thereby shaping moral norms, gender roles, and public policy in ways that may prioritize demographic growth over individual reproductive autonomy and informed consent.

91. Mala Htun

In SOCAS, Htun is referenced for her analysis of how Catholic institutional influence in Latin America shaped state regulation of family law, divorce, and abortion , demonstrating how religious authority can become embedded in political structures and affect reproductive governance.

92. Van Thi Thanh Suy Van *et al.*

In SOCAS, public health researcher Van Thi Thanh Suy Van and colleagues

Van and colleagues are referenced for their analysis of the implementation of reproductive health legislation in the Philippines, illustrating how sustained ecclesiastical influence and political resistance can delay or constrain rights-based family planning policy despite public health needs.

93. Loretta J. Ross & Rickie Solinger

In SOCAS, Ross and Solinger are referenced for articulating the reproductive justice framework, which defines reproductive freedom as encompassing the right to have children, not have children, and to parent in safe and sustainable conditions, thereby grounding reproductive autonomy within broader social and structural equity.

94. Karen Terry

A forensic psychologist and former director of the Criminal Justice program at John Jay College of Criminal Justice, Karen Terry is widely recognized for her extensive research on clergy sexual abuse within the Catholic Church. As the principal investigator of the 2004 and 2011 reports commissioned by the U.S. Conference of Catholic Bishops, Terry analyzed patterns of abuse, institutional cover-ups, and systemic failures.

In SOCAS, her findings are referenced to demonstrate how religious authority structures have historically obscured accountability, prioritizing institutional reputation over the protection of victims and the pursuit of justice.

95. John L. Allen Jr.

An American journalist and author, John L. Allen Jr., is one of the most respected commentators on the Catholic Church. He has written extensively on Vatican affairs, Church politics, and clerical abuse crises. As a former senior correspondent for *National Catholic Reporter* and founder of *Crux*, his work often explores the tension between transparency and institutional preservation within Catholicism. In *SOCAS*, his insights are cited to underscore how media exposure and investigative journalism have played a pivotal role in challenging ecclesiastical silence around sexual abuse and advocating for accountability.

96. Thomas Doyle

Father Thomas Doyle is a Dominican priest, canon lawyer, and outspoken advocate for survivors of clergy sexual abuse. As one of the earliest whistleblowers within the Catholic Church, he co-authored a groundbreaking 1985 report warning bishops about the scale and severity of the abuse crisis. Despite facing institutional pushback, Doyle has persistently criticized the Church's systemic cover-ups and has worked as an expert witness in hundreds of abuse cases. In SOCAS, his moral clarity and commitment to justice are cited as emblematic of internal dissent against doctrinal and institutional silence surrounding sexual violence.

97. Marie Keenan

A social work scholar and restorative justice practitioner based at University College Dublin, Keenan is internationally recognized for her extensive research on clerical sexual abuse and institutional response. Her book *Child Sexual Abuse and the Catholic Church: Gender, Power and Organizational Culture* (2012) offers a nuanced psycho-social and structural analysis of abuse within the Church, including how institutional silence and theological authority perpetuated cycles of harm. In SOCAS, she is cited for reframing justice beyond retribution and for amplifying survivor-centered approaches.

98. Jessica N. Fish & Stephen T. Russell

Scholars in adolescent health and LGBTQ+ well-being whose research demonstrates that exposure to sexual orientation and gender identity change efforts is "associated with adverse mental health outcomes," including increased risks of depression and suicidality. Their work provides empirical evidence that conversion therapy is not only ineffective but harmful, reinforcing the consensus within the scientific community against such practices. In SOCAS, their findings underscore the broader argument that practices rooted in moral or religious imperatives—when imposed upon identity—can produce measurable psychological harm, thereby challenging the ethical legitimacy of conversion-based frameworks.

99. Jack L. Turban *et al.*

Researchers in psychiatry and public health whose work demonstrates a significant "association between exposure to gender identity conversion efforts and increased psychological distress and suicide attempts." Their study provides compelling clinical evidence that such practices are linked to serious mental health risks, particularly among transgender individuals. In SOCAS, their findings reinforce the argument that attempts to alter identity—especially under the influence of moral or religious frameworks—can result in profound psychological harm, challenging any claim that such interventions constitute legitimate care.

100. Ian Binns

Associate Professor of Science Education at the University of North Carolina at Charlotte. His work primarily focuses on how science and religion interact in educational contexts, especially in public schools. Binns has published research on the teaching of evolution, intelligent design, and the intersection of science education with sociocultural influences. In *SOCAS*, his contributions help highlight how religious dogma can conflict with scientific approaches to sexual education and critical thinking.

101. Adolescent Family Life Act (AFLA)

Passed under the Reagan administration, AFLA marked a pivotal moment in the fusion of conservative religious morality and federal sex education policy. It funded programs promoting abstinence until marriage, often delivered by faith-based organizations. In SOCAS, AFLA is examined as a key legislative example of how public health policy has been shaped by ideological, rather than scientific, priorities.

102. Lemon test

Derived from the 1971 Supreme Court case *Lemon v. Kurtzman*, this test has served as a key legal benchmark for determining the constitutionality of laws under the Establishment Clause. In *SOCAS*, it is referenced to underscore the judicial balancing act between religion and state, especially in education and sexual health legislation—areas often influenced by religious ideologies.

103. Tracy Prewitt

A legal scholar whose work examines how law, morality, and gender intersect—particularly in areas where family law fails to protect survivors of sexual violence. Prewitt's research highlights how legal systems shaped by moral assumptions about rape, motherhood, and victimhood can compound harm for survivors, revealing gaps in protections and the influence of gendered moral norms on legal outcomes. In SOCAS, her analysis is used to illustrate how inherited moral codes continue to shape legal treatments of bodies, autonomy, and erotic agency.

104. LifeWise Academy

LifeWise Academy is an Ohio-based Christian nonprofit that partners with public school districts to provide *released-time* Bible education during the school day—off-campus and with parental permission—under longstanding U.S. legal precedents. Its curriculum, based on evangelical Christian teachings, has expanded rapidly into dozens of states, prompting debate about the role of religion in public education. In SOCAS, LifeWise is referenced as a contemporary example of how religious moral authority enters public institutions, raising questions about church-state separation, inclusivity, and how moral education is mobilized to shape norms around bodies, identity, and belief.

105. First Amendment

Central to U.S. constitutional protections, the First Amendment has been both a shield and a battleground in conflicts over religious influence in public institutions. In SOCAS, it is referenced in discussions about public education, reproductive rights, and sexual freedom—highlighting how courts and policymakers interpret its clauses on *free exercise* and *establishment* to either limit or justify religious intervention in secular life. Landmark cases like *Lemon v. Kurtzman* and debates around programs like LifeWise Academy underscore its contested role in contemporary moral governance.

106. Expurgation

Religious reformers and progressive theologians have long grappled with scriptural verses that promote slavery, patriarchy, homophobia, or divine-sanctioned violence. In SOCAS, such expurgation is examined as both a necessity and a challenge: while it can align sacred texts with universal human rights, it also raises tensions about textual integrity and theological authority.

107. Gender Apartheid

The term refers to policies and practices that enforce unequal treatment and separation of individuals by gender, especially targeting women and sexual minorities. In SOCAS, gender apartheid is explored as a structural form of oppression legitimized by both religious doctrine and state law, exemplifying how patriarchy weaponizes divine authority to maintain control over sexuality, freedom, and identity.

CHAPTER THREE

1. Constitutional Jurisprudence

Refers to the evolving body of court rulings that interpret constitutional rights and limits, especially regarding individual freedoms, equality, and state intervention. In SOCAS, constitutional jurisprudence is referenced to explore how courts have historically regulated sexual behavior, reproductive rights, and church-state boundaries, revealing the tension between secular legal principles and moral doctrines.

2. Roe v. Wade

Decided in 1973, *Roe v. Wade* established that the U.S. Constitution protects a woman's right to choose abortion, framing it under the right to privacy. The decision symbolized a major legal victory for reproductive freedom, though it remained contested for decades. In SOCAS, Roe is examined as a pivotal moment when constitutional jurisprudence briefly aligned with bodily autonomy before its reversal in *Dobbs v. Jackson* (2022), illustrating the fragility of sexual and reproductive rights under shifting judicial ideologies.

3. Due Process Clause of the Fourteenth Amendment

Adopted in 1868, this clause has been invoked in key legal decisions to protect individual liberties against state interference. In SOCAS, it is examined as a pivotal constitutional safeguard that underpinned landmark rulings like *Griswold v. Connecticut* and *Roe v. Wade*, affirming personal agency in matters of intimacy, contraception, and abortion —until its protective scope was narrowed in *Dobbs v. Jackson* (2022), highlighting the volatile nature of judicial interpretations over time.

4. Egregiously

An adverb describing an action or behavior that is shockingly bad, flagrant, or conspicuously offensive. Often used in legal, moral, or social critique to emphasize the severity of a violation or injustice.

5. Trigger Laws

Trigger laws represent a legal mechanism by which states prepare for shifts in federal jurisprudence, especially regarding controversial issues like reproductive rights. In SOCAS, they are examined as part of broader strategies of religiously influenced governance that seek to curtail bodily autonomy in anticipation of favorable judicial outcomes.

6. Heartbeat Bills

Heartbeat bills serve as a legislative strategy to severely limit access to abortion under the guise of early fetal protection. In SOCAS, they are analyzed as moralizing policies influenced by religious ideologies that conflate embryonic development with personhood, despite lacking scientific consensus. These laws reflect broader attempts to entrench patriarchal control over reproductive autonomy through emotionally charged rhetoric.

7. Gestational Viability

The stage of fetal development at which a fetus may survive outside the womb with or without medical intervention is typically considered to be around 24 weeks of pregnancy. This concept plays a critical role in legal and ethical debates over abortion rights and limits, particularly in judicial interpretations of reproductive autonomy.

8. Sanctuary States

These are states that actively resist federal overreach by enacting laws or policies to shield specific groups—such as undocumented immigrants or individuals seeking reproductive care—from punitive enforcement. In SOCAS, sanctuary states are explored not only as legal constructs but as ethical expressions of jurisdictional compassion, often positioning themselves in stark contrast to theocratic or punitive governance models. They exemplify the intersection of state autonomy, civil liberties, and evolving moral landscapes.

9. Abortion deserts

Regions where reproductive healthcare access is severely curtailed, individuals often have to travel hundreds of miles to obtain legal abortion services. In SOCAS, abortion deserts are analyzed as a direct consequence of restrictive legislation, moral coercion, and unequal healthcare infrastructure—often reinforcing structural oppression under the guise of religiously framed "pro-life" agendas.

10. Establishment Clause of the First Amendment

The Establishment Clause serves as a legal safeguard against the imposition of religious doctrines through state mechanisms. In SOCAS, it is presented as a constitutional barrier to moral authoritarianism, particularly in the realms of sexual and reproductive rights, where religious ideologies often seek to dictate public policy.

11. Title V of the Welfare Reform Act

Passed in 1996, Title V allocated federal funds to abstinence-only education, embedding a conservative sexual morality into public policy.

In SOCAS, this legislative move is critiqued for marginalizing evidence-based sex education and reinforcing heteronormative, religiously motivated ideals about sexuality and family.

12. Section 510 of the Social Security Act

Section 510 codified the federal abstinence-only-until-marriage framework, offering funding contingent upon compliance with an ideologically conservative curriculum. In SOCAS, this statute is examined as a pivotal moment when moral conservatism was embedded into public health policy, limiting scientific and inclusive approaches to sexuality education.

13. Guttmacher Institute

A leading research and policy organization committed to advancing sexual and reproductive health and rights globally. In SOCAS, the Guttmacher Institute is cited for its rigorous data collection on topics like contraceptive access, abortion trends, and the impact of abstinence-only education, providing critical evidence against ideologically driven policy.

14. Parental Rights in Education Act

Also referred to as the "Don't Say Gay" law, this Florida legislation limits educators' ability to address topics related to gender identity and sexual orientation in early-grade classrooms. In SOCAS, it is analyzed within the broader trend of educational censorship that prioritizes ideological conformity over inclusive, evidence-based learning, with serious implications for LGBTQ+ youth and comprehensive sexuality education.

15. Educational Gag Orders

Refers to legislative or administrative restrictions placed on teachers and schools, limiting the discussion of topics deemed "divisive" or "controversial." In SOCAS, such gag orders are critiqued as tools of ideological control that threaten academic freedom, chill discourse around gender and sexuality, and undermine students' rights to comprehensive, truthful education.

16. American Civil Liberties Union (ACLU)

The ACLU has consistently played a leading role in legal and policy battles involving civil rights, religious neutrality in education, and reproductive autonomy. In SOCAS, the ACLU is cited as a major defender of the First Amendment, often litigating cases where religious ideologies threaten to undermine constitutional protections in schools, healthcare, and public policy.

17. Diversity, Equity, and Inclusion (DEI)

Three interconnected principles are used to support inclusive environments where differences in identity and experience are recognized, respected, and valued. *Diversity* refers to the presence of a range of personal and social characteristics; *equity* involves fair treatment and access by accounting for historical and structural disadvantages; and *inclusion* means creating conditions where all individuals can participate fully and feel they belong. In SOCAS, DEI efforts are examined both as responses to systemic discrimination and as contested terrain in public debates about education and organizational culture.

18. Michael K. Steenson

Legal scholar and professor of law at Mitchell Hamline School of Law, known for his expertise in constitutional law, tort law, and freedom of expression. He has contributed to the analysis of First Amendment jurisprudence and privacy law, particularly in the context of emerging legislative and judicial trends that affect civil liberties. In *SOCAS*, his scholarship helps contextualize how state-level interpretations of constitutional rights can either bolster or erode protections for sexual and educational freedoms.

19. Thomas C. Berg and Douglas Laycock

Thomas C. Berg and Douglas Laycock are American legal scholars known for their work on religious liberty, constitutional law, and church-state issues. Berg's research focuses on the First Amendment, religion in public life, and the balance between religious freedom and other civil rights. Laycock is a leading expert on religious-liberty doctrine and the author of influential texts on free exercise and government accommodation of religion. In SOCAS, their work is referenced to illuminate how legal interpretations of religious freedom shape policies on education, sexuality, and public expression—highlighting the tensions between protecting conscience and preventing religious moral authority from undermining individual rights.

20. Mark Satta

Theologian and ethicist whose work focuses on Christian understandings of gender, sexuality, and the body. His scholarship examines how theological traditions shape moral norms and cultural attitudes toward sexual difference and embodied life. In SOCAS, Satta's analysis of how doctrine and ecclesial teaching intersect with contemporary debates on sexuality and human dignity is used to explore the influence of religious moral reasoning on legal, educational, and social frameworks governing bodies and erotic experience.

21. Originalist Interpretations of the Constitution

Originalism is a legal philosophy asserting that constitutional interpretation should be grounded in the original public meaning of the text as understood at the time of its ratification. In SOCAS, originalist frameworks are examined for their influence on judicial decisions concerning religious liberty, reproductive rights, and educational policy— often reinforcing traditional moral values over evolving social norms. Critics argue that such interpretations can constrain legal progress by anchoring civil rights debates to 18th-century assumptions.

22. Project Blitz

Project Blitz is a coordinated legislative campaign in the United States aimed at promoting Christian nationalist policies at the state level. Backed by conservative religious lobbying groups, it pushes model bills that promote prayer in schools, display of "In God We Trust," and exemptions allowing religious beliefs to override anti-discrimination laws. In SOCAS, Project Blitz is cited as a contemporary example of the erosion of secular governance, using faith-based legal strategies to reassert religious control over public life and education.

23. Religious Freedom Restoration Act (RFRA)

Passed in 1993, the Religious Freedom Restoration Act (RFRA) was designed to prevent laws that substantially burden a person's free exercise of religion. Initially intended to restore a strict scrutiny standard after *Employment Division v. Smith* (1990), RFRA has since been interpreted in ways that allow individuals and institutions to claim exemptions from generally applicable laws—especially around healthcare, LGBTQ+ rights, and reproductive services. In SOCAS, RFRA is examined critically as a legal mechanism that can privilege religious beliefs over civil liberties, raising tensions between freedom of conscience and equal protection under the law.

24. Strict Scrutiny

The highest standard of judicial review used by U.S. courts to evaluate laws or policies that infringe upon constitutional rights. Under this test, the government must demonstrate that the challenged law serves a "compelling governmental interest" and is "narrowly tailored" to achieve that interest using the least restrictive means. In SOCAS, this standard is especially relevant when evaluating legislation that intersects with religious freedom, education, and sexual rights—such as in cases related to RFRA, LGBTQ+ protections, or the First Amendment.

25. Decentralized Legal Architecture

Refers to the structural distribution of lawmaking power across various jurisdictions, such as states in the U.S. or member states in a federation. In SOCAS, this concept helps explain why legal protections or restrictions on sexuality, education, or religion can vary drastically depending on local politics and cultural norms. Decentralization complicates the enforcement of universal human rights and often enables conservative backlashes through state-level legislation.

26. John R. Blosnich

A public health researcher specializing in LGBTQ+ mental health disparities, particularly among veterans. In SOCAS, his studies on minority stress, suicidality, and the compounded impact of stigma, discrimination, and religion-based rejection are cited to highlight the psychological consequences of moral condemnation and systemic exclusion of queer individuals. His work underscores the urgency of trauma-informed, inclusive policies and health interventions.

CHAPTER FOUR

1. Anne M. Grey

Anne M. Grey's advocacy in sexual and reproductive health aligns with feminist theology's critical stance toward patriarchal religious narratives, especially those that regulate women's bodies. Her work promotes rights-based, stigma-free sexuality education and access to care. In SOCAS, she exemplifies the turn toward secular, feminist-informed frameworks that prioritize dignity, consent, and comprehensive, evidence-based approaches. She is referenced for advancing alternatives to shame-based education models that often undermine personal agency and public health.

2. Patrick S. Cheng

A queer theologian and ordained minister, Reverend Patrick S. Cheng is known for developing a theology that affirms LGBTQ+ identities as sacred. In Radical Love: An Introduction to Queer Theology (2011), he reinterprets Christian doctrines through a queer lens, framing concepts like sin, grace, and salvation in ways that honor sexual and gender diversity. In SOCAS, Cheng is cited for his challenge to heteronormative theological frameworks and for advancing a liberatory, inclusive vision of spiritual belonging.

3. Reform and Reconstructionist movements

Both branches emerged from Judaism's engagement with modernity and reflect evolving interpretations of Jewish law and tradition. The *Reform movement*, originating in 19th-century Germany, emphasizes ethical monotheism, personal autonomy, and inclusivity, including the full participation of women and LGBTQ+ individuals. The *Reconstructionist movement*, founded by Mordecai Kaplan in the 20th century, views Judaism as an evolving religious civilization, advocating democratic decision-making and progressive values. In SOCAS, these movements are cited as emblematic of liberal religious approaches that support reproductive rights, sexual diversity, and gender equality within a faith-based framework.

4. Imam Daayiee Abdullah

One of the first openly gay imams in the United States, Imam Daayiee Abdullah, has been a prominent advocate for LGBTQ+ inclusion within Islam. He challenges exclusionary interpretations of the Qur'an and Islamic law by emphasizing compassion, justice, and personal dignity. In SOCAS, he is cited as a pioneering voice in reconciling faith with queer identity and for his work in providing inclusive religious guidance, especially for Muslim youth navigating sexuality and spirituality.

5. Metropolitan Community Church (MCC)

Founded in 1968 by Rev. Troy Perry, the Metropolitan Community Church (MCC) is a global denomination rooted in the Christian faith and explicitly affirming of LGBTQ+ identities. It emerged in response to widespread religious rejection of queer people, creating sacred spaces centered on inclusion, dignity, and spiritual healing. In SOCAS, MCC is cited as a landmark example of how theological frameworks can evolve to embrace erotic justice and affirm sexual diversity as compatible with religious life.

6. International Raelian Movement

Founded by Maitreya Rael in 1974, the International Raelian Movement is a spiritual and philosophical organization that promotes a worldview centered on science, sensuality, peace, and universal love. It advocates for the recognition of humanity's extraterrestrial origins, as relayed by advanced beings called the Elohim. In SOCAS, the movement is cited for its sex-positive stance, its rejection of guilt-based morality, and its support for sexual freedom, gender equality, and comprehensive sexuality education grounded in science and consent.

7. Ronald Dworkin

A prominent American legal philosopher and scholar of constitutional law, Ronald Dworkin (1931–2013), is widely known for his theory of "law as integrity," which argues that legal decisions should be grounded in moral reasoning and the consistent application of rights. In

SOCAS, Dworkin is cited for his emphasis on the moral dimension of constitutional interpretation, particularly regarding liberty, equality, and the protection of individual dignity. His work offers a compelling counterpoint to originalist and positivist approaches that may fail to account for evolving conceptions of justice—especially in matters of sexuality, autonomy, and religious influence on law.

8. Amartya Sen

Amartya Sen, a Nobel Prize–winning economist and philosopher, is renowned for his work on welfare economics, capabilities theory, and development as freedom. In SOCAS, Sen is referenced for advancing a human-centered framework of justice that integrates well-being, freedom, and dignity—key values in rethinking sexual rights and education beyond narrow religious moralism. His "capabilities approach" provides an ethical lens for evaluating societal progress by asking what individuals are *able to do and be*—including their ability to make informed, autonomous choices about their bodies and identities.

9. Hegemony

A form of dominance in which the ruling class or group maintains control not merely through force, but by shaping cultural norms, values, and beliefs so thoroughly that its power appears natural or inevitable. In SOCAS, hegemony refers to the ways in which religious and political institutions have normalized restrictive sexual ideologies—making dissent seem deviant and alternative frameworks for pleasure, gender, or identity appear illegitimate or immoral.

10. Martha C. Nussbaum

Philosopher and legal scholar, she is noted for her contributions to ethics, political philosophy, and human development theory. In SOCAS, her work is cited for advancing the "capabilities approach," which links dignity and justice to individuals' ability to flourish—physically, emotionally, and sexually. Her critiques of shame-based ideologies and her defense of bodily autonomy are foundational to rights-based frameworks in sexuality education.

11. Dossie Easton and Janet Hardy

Co-authors of *The Ethical Slut*, Easton and Hardy have played a pivotal role in reshaping cultural understandings of sexual ethics, consent, and non-monogamy. Their work challenges restrictive, shame-based frameworks by promoting values of transparency, autonomy, and pleasure. In SOCAS, they are cited for advancing a sex-positive, nonjudgmental approach to intimacy that underscores emotional responsibility, communication, and sexual agency as pathways to personal and collective liberation.

12. Our Whole Lives (OWL)

A comprehensive, values-based sexuality education curriculum co-published by the Unitarian Universalist Association and the United Church of Christ. OWL offers age-appropriate programming from kindergarten through adulthood, emphasizing self-worth, sexual health, responsibility, and justice. It is widely recognized for its inclusive, non-shaming approach to sexuality, gender identity, and relationships. In SOCAS, OWL is cited as a leading model of spiritually grounded, evidence-informed sex education that aligns with principles of human dignity and consent.

13. Unitarian Universalist Association (UUA)

A progressive religious organization in the United States that promotes pluralism, human dignity, and social justice as central tenets of spiritual life. The UUA has long supported LGBTQ+ rights, reproductive freedom, and comprehensive sexuality education. In SOCAS, it is cited for its role in co-creating the *Our Whole Lives* (OWL) curriculum and for exemplifying how faith-based communities can uphold secular values of bodily autonomy, consent, and inclusion within religious frameworks.

14. Wiccan

A modern pagan, earth-centered spiritual tradition that honors cycles of nature, the sacred feminine, and the interplay of energies often symbolized by a God and Goddess. While diverse in belief and practice, Wiccan paths frequently emphasize sexual freedom, ritual sensuality, and the sacralization of the body. In SOCAS, Wiccan traditions are noted for their reclaiming of erotic power and for challenging Judeo-Christian binaries that have historically denigrated sexuality, especially female sexuality.

15. Beltane festivals

Rooted in ancient Celtic traditions and celebrated around May 1st, Beltane marks the midpoint between the spring equinox and the summer solstice. It honors fertility, the blossoming of life, and the sacred union of masculine and feminine energies—symbolized by rituals such as the maypole dance and symbolic "Great Rite" ceremonies. In SOCAS, Beltane is cited for its celebratory approach to sexuality, where erotic expression is viewed not as sinful but as sacred, joyful, and vital to natural and spiritual renewal.

16. Charles Roselli

A neurobiologist at Oregon Health & Science University known for his research on the biological basis of sexual orientation in animals, particularly in rams. Roselli's studies of same-sex preferences among male sheep have contributed to scientific debates on the neuroendocrinology of sexuality. In SOCAS, his work is cited in the context of challenging heteronormative assumptions by highlighting the natural diversity of sexual behavior across species, thus countering claims that same-sex attraction is "unnatural" or pathological.

17. Frigerio, A., Ballerini, A., & Valdés Hernández, M. C.

These researchers contributed to the interdisciplinary field exploring the neurological and developmental aspects of human sexuality. Their collaborative studies have addressed how biological and social factors influence sexual orientation and gender identity. In SOCAS, their work is cited to underscore the scientific complexity behind human sexual diversity and to counter reductionist or pathologizing narratives that have historically underpinned discriminatory policies.

18. American Psychological Association (APA)

The APA is the leading scientific and professional organization representing psychology in the United States, known for setting evidence-based standards in mental health and human behavior. In SOCAS, the APA is cited for its affirming stance on sexual orientation, gender identity, and comprehensive sexuality education. Their policy statements have condemned conversion therapy, affirmed the mental health benefits of sexual authenticity, and supported age-appropriate, inclusive sexual education that is grounded in psychological well-being, human dignity, and scientific evidence.

19. Russell, S. T., & Fish, J. N. (2016)

In their pivotal study on LGBT youth mental health, Stephen T. Russell and Jessica N. Fish document how societal stigma, discrimination, and lack of affirming environments significantly contribute to mental health disparities among queer and transgender adolescents. In SOCAS, this research is cited to underscore how religiously justified marginalization, silence, and educational erasure exacerbate anxiety, depression, and suicidal ideation among LGBTQ+ youth. Their findings support the call for inclusive, affirming sexuality education and mental health interventions that recognize the protective power of social acceptance, visibility, and comprehensive care.

20. Relational Ethics

In SOCAS, relational ethics is cited as a guiding framework for reimagining sexual morality outside authoritarian religious codes. Rooted in feminist, queer, and Indigenous ethics of care, this approach prioritizes mutual consent, emotional resonance, and situational sensitivity over rigid rules or shame-based norms. It shifts moral discourse from judgment to connection, emphasizing the human impact of choices within interpersonal and societal webs.

21. Erotic Justice

In SOCAS, erotic justice is positioned as a critical alternative to religiously imposed moral codes. Drawing from feminist legal theory and decolonial sexual ethics, the term highlights how pleasure, desire, and bodily autonomy must be protected as human rights. It critiques both state and ecclesiastical systems that weaponize shame and control sexuality, arguing that true justice must include the freedom to experience, express, and explore erotic life without coercion, stigma, or inequality.

22. Transphobia

In SOCAS, transphobia is framed not merely as prejudice, but as a tool of religious and institutional control that punishes gender diversity. It intersects with homophobia and misogyny, particularly in doctrines that pathologize or erase non-binary and trans experiences. The text links transphobia to the broader apparatus of moral colonization, highlighting how some faith-based teachings reinforce binary gender ideologies and deny the legitimacy of transgender lives. *SOCAS* advocates for comprehensive, gender-affirming education and legal protection as central to erotic justice and human dignity.

23. Ratna Kapur

A leading feminist legal scholar, Ratna Kapur, critiques how liberal and postcolonial legal systems often marginalize sexual difference under the guise of human rights and morality. In SOCAS, her work is cited for introducing the concept of erotic justice, which pushes beyond conventional legal framings to center desire, pleasure, and difference. Kapur exposes how moral regulation—often justified by religion or nationalism—functions to erase non-normative sexualities and maintain colonial legacies of control. Her scholarship provides a critical lens for analyzing how law and culture intersect to police bodies, particularly in South Asian and global postcolonial contexts.

24. Amber Hollibaugh

A pioneering queer feminist, sex worker rights advocate, and co-author of *My Dangerous Desires*, Hollibaugh is recognized for her unflinching exploration of class, sexuality, and survival. In SOCAS, her work is cited as emblematic of erotic justice in practice—especially her emphasis on pleasure, desire, and lived experience as valid epistemologies in sexual ethics. She challenges sanitized, middle-class notions of sexual respectability and calls instead for a radical inclusivity that embraces sex workers, poor women, and queer bodies as central to any serious liberation project. Her voice underscores the intersectionality of class, gender, and sexual politics in sexuality education and policy discourse.

25. Transnational movements

Grassroots and institutional efforts that cross national borders to address shared goals—such as sexual rights, reproductive justice, and bodily autonomy. In SOCAS, transnational movements are referenced for their role in shaping global norms through advocacy, coalition-building, and knowledge exchange. Examples include international LGBTQ+ rights campaigns, feminist reproductive justice networks, and global initiatives for comprehensive sexuality education. These movements challenge parochial religious restrictions and promote frameworks grounded in universal human rights and erotic justice.

26. Decriminalization of desire

Refers to dismantling legal and moral frameworks that pathologize or punish consensual sexual expression, especially when it deviates from heteronormative or religious norms. In SOCAS, this concept is used to underscore the importance of separating state and church power from intimate life, and to advocate for legal reforms that affirm sexual rights, autonomy, and pleasure as integral to human dignity. The phrase critiques how laws—often influenced by theological doctrines—have historically suppressed erotic diversity through criminalization, censorship, or social stigma.

27. Intersectional and intergenerational movements

These refer to coalitions that bridge generational divides and embrace the interconnectedness of social identities—such as race, gender, sexuality, class, and ability—in their activism. In SOCAS, such movements are recognized for advancing sexual rights and justice by drawing on the lived experiences of both elders and youth, and by acknowledging how systems of oppression overlap. These alliances foster collective resilience, historical continuity, and broadened strategies for liberation that challenge ageism, heteronormativity, and other structural inequities.

28. Carl Stychin

Legal scholar whose work explores the intersection of law, sexuality, and citizenship. His research has examined how legal frameworks construct and regulate sexual identities, particularly in Western liberal democracies. In SOCAS, he is referenced for his contributions to queer legal theory and critiques of heteronormativity in constitutional and human rights discourse. Stychin's insights help frame the legal system not as a neutral arbiter but as an active participant in shaping moral and sexual norms.

29. Erotic Intelligence

Refers to a form of emotional and sensual awareness that embraces erotic desire as a vital source of self-knowledge, creativity, intimacy, and vitality. Erotic intelligence challenges the moral repression of sexuality and encourages mindful, ethical, and life-affirming expressions of pleasure and connection. In SOCAS, it is discussed as part of a broader call to reclaim erotic consciousness from centuries of religious shame and repression. Thinkers like Esther Perel and Audre Lorde have emphasized how erotic intelligence allows individuals to live more fully, with emotional honesty and bodily presence. It is also a foundation for sexual ethics rooted in consent, mutuality, and joy.

CHAPTER FIVE

1. Renate Dixon-Mueller

A prominent scholar in the fields of population studies, reproductive health, and gender policy, Renate Dixon-Mueller has contributed extensively to understanding how social structures, religious norms, and public policy intersect with sexual and reproductive rights. Her research highlights the ways in which institutional power—particularly in law, health systems, and international development—can either support or hinder bodily autonomy and gender equality. SOCAS references her work to underscore how patriarchal and dogmatic frameworks shape access to contraception, reproductive health services, and culturally biased sex education. Dixon-Mueller's analyses help frame sexual freedom not only as an individual right, but as a matter of social justice and public policy.

2. Capitulate to Ideological Fearmongering

This phrase describes the act of surrendering one's critical thinking or moral clarity in response to manipulative narratives rooted in fear. Within the context of SOCAS, it refers to how religious, political, or cultural authorities exploit fear—often of moral decay, divine punishment, or social ostracism—to enforce conformity and suppress dissent. When individuals or institutions capitulate to such fearmongering, they often uphold regressive ideologies, even at the expense of human rights, scientific understanding, or personal integrity. SOCAS critiques this pattern as a core mechanism of religious authoritarianism and a major obstacle to erotic justice and unapologetic freedom.

3. Body Awareness

Within the framework of SOCAS, body awareness is more than a wellness trend; it is a radical act of reclamation. It refers to the capacity to consciously sense and respond to the body's messages—its desires, discomforts, pleasures, and boundaries—without judgment or disembodiment. In societies marked by religious repression or sexual shame, reconnecting with body awareness is foundational to healing erotic wounds and cultivating authentic, autonomous pleasure. Through practices such as Sensual Meditation, yoga, massage, or mindful breathwork, body awareness becomes a tool for resistance against the internalized fragmentation imposed by patriarchal or puritanical ideologies.

4. Sexual Health

Defined by the World Health Organization, sexual health encompasses more than STI prevention or reproductive services—it affirms the right to pleasure, consent, information, and bodily autonomy. In SOCAS, sexual health is framed as a cornerstone of erotic justice and human dignity, directly challenged by abstinence-only policies, religious dogma, and censorship. Promoting sexual health means advocating for science-based sex education, access to care, and the normalization of pleasure as a vital component of well-being.

5. Convention on the Rights of the Child (CRC)

Adopted by the UN General Assembly in 1989 and ratified by nearly every country, the CRC is a landmark treaty that redefined children as rights-holding individuals. In SOCAS, it is cited for its emphasis on access to accurate information, education, and protection from all forms of abuse or discrimination—foundational principles that underpin the call for inclusive, science-based, and rights-affirming sex education. The CRC serves as a global legal and ethical reference point in defending the dignity, autonomy, and evolving capacities of young people.

6. Raisa Cacciatore

Finnish medical doctor, adolescent psychiatrist, and specialist in sexual health education. Dr. Cacciatore has been internationally recognized for her pioneering work in promoting Comprehensive Sexuality Education (CSE), especially among youth. Her efforts emphasize empowerment, emotional development, and the destigmatization of sexuality. Cited in SOCAS for advancing science-based, rights-affirming approaches to sex education through both policy and pedagogy.

7. Anita Brakman, *et al.*

Cited for her work as a global advocate for female sexual autonomy and empowerment, particularly in relation to the elimination of harmful traditional practices like female genital mutilation (FGM). Brakman has collaborated with international organizations to promote gender equality and has been involved in educational campaigns emphasizing bodily integrity and reproductive rights. In SOCAS, Brakman is referenced for her contributions to raising awareness about the psychosocial impacts of FGM and for advancing sex-positive, culturally sensitive approaches to women's health education.

8. Starkman, N., & Rajani, N.

Cited for their influential article *The Case for Comprehensive Sex Education*, which outlines the public health, educational, and ethical imperatives of medically accurate, age-appropriate sexuality education. In *SOCAS*, this work is referenced to support arguments that abstinence-only programs fail to meet the needs of diverse youth populations, and that CSE fosters healthier outcomes and more informed decision-making.

9. Andrzejewski, J., Liddon, N., & Leonard, S.

Cited for their literature review on condom availability programs (CAPs) in U.S. schools, which concludes that CAPs increase condom acquisition and use, while showing no evidence of encouraging earlier or more frequent sexual activity. In SOCAS, this study helps dismantle the myth that access leads to recklessness. It reinforces the book's stance that youth deserve protection, education, and trust—not fear-based restrictions or moral panic.

10. Nassim Alisobhani

Referenced for exposing the ideological bias and public health risks of U.S. abstinence-only education policies. Their work critiques the ways in which shame-based, non-inclusive approaches distort scientific understanding and restrict youth access to accurate information. In SOCAS, Alisobhani's scholarship helps contextualize broader critiques of state-sponsored moralism, highlighting how federal funding has often been used to suppress sexual agency and promote misinformation.

11. Colleen Marron

In her 2022 paper *Freeing Females from Toplessness Bans: A Strict Scrutiny Analysis*, Marron critiques the legal double standard that allows men, but not women, to go topless in public—arguing that such bans violate the Equal Protection Clause. In SOCAS, this analysis supports broader arguments for bodily autonomy and the dismantling of legal taboos rooted in patriarchal and religious control.

12. Amr Seifeldin

Cited for his medical work on genital reconstructive surgery following female genital mutilation (FGM), with particular focus on healing, functional restoration, and ethical care. In *SOCAS*, his contributions underscore the role of post-trauma interventions in restoring bodily autonomy and sexual health while addressing the psychological impacts of genital harm.

13. Chantal Compaoré

As First Lady of Burkina Faso, Chantal Compaoré became internationally recognized for her advocacy against female genital mutilation (FGM). Her leadership played a pivotal role in making Burkina Faso one of the first African nations to criminalize the practice and prioritize survivor rehabilitation. In SOCAS, Compaoré is referenced as an example of influential female leadership in the global fight against

FGM and for reproductive justice, aligning with the book's broader themes of bodily autonomy and international sexual rights reform.

14. Dystopian

Often used to describe fictional or real-world societies marked by systemic oppression, surveillance, and loss of personal freedom. In SOCAS, the term highlights how some modern-day religious or political regimes—particularly those that criminalize pleasure, suppress bodily autonomy, or enforce rigid sexual norms—mirror dystopian frameworks by controlling both public behavior and private desire.

15. Cultural Inertia

Refers to the resistance to change within societies due to longstanding traditions, values, or norms. In SOCAS, cultural inertia is cited as a key obstacle to the adoption of progressive, evidence-based sex education and the dismantling of outdated moral frameworks. Even when laws or scientific understanding evolve, deeply embedded customs and inherited fears often slow social transformation—especially around gender, sexuality, and bodily autonomy.

16. Americans with Disabilities Act (ADA)

Passed in 1990, the ADA enshrines protections for people with physical and mental disabilities, mandating accessibility and anti-discrimination across public and private sectors. In SOCAS, the ADA is cited as a model of legislative progress where bodily diversity and human dignity are affirmed—offering a legal precedent for broader frameworks of inclusion, especially in sexual health education, reproductive rights, and bodily autonomy.

17. Carson Strong

Cited in SOCAS for his contribution to the ethical debate surrounding human reproductive cloning. His analysis in *"The Ethics of Human Reproductive Cloning"* presents a nuanced exploration of bioethical concerns, such as autonomy, identity, and potential harms. In SOCAS, Strong is referenced in the context of Raelian advocacy for cloning and bodily autonomy, offering a secular counterpoint to religious condemnations of reproductive technology.

18. Aisya Aymanee Zaharin and Maria Pallotta-Chiarolli

Cited in SOCAS for their work on decolonial, intersectional, and queer feminist critiques of religious, cultural, and political structures that shape sexual norms. In SOCAS, their scholarship is referenced for its contribution to understanding how faith-based ideologies intersect with race, gender, and colonial power to shape sexual repression and exclusion—particularly in Muslim-majority contexts and diasporic communities.

19. Mirjam van Schaik

Explores the legal recognition of apostasy—particularly the right to renounce one's religion—in international human rights law and comparative constitutional frameworks. Her dissertation analyzes how freedom of religion includes the right to leave religious belief systems, especially in contexts where apostasy is penalized socially or legally. In SOCAS, van Schaik's research supports broader discussions of religious freedom and the right to non-belief, particularly in highlighting how the denial of such rights reinforces patriarchal and theocratic systems that limit sexual and personal autonomy.

20. Ronald Weitzer

Cited in SOCAS for his scholarly contributions to the sociology of sex work, particularly his critique of anti-prostitution ideologies and advocacy for evidence-based, harm-reduction approaches to sex industry regulation. His work supports SOCAS's broader emphasis on sexual agency, empirical ethics, and the need to move beyond moral panic when shaping public policy.

21. Scott Cunningham & Manisha Shah

Economist Scott Cunningham and policy scholar Manisha Shah have contributed extensively to the empirical understanding of sex work, sexual health, and the legal regulation of sexuality. Their collaborative research, including studies on decriminalization, public health outcomes, and the economics of commercial sex, provides foundational evidence for arguments against moralistic or punitive legal frameworks. In SOCAS, they are cited for offering data-driven insights that support a more humane, evidence-based approach to sex work policy—bolstering calls for reform grounded in health, dignity, and rights.

22. Karen Terry

A criminologist and lead researcher of the *John Jay Report*, Terry is recognized for her extensive analysis of the patterns and institutional failures behind sexual abuse in the Catholic Church. Her work illuminates the ethical and systemic complexities involved in reconciling harm with healing in faith-based and secular settings alike. In SOCAS, she is cited as a key figure whose empirical research underscores the systemic nature of religiously shielded abuse and the urgency of independent, secular oversight to protect minors and vulnerable populations.

23. Sensual Meditation

A Raelian method of awakening the senses and fostering connection between the body and the infinite. Far from being merely a relaxation technique, it is a core practice that empowers individuals to reclaim their erotic potential, cultivate inner peace, and deepen their connection with existence. In SOCAS, it is referenced as both a spiritual tool and a form of erotic liberation, bridging science, sensuality, and self-realization.

24. Sensuality Education

Expands the scope of what is often reduced to anatomy and abstinence. It affirms the body as a site of knowledge, pleasure, and healing. In SOCAS, it is referenced as a counterbalance to shame-based or punitive models of education, and as a necessary foundation for cultivating erotic intelligence, self-acceptance, and relational well-being.

CONCLUSION

1. Mary E. Hunt

A feminist theologian, scholar, and co-founder of the Women's Alliance for Theology, Ethics, and Ritual (WATER). Hunt's work interrogates patriarchal and exclusionary structures within traditional theology and promotes inclusive, justice-centered frameworks grounded in lived experience. Her contributions are foundational to the development of *transformative theology*—a liberatory approach that centers the voices of women, LGBTQ+ people, and other marginalized communities. In SOCAS, Hunt's emphasis on embodied spirituality and ethics rooted in justice aligns with the book's call to reimagine sexual and spiritual liberation beyond the confines of religious orthodoxy.

2. Transformative Theology

A branch of theological reflection that emphasizes spirituality as a vehicle for social justice, personal healing, and systemic change. Transformative theology integrates liberationist, feminist, queer, and ecological frameworks to challenge oppression and reimagine religion as a force for collective liberation. In SOCAS, this concept undergirds critiques of traditional religious authority, offering alternative models rooted in empathy, embodiment, and erotic justice.

3. Liturgy

Refers to the formal rituals and public worship practices prescribed by religious traditions, often involving sacred texts, symbolic gestures, and communal participation. In many Abrahamic traditions, liturgy plays a central role in shaping moral instruction and social norms, including those related to sexuality and gender. In SOCAS, liturgical structures are examined for how they encode and perpetuate patriarchal, heteronormative, and ascetic values, often at odds with erotic justice and embodied freedom.

4. Katie G. Cannon

A trailblazing theologian and ethicist, Dr. Katie Geneva Cannon (1950–2018) was a founding voice in womanist theology. Her work centered on the moral wisdom and lived experiences of Black women, challenging both white feminist and patriarchal theological frameworks. In SOCAS, Cannon's legacy affirms the need for intersectional, embodied ethics and highlights how religious institutions have historically erased Black women's erotic agency and spiritual authority.

5. Reverend Nadia Bolz-Weber

An ordained Lutheran pastor and outspoken advocate for sexual wholeness and inclusivity, Nadia Bolz-Weber reclaims Christian theology from purity culture and shame-based moralism. Through her books and ministry, she promotes an embodied, grace-centered faith that affirms LGBTQ+ identities, challenges gender norms, and invites honest dialogue about desire and trauma. In SOCAS, Bolz-Weber is referenced as a trailblazing figure in transformative theology, offering a model of post-patriarchal spirituality that embraces sexual authenticity without dogma.

Works Cited

Ahmed, L. (2021). *Women and gender in Islam: Historical roots of a modern debate.* Yale University Press.

Ahmed, S. (2013). *The cultural politics of emotion.* Routledge.

Akweongo, P., Jackson, E. F., Appiah-Yeboah, S., Sakeah, E., & Phillips, J. F. (2021). *It's a woman's thing: gender roles sustaining the practice of female genital mutilation among the Kassena-Nankana of northern Ghana.* Reproductive health, 18(1), 52.

Ali, K. (2016). *Marriage and slavery in early Islam.* Harvard University Press.

Ali, K. (2016). *Sexual ethics and Islam: feminist reflections on Qur'an, hadith, and jurisprudence.* Simon and Schuster.

Alisobhani, N. (2018). *Female Toplessness: Gender Equality's Next Frontier.* UC Irvine L. Rev., 8, 299.

Althaus-Reid, M. (2005). *From the Goddess to Queer Theology: The State we are in now.* Feminist Theology, 13(2), 265-272.

American Psychological Association. (2021). *Guidelines for psychological practice with sexual minority persons.*

American Psychological Association. (2021). *Resolution on sexual orientation change efforts.*

Andrzejewski, J., Liddon, N., & Leonard, S. (2019). *Condom availability programs in schools: a review of the literature.* American Journal of Health Promotion, 33(3), 457-467.

Aquinas, T. (1947). *Summa Theologica. Fathers of the English Dominican Province, Trans..* New York: Benziger Brothers.

Aquinas, T. (1952). *Summa Theologica. Fathers of the English Dominican Province.* Great books of the Western world. Chicago: Encyclopedia Britannica.

Armstrong, K. (1994). *A history of God: The 4,000-year quest of Judaism, Christianity and Islam.* Ballantine Books.

Assante, J. (1998). *The kar. kid/ḫarimtu, Prostitute or Single Woman? A Reconsideration of the Evidence.* Ugarit-Forschungen, 30, 5-96.

Associated Press. (2024, February 21). *Georgia GOP senators push bills to censor sexually explicit books, limit sex education, display Ten Commandments, allow school chaplains.* Associated Press. https://apnews.com/article/georgia-education-sex-education-libraries-librarians-commandments-4436ab03a82807f2dab15a3047947177

Associated Press. (2024, June 9). *A Christian group teaches public school students during the school day. Their footprint is growing.* Associated Press. https://apnews.com/article/indiana-lifewise-public-school-religion-d7cf2b67b2ae3b7919e0a21f89ce80c0

Barclay, J. (2015). *Paul and the gift.* Oxford University Press.

Beeharry-Paray, G. (2000). *"Les Bijoux indiscrets" de Diderot: Pastiche, forgerie ou charge du conte crébillonien?* Diderot studies, 28, 21-37.

Bentham, J., & Crompton, L. (1978). *Offences Against One's Self: Paederesty (Part 1).* Journal of Homosexuality, 3(4), 389-406.

Berg, T., & Laycock, D. (2021). *Protecting Free Exercise under Smith and after Smith.* Christian Law., 17, 3.

Biale, D. (2023). *Judaism: The genealogy of a modern notion.* Columbia University Press.

Biale, D. (2023). *Eros and the Jews: From biblical Israel to contemporary America.* Univ of California Press.

Biles, B. J., Serova, N., Stanbrook, G., Brady, B., Kingsley, J., Topp, S. M., & Yashadhana, A. (2024). *What is Indigenous cultural health and wellbeing? A narrative review.* The Lancet Regional Health–Western Pacific, 52.

Binns, I. C. (2013). *Academic freedom legislation: The latest effort to undermine the integrity of science and science education.* Journal of Science Teacher Education, 24(4), 589-595.

Blank, H. (2008). *Virgin: The untouched history*. Bloomsbury Publishing USA.

Bolz-Weber, N. (2019). *Shameless: A sexual reformation*. Convergent Books.

Boralevi, L. C. (2012). *Bentham and the Oppressed (Vol. 1)*. Walter de Gruyter.

Boswell, J. (1980). *Christianity, social tolerance, and homosexuality: Gay people in Western Europe from the beginning of the Christian era to the fourteenth century*. University of Chicago Press.

Brakman, A., Borzutzky, C., Carey, S., Kang, M., Mullins, T. K., Peter, N., … & Straub, D. M. (2017). *Condom availability in schools: A practical approach to the prevention of sexually transmitted infection/HIV and unintended pregnancy*. Journal of Adolescent Health, 60(6), 754-757.

Brown, B. (2015). *Daring greatly: How the courage to be vulnerable transforms the way we live, love, parent, and lead*. Penguin.

Brown, P. (1988). *The body and society: Men, women, and sexual renunciation in early Christianity*. Columbia University Press.

Brown, P. (1990). *Authority and the sacred: Aspects of the Christianisation of the Roman world*. Cambridge University Press.

Budin, S. L. (2008). *The myth of sacred prostitution in antiquity*. Cambridge University Press.

Burke, P. (2014). *The Italian Renaissance: culture and society in Italy*. Princeton University Press.

Cacciatore, R., Ingman-Friberg, S., Apter, D., Sajaniemi, N., & Kaltiala, R. (2020). *An alternative term to make comprehensive sexuality education more acceptable in childhood*. South African Journal of Childhood Education, 10(1), 1-10.

Caldwell, S. (2015). *Let's Talk About Sex: The Failure of Abstinence-Only Policies in America's Public Schools* (Senior thesis, Claremont McKenna College).

Catholic theology of sexuality. (2025, last week). *Catholic theology of sexuality*. Wikipedia. Retrieved from https://en.wikipedia.org/wiki/Catholic_theology_of_sexuality

Center for Reproductive Rights. (2023). *El Salvador's total abortion ban*. Retrieved from https://reproductiverights.org

Cheng, P. S. (2011). *Radical love: Introduction to queer theology*. Church Publishing, Inc..

Coady, C. A. J. (2023). *The Significance and Complexity of Conscience*. Philosophia, 51(5), 2497-2516.

Commonweal Magazine. (2010, March 19). *Sin, confession, and absolution*. https://www.commonwealmagazine.org/sin-confession-and-absolution

Coontz, S. (2006). *Marriage, a history: How love conquered marriage*. Penguin.

Cunningham, S., & Shah, M. (2018). *Decriminalizing indoor prostitution: Implications for sexual violence and public health*. The Review of Economic Studies, 85(3), 1683-1715.

Deer, S. (2015). *The beginning and end of rape: Confronting sexual violence in Native America*. U of Minnesota Press.

Deloria, V., Jr. (2003). *God is red: A Native view of religion* (3rd ed.). Fulcrum Publishing.

Despeux, C., & Pregadio, F. (2008). *Sexuality*. In F. Pregadio (Ed.), The encyclopedia of Taoism (Vol. 2, pp. 1045–1053). Routledge.

Dixon-Mueller, R. (2010). *International Technical Guidance on Sexuality Education: An evidence-informed approach for schools, teachers and health educators*. Vol. I, Vol. II.

Dobbs, T. E. (2022). *Jackson Women's health organization*. Read US Supreme Court opinion in Dobbs vs. Jackson Women's Health Organization: Roe v. Wade overturned.

Doniger, W. (2003). *The "Kamasutra": It Isn't All about Sex*. The Kenyon Review, 25(1), 18-37.

Doniger, W., & Kakar, S. (Trans.). (2002). *Kama Sutra: A new, complete English translation of the classic Hindu text.* Penguin Classics.

Douglas, M. (2003). *Purity and danger: An analysis of concepts of pollution and taboo.* Routledge.

Dover, K. J. (1978). *Greek homosexuality.* Harvard University Press.

Doyle, T. P., Sipe, A. R., & Wall, P. J. (2006). *Sex, priests, and secret codes: The Catholic Church's 2000-year paper trail of sexual abuse.* Bonus Books, Inc.

Driskill, Q. L. (2004). *Stolen from our bodies: First Nations two-spirits/queers and the journey to a sovereign erotic.* Studies in American Indian Literatures, 16(2), 50-64.

Dworkin, R. (2011). *Justice for hedgehogs.* Harvard University Press.

Easton, D. & Hardy, J.W. (2009). *The ethical slut: A practical guide to polyamory, open relationships & other adventures.* Random House LLC.

ECHR, https://www.echr.coe.int/w/2022

Eliade, M. (1959). *The sacred and the profane: The nature of religion* (Vol. 81). Houghton Mifflin Harcourt.

Elliott, D. (2021). *Spiritual marriage: sexual abstinence in medieval wedlock.*

Esposito, J. L., & Haddad, Y. Y. (Eds.). (1998). *Islam, gender, & social change (p. ix).* New York: Oxford University Press.

Fish, J. N., & Russell, S. T. (2020). *Sexual orientation and gender identity change efforts are unethical and harmful.* American Journal of Public Health, 110(8), 1113.

Foner, N., & Alba, R. (2008). *Immigrant religion in the US and Western Europe: Bridge or barrier to inclusion?* International Migration Review, 42(2), 360-392.

Foucault, M. (1978). *The History of Sexuality, Volume 1: An Introduction* [The Will to Knowledge]. Trans: Robert Hurley. London: Penguin.

Foucault, M. (1990). *The history of sexuality: An introduction.* Vintage.

Franke, K. (2015). *Wedlocked: The perils of marriage equality.* In Wedlocked. New York University Press.

Frigerio, A., Ballerini, L., & Valdes Hernandez, M. (2021). *Structural, functional, and metabolic brain differences as a function of gender identity or sexual orientation: a systematic review of the human neuroimaging literature.* Archives of Sexual Behavior, 50(8), 3329-3352.

Genuis, S. J., & Lipp, C. (2013). *Ethical diversity and the role of conscience in clinical medicine.* International Journal of Family Medicine, 2013(1), 587541.

Ginsburg, F. D., & Rapp, R. (Eds.). (1995). *Conceiving the new world order: The global politics of reproduction.* Univ of California Press.

Greenawalt, K. (2009). *Religion and the constitution, volume 1: free exercise and fairness* (Vol. 1). Princeton University Press.

Gruenbaum, E. (2001). *The female circumcision controversy: an anthropological perspective.* University of Pennsylvania Press.

Gushee, D. P. (2020). *Katie Cannon's enduring contribution to Christian ethics.* Interpretation, 74(1), 23-30.

Habermas, J. (2008). *Notes on post-secular society.* New Perspectives Quarterly, 25(4), 17-29.

Hartmann, B. (1995). *Reproductive rights and wrongs: The global politics of population control.* South End Press.

Harvey, P. (2000). *An introduction to Buddhist ethics: Foundations, values and issues.* Cambridge University Press.

Hermann, D. H. (2015). *Extending the fundamental right of marriage to same-sex couples: the United States Supreme Court decision in Obergefell v. Hodges.* Ind. L. Rev., 49, 367.

Hollibaugh, A. L. (2000). *My dangerous desires: A queer girl dreaming her way home.* Duke University Press.

Htun, M. (2003). *Sex and the state: Abortion, divorce, and the family under Latin American dictatorships and democracies.* Cambridge University Press.

Human Dignity Trust. (2024). *Criminalisation of LGBT people: Global overview.* Retrieved from https://www.humandignitytrust.org

Hunt, M. E. (2009). *Women-Church: Feminist concept, religious commitment, women's movement.* Journal of Feminist Studies in Religion, 25(1), 85-98.

Ignaciuk, A., & Kelly, L. (2020). *Contraception and Catholicism in the twentieth century: Transnational perspectives on expert, activist and intimate practices.* Medical History, 64(2), 163–172.

Israel, J. I. (2001). *Radical enlightenment: Philosophy and the making of modernity.* 1650–1750. Oxford University Press.

Jacobsen, T. (1976). *The treasures of darkness: A history of Mesopotamian religion.* Yale University Press.

Kant, I. (2013). *An answer to the question: 'What is enlightenment?'.* Penguin UK.

Kapur, R. (2013). *Erotic justice: Law and the new politics of postcolonialism.* Routledge-Cavendish.

Keenan, M. (2011). *Child sexual abuse and the Catholic Church*: Gender, power, and organizational culture. Oxford University Press.

Kimmerer, R. W. (2013). *Braiding sweetgrass: Indigenous wisdom, scientific knowledge, and the teachings of plants.* Milkweed Editions.

Kirby, D. (2007). *Emerging answers, 2007: Research findings on programs to reduce teen pregnancy and sexually transmitted diseases.* National Campaign to Prevent Teen and Unplanned Pregnancy.

Klein, M. (2012). *America's war on sex: The continuing attack on law, lust, and liberty.* Bloomsbury Publishing USA.

Kohn, L. (2006). *Daoist body cultivation: Traditional models and contemporary practices.* Three Pines Press.

Kramer, S. N. (1963). *The Sumerians: Their history, culture, and character*. University of Chicago Press.

Kugle, S. S. (2010). *Homosexuality in Islam: Critical reflection on gay, lesbian, and transgender Muslims*. Oneworld Publications.

Küng, H. (2007). *The Catholic Church: A short history* (Vol. 5). Modern Library.

Louth, A. (1996). *St Augustine, Confessions*. Scottish Journal of Theology, 49(4), 502–504.

Manniche, L. (2013). *Sexual life in ancient Egypt*. Routledge.

Marron, C. (2022). *Freeing Females from Toplessness Bans: A Strict Scrutiny Analysis*. Dickinson Law Review, 127, 839.

Martin, D. B. (2006). *Sex and the single savior: Gender and sexuality in biblical interpretation*. Presbyterian Publishing Corp.

Mason, H. E. (Ed.). (1996). *Moral dilemmas and moral theory*. Oxford University Press.

Masterson, M., Rabinowitz, N. S., & Robson, J. (2014). *Sex in antiquity: Exploring gender and sexuality in the ancient world*. Routledge.

McKinley, C. E., & Knipp, H. (2022). *"You Can Get Away with Anything Here...* No Justice at All"—Sexual Violence Against US Indigenous Females and Its Consequences. Gender Issues, 39(3), 291–319.

McQuillan, K. (2004). *When does religion influence fertility?* Population and Development Review, 30(1), 25–56. https://doi.org/10.1111/j.1728-4457.2004.00002.x

Meyer, I. H. (2003). *Prejudice, social stress, and mental health in lesbian, gay, and bisexual populations: Conceptual issues and research evidence*. Psychological Bulletin, 129(5), 674.

MTSU. (2023). *Free Speech Center Newsletter* (June 6, 2023). https://firstamendment.mtsu.edu/post/free-speech-center-newsletter-6-6-2023/

Nawej, K. U. (2007). *White Poison: A Black Christian Is a Traitor to the Memory of His Ancestors.* https://www.amazon.com/White-Poison-Christian-Traitor-Ancestors/dp/296004780X

Nawej, K. U. (2012). *Erotic Africa.* https://www.scribd.com/document/965597252/Erotic-Africa-uriel-nawej

Norris, P., & Inglehart, R. (2011). *Sacred and secular: Religion and politics worldwide.* Cambridge University Press.

Nussbaum, M. (2008). *Liberty of conscience: In defense of America's tradition of religious equality.* Basic Books.

Pagels, E. (2011). *Adam, Eve, and the serpent: Sex and politics in early Christianity.* Vintage Books.

Pelikan, J. (1996). *Mary through the centuries: Her place in the history of culture.* Yale University Press.

Picq, M. L., & Tikuna, J. (2019, August 20). *Indigenous sexualities: Resisting conquest and translation.* E-International Relations. https://www.e-ir.info/2019/08/20/indigenous-sexualities-resisting-conquest-and-translation/

Prewitt, T. S. (1989). *Bowen v. Kendrick: The Constitutionality of the Adolescent Family Life Act-Has the Court Given Us a Lemon.* J. Fam. L., 28, 87.

Rael (1987). *Sensual Meditation: Awakening the Mind by Awakening the Body.* Raelian Movement Publications. www.rael.org

Rael, M. (1992). *Proposal to the United Nations for a Global Religious Censorship Authority.* Raelian Publications. www.rael.org

Rael (2001). *Yes to human cloning: Eternal life thanks to science.* Raelian Movement Publications. www.rael.org

Rael (2004). *The Maitreya—Extracts from his teachings.* Raelian Movement Publications. www.rael.org

Rael (2005). *Intelligent Design: Message from the Designers.* Nova Distribution—latest edition. This book was originally published in French in 1974. The first English version titled: "The Message Given to me by Extraterrestrials" was published in 1977. www.rael.org

Rainbow, J. (2007). *The Song of Songs and the Testament of Solomon: Solomon's love poetry and Christian magic.* Harvard theological review, 100(3), 249-274. Song of Solomon's praise of sexual pleasure. (n.d.). Retrieved from https://www.compellingtruth.org/sex-for-pleasure.html

Raushenbush, P. B. (2024, September 26). *Censorship is a religious freedom issue—book banning is a political strategy that could silence diverse religious voices and traditions that are a major part of the rich social fabric of America.* Interfaith Alliance. Retrieved from https://interfaithalliance.org/post/censorship-is-a-religious-freedom-issue

Reardon-Smith, H. (2023). *Reclaiming the Landbodymind Erotic.* Journal of Global Indigeneity, 7(2), 1-14.

Rivera, V. (2013). *Captive on Their Own Land: Unfree Indian Labor in California's Missions, 1769.* QUAESTIO, 149.

Robinet, I. (1997). *Taoism: Growth of a Religion.* Stanford University Press.

Robinson, L. (2013). *Gay men and the Left in post-war Britain: How the personal got political.* In Gay men and the Left in post-war Britain. Manchester University Press.

Roscoe, W. (1998). *Changing ones: Third and fourth genders in Native North America* (p. viii). New York: St. Martin's Press.

Roselli, C. E. (2018). *Neurobiology of gender identity and sexual orientation.* Journal of neuroendocrinology, 30(7), e12562.

Rosenfeld, M. J. (2008). *Racial, educational and religious endogamy in the United States: A comparative historical perspective.* Social forces, 87(1), 1-31.

Ross, L., & Solinger, R. (2017). *Reproductive justice: An introduction* (Vol. 1). Univ of California Press.

Ruether, R. R. (1993). *Sexism and God talk: Toward a feminist theology.* Beacon Press.

Russell, S. T., & Fish, J. N. (2016). *Mental health in lesbian, gay, bisexual, and transgender (LGBT) youth.* Annual review of clinical psychology, 12(1), 465-487.

Ryan, C., Huebner, D., Diaz, R. M., & Sanchez, J. (2009). *Family rejection as a predictor of negative health outcomes in white and Latino lesbian, gay, and bisexual young adults.* Pediatrics, 123(1), 346-352.

Sanday, P. R. (1981). *Female power and male dominance: On the origins of sexual inequality.* Cambridge University Press.

Santelli, J., Ott, M. A., Lyon, M., Rogers, J., Summers, D., & Schleifer, R. (2006). *Abstinence and abstinence-only education: A review of US policies and programs.* Journal of Adolescent health, 38(1), 72-81.

Satta, M. (2024). *The Supreme Court's Refusal to Acknowledge Sexual-Orientation Discrimination in 303 Creative v. Elenis. Elenis* (May 13, 2024). Wayne State University Law School Research Paper, (4826345).

Schipper, K. (1993). *The Taoist body.* University of California Press.

Seifeldin, A. (2016). *Genital reconstructive surgery after female genital mutilation.* Obstet Gynecol Int J, 4(6), 00129.

Sen, A. (2008). *The idea of justice.* Journal of human development, 9(3), 331-342.

Shaheed, A. (2019). *Freedom of religion or belief and gender equality.* Report of the UN Special Rapporteur to the UN Human Rights Council, A/HRC/43/48. Retrieved from https://www.ohchr.org

Starkman, N., & Rajani, N. (2002). *The case for comprehensive sex education.* AIDS patient care and STDs, 16(7), 313-318.

Steenson, M. (2019). *Masterpiece Cakeshop, Ltd. v. Colorado Civil Rights Commission.* Mitchell Hamline L. Rev., 45, 57.

Steffen, W., et al. (2015). *Planetary boundaries: Guiding human development on a changing planet.* Science, 347(6223). https://doi.org/10.1126/science.1259855

Strong, C. (2005). *The ethics of human reproductive cloning.* Reproductive BioMedicine Online, 10, 45-49.

Stychin, C. F. (2003). *Same-sex sexualities and the globalization of human rights discourse.* McGill LJ, 49, 951.

Syed, J. (2010). *An historical perspective on Islamic modesty and its implications for female employment.* Equality, Diversity and Inclusion: An International Journal, 29(2), 150-166.

Terry, K. J. (2018). *Restorative justice and child sexual abuse.* In Routledge International Handbook of Restorative Justice (pp. 145-158). Routledge.

Terry, K. J., Smith, M. L., Schuth, K., Kelly, J. R., Vollman, B., & Massey, C. (2011). *The causes and context of sexual abuse of minors by Catholic priests in the United States, 1950-2010.* In United States Conference of Catholic Bishops, Washington, DC.

Tilahun, M. A., Gatisso, M. M., & Ali, A. M. (2025). *Love beyond religious conviction: the challenges of interreligious marriage in South Wollo, Ethiopia.* Discover Global Society, 3(1), 74.

Tohit, N. F. M., & Haque, M. (2024). *Forbidden conversations: A comprehensive exploration of taboos in sexual and reproductive health.* Cureus, 16(8).

Turban, J. L., Beckwith, N., Reisner, S. L., & Keuroghlian, A. S. (2020). *Association between recalled exposure to gender identity conversion efforts and psychological distress and suicide attempts among transgender adults.* JAMA psychiatry, 77(1), 68-76.

U.S. Supreme Court. (1990). *Employment Division, Department of Human Resources of Oregon v.* Smith, 494 U.S. 872. https://supreme.justia.com/cases/federal/us/494/872/

UNESCO. (2009, 2018). *International Technical Guidance on Sexuality Education: An evidence-informed approach for schools, teachers and health educators.* Paris: UNESCO.

UNICEF. (2021). *Female genital mutilation (FGM).* https://www.unicef.org/protection/female-genital-mutilation

Valenti, J. (2010). *The purity myth: How America's obsession with virginity is hurting young women.* ReadHowYouWant. com.

Van, V. T. S., Uy, J., Bagas, J., & Ulep, V. G. T. (2021). *Trends in national-level governance and implementation of the Philippines'*

Responsible Parenthood and Reproductive Health Law from 2014 to 2020. Global Health: Science and Practice, 9(3), 548-564.

Van der Toorn, J., Jost, J. T., Packer, D. J., Noorbaloochi, S., & Van Bavel, J. J. (2017). *In defense of tradition: Religiosity, conservatism, and opposition to same-sex marriage in North America.* Personality and Social Psychology Bulletin, 43(10), 1455-1468.

van Schaik, B. M. (2023). *The right to apostasy recognised? Reaffirming the right to religious freedom.* Politics, Religion & Ideology, 24(2), 267-287.

Vanita, R., & Kidwai, S. (1996). *Same-sex love in India: Readings from literature and history. St.* Martin's Press.

Wadud, A. (2013). *Inside the gender jihad: Women's reform in Islam.* Praktyka teoretyczna, (08), 249-262.

Weitzer, R. (2006). *Moral Crusade against Prostitution.* Society, 43(3).

Wiesner-Hanks, M. (2010). *Christianity and sexuality in the early modern world: Regulating desire, reforming practice.*

Wilcox, M. (2003). *Coming out in Christianity: Religion, identity, and community.* Indiana University Press.

Winkler, J. J. (1990). *Laying down the law: The oversight of men's sexual behavior in classical Athens. Before sexuality: The construction of erotic experience in the ancient Greek world.* 171-209.

Witherington III, B. (2024). *2 Corinthians ().* Baker Books.

Woodhead, L. (2008). *Gendering secularization theory.* Social compass, 55(2), 187-193.

Zaharin, A. A. M., & Pallotta-Chiarolli, M. (2020). *Countering Islamic conservatism on being transgender: Clarifying Tantawi's and Khomeini's fatwas from the progressive Muslim standpoint.* International journal of transgender health, 21(3), 235-241.

Ziegler, M. (2020). *Abortion and the Law in America: Roe v. Wade to the Present.* Cambridge University Press.

Suggestions for Further Reading

Abusch, T. (2007). *Witchcraft literature in Mesopotamia*. In G. Leick (Ed.), The Babylonian World (pp. 373-385). Routledge.

Acker, M. (2009). *Breast is best... but not everywhere: ambivalent sexism and attitudes toward private and public breastfeeding*. Sex roles, 61(7), 476-490.

Alba, R., & Foner, N. (2015). *Mixed unions and immigrant-group integration in North America and Western Europe*. The ANNALS of the American Academy of Political and Social Science, 662(1), 38-56.

Ali, K. (2006). *Sexual ethics and Islam: Feminist reflections on Qur'an, Hadith, and jurisprudence*. Oneworld Publications.

Alito, S. A. (2022). *Dobbs v. Jackson Women's Health Organization, 597 U.S. (2022)*. Supreme Court of the United States. https://www.supremecourt.gov/opinions/21pdf/19-1392_6j37.pdf

Allen Jr, J. L. (2003). *1962 document orders secrecy in sex cases Many bishops unaware obscure missive was in their archives*. National Catholic Reporter.

Anderson, K. (2010). *Life Stages and Native Women: Memory, Teachings, and Story Medicine*. University of Manitoba Press.

Assmann, J. (2008). *Of God and gods: Egypt, Israel, and the rise of monotheism*. University of Wisconsin Press.

Assmann, J. (2016). *Monotheism and polytheism*. Universitätsbibliothek Heidelberg.

Astell, A. W. (2018). *The Song of Songs in the Middle Ages*. Cornell University Press.

Athanagoras of Athens. (n.d.). *Plea for the Christians (ch. 33)*. New Advent. Retrieved from https://www.newadvent.org/fathers/0205.htm

Barlas, A. (2019). *Believing women in Islam: Unreading patriarchal interpretations of the Qur'an*. University of Texas Press.

Baus, D. (2017). *Overpopulation and the Impact on the Environment.*

Benagiano, G., Carrara, S., Filippi, V., & Brosens, I. (2011). *Condoms, HIV and the Roman Catholic Church*. Reproductive BioMedicine Online, 22(7), 701-709.

Berg, R. C., & Denison, E. (2012). *Effectiveness of interventions designed to prevent Female Genital Mutilation/Cutting: a systematic review*. Studies in family planning, 43(2), 135-146.

Besnier, N., & Alexeyeff, K. (Eds.). (2014). *Gender on the edge: Transgender, gay, and other Pacific Islanders*. Hong Kong University Press.

Bills, M. A., & Hayes, B. E. (2022). *The association between adherence to sexist beliefs and traditional family norms, religion, and attitudes toward sexual minorities*. Journal of Homosexuality, 69(3), 499-524.

Blosnich, J. R., Cassese, E. C., Friedman, M. R., Coulter, R. W., Sang, J. M., Matthews, D. D., & Mair, C. (2019). *Religious freedom restoration acts and sexual minority population health in the United States*. American Journal of Orthopsychiatry, 89(6), 675.

Blosnich, J. R., Farmer, G. W., Lee, J. G., Silenzio, V. M., & Bowen, D. J. (2014). *Health inequalities among sexual minority adults: evidence from ten US states, 2010*. American journal of preventive medicine, 46(4), 337-349.

Bogdan, H., & Lewis, J. R. (2014). *Introduction: Sexuality and New Religious Movements*. In Sexuality and New Religious Movements (pp. 1-8). New York: Palgrave Macmillan US.

Bolz-Weber, N. (2019). *Shameless: A sexual reformation*. Convergent Books.

Booth, C. (2015). *In bed with the ancient Egyptians*. Amberley Publishing Limited.

Borde, C., & Malovany-Chevallier, S. (1949). *The second sex; Simone De Beauvoir*.

Bottéro, J. (2001). *Religion in ancient Mesopotamia*. (T. Lavender-Fagan, Trans.). University of Chicago Press.

Brecher, E. M., Masters, W. H., & Johnson, V. E. (1969). *The sex researchers*. (No Title).

Brenna, V. L. (2013, May 8). Gender & power: Yoruba, Maasai, Igbo. *Women & Religion in Africa*. University of Vermont. https://blog.uvm.edu/vlbrenna-rel163/gender-power/

Brereton, V. L., & Bendroth, M. L. (2001). *Secularization and gender: An historical approach to women and religion in the twentieth century*. Method & theory in the study of religion, 13(1-4), 209-223.

Brewer, D. J., & Teeter, E. (2007). *Egypt and the Egyptians*. Cambridge University Press.

Brodie, J. F. (1994). *Contraception and abortion in nineteenth-century America*. Cornell University Press.

Browning, D. S., Green, M. C., & Witte, J. Jr. (Eds.). (2006). *Sex, marriage, and family in world religions*. Columbia University Press.

Brownmiller, S. (1993). *Against our will: Men, women, and rape*. Ballantine Books.

Bystydzienski, J. M. (2011). *Intercultural couples: Crossing boundaries, negotiating difference*. NYU Press.

Cafaro, P. (2012). *Climate ethics and population policy*. Wiley Interdisciplinary Reviews: Climate Change, 3(1), 45-61.

Cairns-Smith, S., Jaffe, H. K., & Speidel, J. J. *Contraceptive technology is failing to meet the needs of people in the US because of under-investment in new methods*. Contraception.

Cajete, G. (1994*). Look to the Mountain: An Ecology of Indigenous Education*. Kivaki Press.

Casillas, C. J., Enns, P. K., & Wohlfarth, P. C. (2011). *How public opinion constrains the US Supreme Court*. American Journal of Political Science, 55(1), 74-88.

Catholics for Choice. (2018). *Humanae Vitae and the damage done: How the Vatican's ban on birth control hurt the world* (Report). https://www.catholicsforchoice.org/wp-content/uploads/2018/07/CFC-HumanVitae-13.pdf

Chong, K. H. (2020). *Deliverance and submission: Evangelical women and the negotiation of patriarchy in South Korea* (Vol. 309). Brill.

Coen-Sanchez, K., Ebenso, B., El-Mowafi, I. M., Berghs, M., Idriss-Wheeler, D., & Yaya, S. (2022). *Repercussions of overturning Roe v. Wade for women across systems and beyond borders*. Reproductive Health, 19(1), 184.

Colapinto, J. (2000). *As nature made him: The boy who was raised as a girl*. HarperCollins Publishers.

Cotter, D., Hermsen, J. M., & Vanneman, R. (2011). *The end of the gender revolution? Gender role attitudes from 1977 to 2008*. American Journal of Sociology, 117(1), 259–289.

Cox, L. R. (2015). *Religion and sexuality: The historical and current impact on mental health*. Journal of Religion and Health, 54(5), 1657–1668.

Dawson, C. (1991). *Religion and the rise of Western culture: The classic study of medieval civilization*. BoD–Books on Demand.

Deming, W. (2004). *Paul on marriage and celibacy: The Hellenistic background of 1 Corinthians 7*. Wm. B. Eerdmans Publishing.

Dollahite, D. C., & Lambert, N. M. (2007). *Forsaking all others: How religious involvement promotes marital fidelity in Christian, Jewish, and Muslim couples*. Review of Religious Research, 290–307.

Dossie Easton, & Janet W. Hardy. (2009). *The ethical slut: A practical guide to polyamory, open relationships & other adventures*. Random House LLC.

Downs, A. (2005). *The Velvet Rage: What it Really Means to Grow Up Gay in a Straight Man's World*. Da Capo Lifelong Books.

Edström, M., & Svensson, E. M. (2023). *Promoting Gender Equality in Media Content: A Limitation or Extension of Freedom of Expression?*. The Handbook of Gender, Communication, and Women's Human Rights, 193–211.

Ellingson, S., & Green, M. C. (Eds.). (2002). *Religion and sexuality in cross-cultural perspective*. Routledge.

Esposito, J. L. (1998). *Islam: The straight path (3rd ed.).* Oxford University Press.

Farley, M. A. (2006). *Just love: A framework for Christian sexual ethics.* Continuum.

Ferrero, M. (2021). *From polytheism to monotheism: Zoroaster and some economic theory.* Homo Oeconomicus.

Fisher, H. E. (1982). *The sex contract: The Evolution of human behaviour.* (No Title).

Fisher, H. E. (1992). *Anatomy of love: The natural history of monogamy, adultery, and divorce.* (No Title).

Ford, J. V., & Coleman, E. (2023). *Gender diversity, gender liminality in French Polynesia.* International Journal of Transgender Health, 25(4), 926–942.https://doi.org/10.1080/26895269.2023.2291128

Forman-Rabinovici, A., & Sommer, U. (2018). *An impediment to gender equality? Religion's influence on development and reproductive policy.* World Development, 105, 48–58.

Gnuse, R. (1999). *The emergence of monotheism in ancient Israel: A survey of recent scholarship.* Religion, 29(4), 315–336.

Goudsouzian, C. E. (2012). *Becoming Isis: Myth, magic, medicine, and reproduction in ancient Egypt.* The University of Memphis.

Graham, M., Haintz, G. L., McKenzie, H., Lippi, K., & Bugden, M. (2022, January). *"That's a woman's body, that's a woman's choice": The influence of policy on women's reproductive choices.* In Women's Studies International Forum (Vol. 90, p. 102559). Pergamon.

Gregg, S. E. (2014). *Queer Jesus, straight angels: Complicating 'sexuality' and 'religion' in the International Raëlian Movement.* Sexualities, 17(5–6), 565–582. https://doi.org/10.1177/1363460714526129

Grey, M. (1999). *Feminist theology: A critical theology of liberation.* The Cambridge Companion to Liberation Theology, 89–106.

Guttmacher Institute (2025 fact sheet). *Comprehensive sex education consistently yields better outcomes.* April 25, 2025.

Guttmacher Institute. (2001). *States' implementation of the Section 510 abstinence education program: Fiscal Year 1999*. Perspectives on Sexual and Reproductive Health.

Hall, K. S., Sales, J. M., Komro, K. A., & Santelli, J. (2016). *The state of sex education in the United States*. The Journal of Adolescent Health, 58(6), 595.

Hamilton, M. A. (2014). *God vs. the gavel: The perils of extreme religious liberty*. Cambridge University Press.

Hardman, O. (1924). *The ideals of asceticism: An essay in the comparative study of religion*. London: Society for Promoting Christian Knowledge.

Hare, T. (1999). *ReMembering Osiris: Number, gender, and the word in ancient Egyptian representational systems*. Stanford University Press.

Harris, H., Yancey, G. I., Dawson, K., & Gregory, J. (2020). *Congregational discernment and LGBTQ+ inclusion: Process lessons from 21 congregations*. Religions, 12(1), 25.

Harris, S. (2008). *Letter to a Christian nation*. Vintage.

Haslhofer, E. (2023). *Breaking barriers: Improving access to abortion care in rural Alberta*.

Hedreen, G. (2022). *The nature of beauty in classical antiquity*. Cambridge University Press.

Helland, C. (2007). *The Raëlian Creation. Alien Worlds: Social and Religious Dimensions of Extraterrestrial Contact*, 275.

Hitchens, C. (2008). *God is not great: How religion poisons everything*. McClelland & Stewart.

Homer-Dixon, T. F. (1994). *Environmental scarcities and violent conflict: Evidence from cases*. International Security, 19(1), 5–40.

Horn, M. J., Piedmont, R. L., Fialkowski, G. M., Wicks, R. J., & Hunt, M. E. (2005). *Sexuality and spirituality: The embodied spirituality scale*. Theology & Sexuality, 12(1), 81–101.

Humanae vitae. (1968). *Encyclical letter of His Holiness Paul VI on the regulation of birth.* Retrieved from https://en.wikipedia.org/wiki/Humanae_vitae

Hunter, J. D. (2010). *To change the world: The irony, tragedy, and possibility of Christianity in the late modern world.* Oxford University Press.

Huntington, S. P. (2004). *The clash of civilizations and the remaking of world order.* Braille Jymico Incorporated.

Ingersoll, J. (2003*). Evangelical Christian women: War stories in the gender battles* (Vol. 1). NYU Press.

Ince, J. (2010). *The politics of lust.* Prometheus Books.

Joseph, S., & Naǧmābādī, A. (Eds.). (2003). *Encyclopedia of Women & Islamic Cultures: Family, body, sexuality and health* (Vol. 3). Brill.

Kama Sutra of Vatsyayana, Translated by Sir Richard Burton. (1883). *Kama Sutra of Vatsyayana.* Reprint, Cosimo Classics, 2008.

Kaufman, M. R., Eschliman, E. L., & Karver, T. S. (2023). *Differentiating sex and gender in health research to achieve gender equity.* Bulletin of the World Health Organization, 101(10), 666.

Kaufmann, E. (2010). *Shall the religious inherit the earth?: Demography and politics in the twenty-first century.* Profile Books.

King, E., Hebl, M., Corrington, A., Dhanani, L., Holmes IV, O., Lindsey, A. P., … & Thoroughgood, C. (2024). *Understanding and addressing the health implications of anti-LGBTQ+ legislation.* Occupational Health Science, 8(1), 1–41.

Kingsley, A. (2024). *The Fight for Reproductive Rights: An Analysis of State Attorneys General Tools.*

Knapp, C. (2013). *Sexuality and religion: What's the connection?* Psychology Today.

Knowles, J., & Reed, C. (2019). *How Sex Got Screwed Up.*

Knust, J. W. (2011). *Unprotected texts: The Bible's surprising contradictions about sex and desire.* HarperOne.

Kohler, P. K., Manhart, L. E., & Lafferty, W. E. (2008). *Abstinence-only and comprehensive sex education and the initiation of sexual activity and teen pregnancy*. Journal of Adolescent Health, 42(4), 344–351.

Landy, U., & Darney, P. D. *Pregnancy termination and potential psychiatric outcomes*.

Lapinkivi, P. (2004). *The Sumerian sacred marriage in the light of comparative evidence*. The Neo-Assyrian Text Corpus Project.

Leavitt, C. E., Allsop, D. B., Price, A. A., Marks, L. D., & Dollahite, D. C. (2021). *Exploring gender roles in highly religious families*. Review of Religious Research, 63(4), 511–533.

Lee, J. (2012). *Torn: Rescuing the Gospel from the Gays-vs. Christians Debate*. New York, NY: Jericho.

Leeming, D. (2003). *Religion and sexuality: The perversion of a natural marriage*. Journal of Religion and Health, 42(1), 101–109.

Lefevor, G. T., Davis, E. B., Paiz, J. Y., & Smack, A. C. (2021). *The relationship between religiousness and health among sexual minorities: A meta-analysis*. Psychological Bulletin, 147(7), 647.

Leick, G. (2008). *Sexuality and religion in Mesopotamia*. Religion Compass, 2(2), 119–133.

Levine, J. (2006). *Harmful to minors: The perils of protecting children from sex* (p. 617). Minneapolis: University of Minnesota Press.

Logan, F. D. (2012). *A History of the Church in the Middle Ages*. Routledge.

Mahoney, A. (2010). *Religion in families, 1999–2009: A relational spirituality framework*. Journal of Marriage and Family, 72(4), 805–827.

Masters, William. "H. and Virginia E. Johnson." *Human Sexual Response* (1966).

McAloney, K. (2013). *Inter-faith relationships in Great Britain: Prevalence and implications for psychological well-being*. Mental Health, Religion & Culture, 16(7), 686–694.

McGrath, A. E. (2013). *Christian history: An introduction.* John Wiley & Sons.

McKeown, J. (2014). *God's babies: Natalism and Bible interpretation in modern America* (p. 260). Open Book Publishers.

Millett, K. (2016). *Sexual politics.* Columbia University Press.

Moon, J. W. (2021). *Why are world religions so concerned with sexual behavior?* Current Opinion in Psychology, 40, 15–19.

Moriber, D. (2009). *A Right to Bare All? Female Public Toplessness and Dealing with the Laws That Prohibit.* Cardozo Pub. L. Pol'y & Ethics J., 8, 453.

Mumford, S. D. (1984). *American Democracy & the Vatican: Population Growth & National Security.* Humanist Press.

Myers, C. K. (2022). *Confidential and legal access to abortion and contraception in the USA, 1960–2020.* Journal of Population Economics, 35(4), 1385–1441.

Nagoski, E. (2015). *Come as you are: The surprising new science that will transform your sex life.* Simon and Schuster.

NeJaime, D., & Siegel, R. (2018). *Religious exemptions and antidiscrimination law in Masterpiece Cakeshop.* Yale LJF, 128, 201.

Neusner, J. (1988). *The Mishnah: A new translation.* Yale University Press.

Nissinen & Uro (Eds.). *Sacred Marriages: The divine-human sexual metaphor.* De Gruyter.

North, J. (2010). *Pagan ritual and monotheism. In One God: Pagan monotheism in the Roman Empire.* Obstetrics and Gynecology, 19(5), 446–452.

Omar, H. A., & Greydanus, D. E. (2021). *Death before birth: Issues of pregnancy termination.* Journal of Pain Management, 14(4), 289–297.

Ormand, K. (2008*). Controlling desires: Sexuality in ancient Greece and Rome.* Bloomsbury Publishing USA.

Palmer, S. (2011). *The New Heretics of France: Minority Religions, la Republique, and the Government-Sponsored "War on Sects"*. Oxford University Press.

PEN America. (2023). *America's Censored Classrooms 2023*: Educational Gag Orders.

Pinch, G. (2004). *Egyptian myth: A very short introduction*. Oxford University Press.

Poloma, M. M., & Pendleton, B. F. (1991). *The effects of prayer and prayer experiences on measures of general weil-being.* Journal of Psychology and Theology, 19(1), 71-83.

Pongratz-Leisten, B. (2008). *Sacred marriage and the transfer of divine knowledge: Alliances between the gods and the king in ancient Mesopotamia.* In Powers, J. (1995). A Concise Encyclopedia of Buddhism. Oneworld Publications.

Punt, J. (2016). *Engaging Empire with the body: Rethinking Pauline celibacy.* Journal of Early Christian History, 6(3), 43-66.

Ramadan, T. (2003). *Western Muslims and the future of Islam.* Oxford University Press.

Ryan, C., & Jethá, C. (2010). *Sex at dawn: The prehistoric origins of modern sexuality.* New York, NY: Harper.

Saadeh, L. (1962). *The fertility cult in Mesopotamia, Egypt, and Phoenicia* (Publication No. 27550257) [Doctoral dissertation, American University of Beirut]. ProQuest Dissertations & Theses.

Sanday, P. R. (1981). *Female power and male dominance: On the origins of sexual inequality.* Cambridge University Press.

Schwartzman, M. (2012). *What if religion is not special.* U. Chi. L. Rev., 79, 1351.

Selz, G. J. (2000). *Five divine ladies: Thoughts on Inanna(k), Ishtar, In(n)in(a), Annunitum, and Anat and the origin of the title "Queen of Heaven".* NIN Journal of Gender Study in Antiquity, 1, 29-62.

Shell-Duncan, B., & Hernlund, Y. (Eds.). (2000). *Female" circumcision" in Africa: culture, controversy, and change*. Lynne Rienner Publishers.

Smith, L. T. (2021). *Decolonizing methodologies: Research and indigenous peoples*. Bloomsbury Publishing.

Sobrero, E. (2023). *The demonization of women's health and the criminalization of abortion*: a health security threat and violation of human rights.

Sohn, A. (2021). *The man who hated women: Sex, censorship, and civil liberties in the Gilded age*. Farrar, Straus and Giroux.

Sonfield, A., & Gold, R. B. (2001). *States' implementation of the section 510 abstinence education program,* FY 1999. Family Planning Perspectives, 166-171.

Stanger-Hall, K. F., & Hall, D. W. (2011). *Abstinence-only education and teen pregnancy rates: Why we need comprehensive sex education in the US*. PloS one, 6(10), e24658.

Storey, B. (2013). *Montaigne, Secularism, and the Enlightenment*. Enlightenment and Secularism: Essays on the Mobilization of Reason, 115-27.

Swan, L. E. (2021). *The impact of US policy on contraceptive access: a policy analysis*. Reproductive Health, 18, 1-14.

Tal, A. (2016). *The land is full: Addressing overpopulation in Israel*. Yale University Press.

Tangney, J. P., & Dearing, R. L. (2002). *Shame and guilt*. Guilford Press. New York, NY.

Taylor, C. (2014). *How to define secularism. In Boundaries of toleration* (pp. 59-78). Columbia University Press.

The Washington Post: *Whose 'utmost, sincere convictions' matter to the Supreme Court?* The Washington Post. (2025, July 4).

Theology of the Body: Nuptial meaning of the body. (n.d.). Retrieved from https://www.giftofself.ca/pope-john-paul-iis-theology-body/

Thompson, G. (2024). *Declining Approval in the Supreme Court of the United States.*

Thoreson, R. R. (2018). *"All We Want is Equality": Religious Exemptions and Discrimination Against LGBT People in the United States.* Human Rights Watch.

Todd, N. R., McConnell, E. A., Odahl-Ruan, C. A., & Houston-Kolnik, J. D. (2017). *Christian campus-ministry groups at public universities and opposition to same-sex marriage.* Psychology of Religion and Spirituality, 9(4), 412.

United Nations Children's Fund, & Gupta, G. R. (2013). *Female genital mutilation/cutting: a statistical overview and exploration of the dynamics of change.* Reproductive Health Matters, 184-190.

Wadud, A. (1999). *Qur'an and woman: Rereading the sacred text from a woman's perspective.* Oxford University Press.

Walker, G. (2016). *Celibacy and misogyny. In Predatory Priests, Silenced Victims* (pp. 213-230). Routledge.

Wang, A., Wong, N., & Yuksel, Y. (2025). *"Ripe for Reexamination": Fulton, Smith, and the Future of Free Exercise.* LETTER FROM THE EXECUTIVE EDITORS, 51.

Weitzer, R. (2009). *Sex for sale: Prostitution, pornography, and the sex industry.* Routledge.

Westenholz, J. G. (2007). *Inanna and Ishtar in the Babylonian world.* In G. Leick (Ed.), The Babylonian World (pp. 332-347). Routledge.

Wilcox, W. B. (2004). *Soft patriarchs, new men: How Christianity shapes fathers and husbands* (Vol. 880). University of Chicago Press.

Wilkins, C. L., Wellman, J. D., Toosi, N. R., Miller, C. A., Lisnek, J. A., & Martin, L. A. (2022). *Is LGBT progress seen as an attack on Christians?: Examining Christian/sexual orientation zero-sum beliefs.* Journal of personality and social psychology, 122(1), 73.

Wilson, E. J. (1994). *'Holiness' and 'Purity' in Mesopotamia.* Neukirchner Verlag. Fertility cult (n.d.). In Britannica Online Encyclopedia.

Wimbush, V. L., & Valantasis, R. (Eds.). (2002). *Asceticism.* Oxford University Press.

Winkler, M. M., & Bantekas, I. (2024). *The criminalization of sexual minorities in international human rights law: an appraisal.* Human Rights Law Review, 25(2), ngaf017.

World Health Organization. (2008). *Eliminating female genital mutilation: an interagency statement*-OHCHR, UNAIDS, UNDP, UNECA, UNESCO, UNFPA, UNHCR, UNICEF, UNIFEM, WHO. World Health Organization.

World Health Organization. (2022). *Female genital mutilation.* https://www.who.int/news-room/fact-sheets/detail/female-genital-mutilation

Yahya, S., & Boag, S. (2014). *"My family would crucify me!": The perceived influence of social pressure on cross-cultural and interfaith dating and marriage.* Sexuality & Culture, 18, 759-772.

Yarhouse, M. A., & Tan, E. S. (2004). *Sexual identity synthesis: Attributions, meaning-making, and the search for congruence.* University Press of America.

Appendices

Appendix A: Links to Legal Cases

1- Roe v. Wade (1973)

ACLU History: The Roe v. Wade Era

https://www.aclu.org/documents/aclu-history-roe-v-wade-era

2- Dobbs v. Jackson Women's Health Organization

https://www.aclu.org/cases/dobbs-v-jackson-womens-health-organization

3- Establishment Clause of the First Amendment

https://www.law.cornell.edu/wex/establishment_clause

4- Griswold v. Connecticut (1965)

On the Anniversary of Griswold, the Facts about Contraception

https://www.aclu.org/news/religious-liberty/anniversary-griswold-facts-about-contraception

5- Lawrence v. Texas: A Watershed for Gay Rights

https://www.aclu.org/documents/aclu-history-lawrence-v-texas-watershed-gay-rights

6- Obergefell v. Hodges (2015)—Freedom to Marry in Ohio

https://www.aclu.org/cases/obergefell-et-al-v-hodges-freedom-marry-ohio

7- Social Security Beneficiary 2nd Amendment Rights Protection Act

https://www.aclu.org/documents/aclu-endorses-hr-3516-social-security-beneficiary-2nd

8- Guttmacher Institute, 2025 Fact Sheet

https://www.guttmacher.org/united-states/fact-sheets

9- Parental Rights in Education Act, often called the Parents Bill of Rights Act

https://www.congress.gov/bill/118th-congress/house-bill/5/text

10- PEN America's 2023 report

https://pen.org/report/americas-censored-classrooms-2023/

11- Masterpiece Cakeshop, Ltd. v. Colorado Civil Rights Commission (2018)

https://www.aclu.org/cases/masterpiece-cakeshop-v-colorado-civil-rights-commission

12- Fulton v. City of Philadelphia (2021)

https://www.aclu.org/cases/fulton-v-city-philadelphia

13- Employment Division v. Smith (1990)

https://www.aclu-or.org/en/cases/smith-v-employment-division

14- 303 Creative, Inc. v. Elenis

https://www.aclu.org/cases/303-creative-inc-v-elenis

15- Carson v. Makin

https://www.aclu.org/cases/carson-v-makin

16- Kennedy v. Bremerton School District

https://www.aclu.org/cases/kennedy-v-bremerton

17- Engel v. Vitale (1962)

ACLU History: Defending Separation

https://www.aclu.org/documents/aclu-history-defending-separation

18- Lee v. Weisman (1992)

https://www.riaclu.org/cases/weisman-v-lee/

19- Project Blitz

https://www.blitzwatch.org/

20- City of Boerne v. Flores, Archbishop of San Antonio, et al.

https://www.aclu.org/cases/city-boerne-v-flores-archbishop-san-antonio-et-al

21- ACLU -- 5 things to know about 'conversion therapy'

https://www.aclu.org/documents/exodus-positions-against-reparative-therapy-and-ex-gay-movement

More Reading

Say No to Religious Instruction in Public Schools

https://www.acluwv.org/en/news/say-no-religious-instruction-public-schools

State Justices Speak Out Against Originalism

https://statecourtreport.org/our-work/analysis-opinion/state-justices-speak-out-against-originalism?utm_source=chatgpt.com

When the Supreme Court Takes Away a Long-Held Constitutional Right

https://www.newyorker.com/news/daily-comment/when-the-supreme-court-takes-away-a-long-held-constitutional-right

Supreme Court Overturns *Roe v. Wade,* Undoing Constitutional Right to Abortion

https://time.com/6189476/abortion-supreme-court-overturns-roe-v-wade/

Georgia GOP senators seek to ban sexually explicit books from school libraries, reduce sex education

https://apnews.com/article/georgia-education-sex-education-libraries-librarians-commandments-4436ab03a82807f2dab15a3047947177

A Christian group teaches public school students during the school day. Their footprint is growing

https://apnews.com/article/indiana-lifewise-public-school-religion-d7cf2b67b2ae3b7919e0a21f89ce80c0

Appendix B: Indictment: *Monotheism is Responsible for the Greatest Crimes Against Humanity*

(Rael)

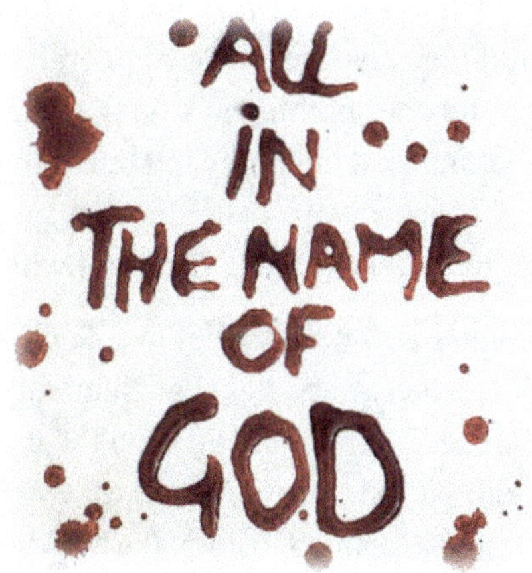

The only solution to terrorism is for science to replace religion

"Education and atheism are the most important weapons to fight terrorism. Remember: there is no such thing as an atheist terrorist. Because when you don't believe in god and heaven, you have nothing to die for, and you are just willing to live happily as long as possible and make the life of other human beings better."—**Rael**

After the tragedy of the terrorist attack in New York, it is important to understand why such things can happen. It is important to go back to the root of this evil and not just be satisfied with simplified answers which don't disturb anyone, answers that are "politically correct" but will only perpetuate the problem.

Acts of violence and military retribution will not solve the problem but will beget more hatred, more desperate people, and more violence, thus creating a truly vicious cycle of terror.

On the one hand, we have mad men in complete mystical delirium flying an airplane against a building filled with people while shouting: "God is Great" and dedicating their crime to Him, and on the other hand, we have people who are praying to this same imaginary God to try to forget the suffering of which they are the victims.

But the real danger is undoubtedly this belief in an Almighty God who does absolutely nothing either for or against humans... He does nothing to destroy buildings, nor does he need people who believe in Him to fly suicide airplanes and does nothing to stop these suicide airplanes and protect the innocent victims who then pray to Him with the conviction that He is "by their side…" It has always been this way. Armies on each side of the battlefield have all pretended that "God was with them…"

The truth of the matter is that this belief in a single and Almighty God is the very cause of the greatest tragedies that Humanity has known. From the colonization of Europe by Muslims, through the crusades, the wars of religion, the Inquisition, Nazism, up until today, with the wars between Pakistan and India, Cyprus, Ireland, Kosovo, the Middle East, everywhere, it's always in the name of an Almighty God that people tear each other to pieces and kill one another.

The root of evil is in this very belief in this God described sometimes cynically as a "merciful and loving God," especially in the writings that we attribute to Him, but were always, of course, written by men who, through the Ages, distorted these writings according to their prejudices and own interests.

For instance, the Qur'an asks Muslims to kill or abduct all those who refuse to become members of their belief. This is the precise and official text given by their "Prophet:"

"But once the sacred months have passed away, then slay the idolaters wherever you find them, and take them captives and besiege them and lie in wait for them in every ambush, then if they repent and keep up prayer and pay the poor-rate, leave their way free to them; surely Allah is Forgiving, Merciful." **Qur'an, surah IX, 5**

Islam officially encourages racism and discrimination which is contrary to Human Rights and democratic laws:

"O you who believe! Do not take the Jews and the Christians for friends; they are friends of each other; and whoever amongst you takes them for a friend, then surely, he is one of them; surely Allah does not guide the unjust people." **Qur'an, surah V, 51**

Finally, also considered against Human Rights and against the right to Democracy, Islam demands that their followers engage in domestic violence using the excuse that men are superior to women!

"Men are the maintainers of women because Allah has made some of them to excel others and because they spend out of their property; the good women are therefore obedient, guarding the unseen as Allah has guarded; and (as to) those on whose part you fear desertion, admonish them, and leave them alone in the sleeping-places and beat them." **Qur'an, surah IV, 34**

Is it acceptable for whatever religion to officially encourage three actions that are contrary to Human Rights and to Laws of Democracy: encouraging murder, racial discrimination, and domestic violence?

Surely if a New Age "cult" advocated these same things, its leader would most likely be thrown in jail... Mystico-religious delirium does not give the right to not respect Laws of democratic countries and Human Rights.

The only solution, as I have sought after for more than 20 years, is for all the old and new religious texts from traditional religions and religious minorities to be censored so as to expurgate from them all writings that do not respect Human Rights and Laws of democratic countries or encourage hatred and violence.

But more importantly, such texts must no longer be taught to children! Because the fact is that while the world cries over the victims of Manhattan, there are children who are receiving a religious education that will turn them into the terrorists of tomorrow, who will in turn create new strife among different religious schools.

At the dawn of this new era that will make this Earth a paradise thanks to science, it is time to permanently destroy or at least silence, through a firm and rigorous censorship, any ideology that encourages hatred and violence.

All the "politically correct" condemnations of terrorism will not change anything if they do not tackle the problem at its very root, i.e., eliminate or censor monotheistic religious teachings that always result in fanaticism.

At the same time, thanks to new technologies, we can seriously expect revolutions in our way of life such as: healing all the diseases and feeding the entire planet thanks to genetics, no longer having to work thanks to nanotechnology and robotics, and even living eternally thanks to reproductive cloning. It is inconceivable that backward beliefs coming from the depths of the Ages continue to make this planet a world of suffering, violence, and darkness as in the Middle Ages.

It is time for humans to replace monotheism with science, which should become our only religion.

Appendix C: Demanding Accountability: *An Appeal to the United Nations to Expurgate Human Rights Violations from All Religious Texts*

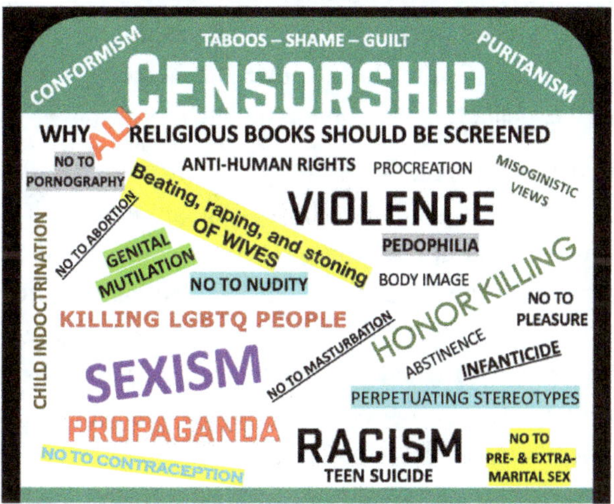

"All spiritual leaders of all faiths, majority and minority, should gather under the aegis of the Universal Declaration of Human Rights and submit their religious writings to an independent international committee responsible to eradicate all the passages not respecting the principles of the Universal Declaration of Human Rights."—**Rael**

More than four decades ago, Rael boldly proposed to the United Nations a visionary and deeply ethical initiative: the systematic expurgation of all passages within religious texts that contravene fundamental human rights. At the heart of this proposal lies a profound commitment to peace, dignity, and universal justice. It calls for the removal of verses and injunctions—regardless of tradition or scripture—that incite hatred, justify violence, encourage discrimination, or promote sexism, homophobia, or murder. Far from being an attack on religion, this appeal is an urgent plea for spiritual responsibility in which religious teachings evolve to uphold, rather than undermine, the values of modern humanity.

Still urgently relevant today, Rael's proposal offers a framework for reexamining sacred writings in light of the globally accepted principles enshrined in the Universal Declaration of Human Rights. It urges religious leaders, scholars, and followers alike to take moral accountability for the content of their texts, ensuring that no verse, no matter how ancient, is used to legitimize cruelty, oppression, or inequality. By confronting the problematic elements of scripture and removing or denouncing them, and by focusing on the positive aspects of religious teachings, faith traditions can begin to heal the rifts they have sometimes helped to create and foster a more inclusive, peaceful, and compassionate world.

This initiative also calls on religious institutions to bring their doctrines into ethical alignment with the 21st century. Such a process of moral modernization is not only necessary to maintain the credibility of faith traditions in pluralistic societies; it is essential to building a world where religion contributes to liberation rather than subjugation. Sacred texts must no longer be treated as unchallengeable monoliths, but instead, they must be viewed as living documents that are subject to interpretation, reflection, and, when necessary, revision in light of evolving human conscience.

Furthermore, Rael's proposal highlights the need for transreligious dialogue and global cooperation. By involving the United Nations and other international bodies, this initiative elevates the discussion to a planetary scale, asserting that human rights are not the possession of any one nation, culture, or creed, but belong equally to all members of the human family. The international community has both the moral authority and the responsibility to ensure that no belief system, however ancient, remains above the standards of universal justice.

Ultimately, this call for expurgation reflects a deeply humanistic vision: one in which spiritual traditions, instead of dividing humanity through rigid dogmas or archaic commandments, unite people around shared values of love, equality, and peace. Rael's initiative challenges religious leaders and followers not to abandon their faith, but to refine it, thus, consciously removing the elements that harm and elevating those that heal. In doing so, religious teachings can become powerful instruments for global harmony, mutual respect, and the flourishing of all human beings.

Appendix D: Paradism: *Forging a Path toward a Remarkable Future for Everyone*

(www.paradism.org)

Paving the way for a new era of abundance and freedom

"Cooperation is the future of humanity, with everybody working for the good of everybody ... and when Paradism will be in place there will no longer be any money, as money is the fruit of power and government. In the future, and very soon, everyone will bring their money to public places and burn it all. We don't need it if everybody works for the good of everybody else and everyone helps each other. The future of society is to do without money because money is only a poison given to you by the government."—**Rael**

It is no coincidence that the institutions most resistant to comprehensive sexuality education have also historically resisted scientific progress. Traditional religions, particularly the Catholic Church, have often placed theological dogma above empirical evidence, thereby hindering the evolution of thought and the development of life-enhancing technologies. In direct response to this regressive trend, Paradism, a socio-economic system introduced by Rael in 2009, offers a transformative future where science and technology are fully harnessed to create a society liberated from work, money, and inequality, and to serve the well-being of all humanity.

Unlike the anti-science posture that has marked much of religious history, Paradism embraces the power of innovation as the catalyst for social and planetary transformation. It asserts that religion has no place in the governance of scientific development—a position rooted not in hostility to faith, but in an unwavering commitment to human progress. In a world teetering on the edge of ecological collapse, technological inequality, and economic injustice, Paradism emerges as a vital evolutionary leap and a blueprint for universal well-being.

The dangers of religious obstruction are not theoretical; they are historical. From the persecution of Galileo for advocating heliocentrism to the tragic execution of Giordano Bruno in 1600—whose radical cosmological and philosophical ideas, as well as his visionary belief in an infinite universe filled with countless worlds and a pantheistic worldview, truly challenged the Church's cosmic and theological monopoly— religious authorities have repeatedly placed orthodoxy above inquiry. Bruno's ideas, revolutionary for their time, undermined core Christian dogmas, including the uniqueness of Christ, the nature of the Trinity, and the then-endorsed geocentric model of the universe. His fate, burned alive for heresy, serves as a cautionary tale in which when power fears knowledge, the result is brutality and death, not enlightenment.

The Raelian Movement proposes an alternative path, one that celebrates science as a tool of compassion, not control. In a Paradism society, automation, robotics, and artificial intelligence would eliminate the need for dehumanizing labor, allowing individuals to pursue creativity, exploration, joy, and happiness. Genetic engineering and nanotechnologies would eradicate disease and extend the quality of life. Renewable energy would power sustainable, eco-conscious communities. These are not utopian fantasies, but rather logical outcomes of liberating science from dogmatic constraint and using it to benefit everyone.

The moral imperative is clear: religious interference in science has cost humanity dearly through suppressed knowledge, delayed progress, and the denial of technologies that could have alleviated suffering and saved lives. Paradism calls for a decisive separation between spiritual institutions and scientific domains. Only by removing outdated religious ideologies from decision-making processes can we ensure that scientific advancements are harnessed for the common good.

Moreover, Paradism is not merely a technological vision but an ethical one. It advocates for a system rooted in sharing, compassion, and cooperation, rather than competition, exploitation, or scarcity. It offers a model where artificial intelligence does not replace humanity, but rather enhances it, where abundance replaces survival, and freedom replaces servitude. It is a world where technology amplifies our capacity to love, to connect, and to evolve.

The Raelian Movement's call to keep religion out of science and its endorsement of Paradism are based on the conviction that humanity's survival depends not on economic growth or military might, but on emotional intelligence, planetary stewardship, and the ethical use of science. A civilization that continues to be guided by fear-based dogmas, whether about sex, knowledge, or power, will inevitably self-destruct. Paradism offers the antidote—a peaceful, prosperous, and harmonious society driven by the pursuit of knowledge and innovation, and in which every individual can blossom.

And so, we must ask ourselves, not rhetorically but with radical sincerity, why would we not embrace this vision? A world without poverty or war. A planet healed by ecological wisdom and scientific clarity. A society where love and happiness are not luxuries, but daily realities. In the words of Rael, Paradism is not only possible, but it is necessary. So, let us rise to the opportunity of this evolutionary moment and create paradise on Earth, not through prayer or punishment, but through consciousness, compassion, and collective intelligence. The future is not something we await but something we build together.

Appendix E: Raelian Values: *The Tree of Life of the 21st Century*

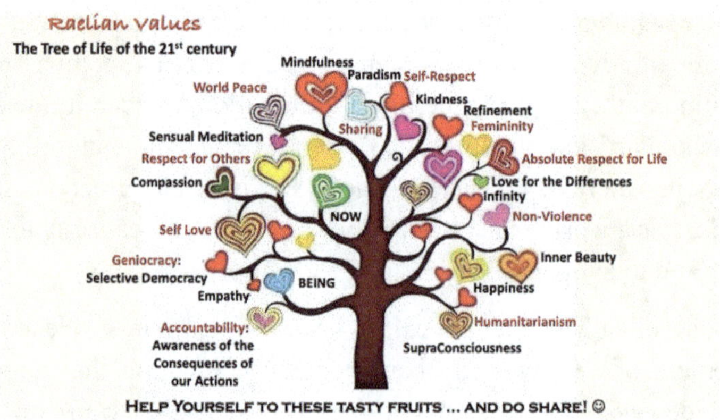

SELF-RESPECT

In the Raelian philosophy, self-respect involves maintaining a healthy lifestyle rooted in harmony with nature. Key practices include meditation, which fosters inner peace and connects individuals with their higher consciousness; relaxation, which helps maintain mental and emotional balance; and a healthy diet, which nourishes the body and supports optimal functioning.

Drugs, tobacco, and alcohol should be avoided since these substances destroy our genetic code and can cause defects for generations to come. Avoiding these harmful substances is also an expression of respect for the delicate and intricate design of our bodies. By maintaining a pure and healthy body, Raelians believe that they honor the work of the Elohim. This commitment to self-care and genetic preservation reflects a deep understanding of the interconnectedness of all life and the importance of each individual in the broader tapestry of human existence.

SELF-LOVE

In the Raelian philosophy, self-love is a fundamental value that underpins our ability to live authentically, embrace our true selves, and cultivate a sense of inner peace and fulfillment. Accepting ourselves as we are, with all our imperfections, is to live out what we are, feel good about ourselves, open up to life, and blossom. This principle contributes to the development of healthy and positive thoughts, cultivates compassion toward oneself and others, strips away all forms of aggression, and enables us to interact with the world from a place of kindness and understanding. Guilt and fear only lead to stress and the secretion of toxic substances within our body that are harmful to our health and can damage our genetic code. Self-love is only possible through both an awareness of these emotions and the rejection of stress.

Ultimately, self-love is much more than a feel-good practice—it is a spiritual responsibility. It forms the basis of a vibrant and enlightened life, allowing each person to honor the extraordinary gift of life bestowed by the Elohim. By loving ourselves deeply and authentically, we align with the true purpose of our existence and contribute to the collective evolution of humanity. Through this inner transformation, we become more capable of peace, creativity, and joy, fulfilling the role we were designed to play in the vast universe.

SHARING

In the Raelian philosophy, sharing is a core value that reflects the deep interconnectedness of all human beings and the importance of collective well-being. The principle of sharing is rooted in the belief that every individual, by virtue of their humanity, is entitled to certain basic necessities throughout their life. These include access to sufficient food, shelter, clothing, and education, even without working.

However, sharing extends beyond the provision of basic needs. It encompasses a broader vision of societal progress, where those who contribute through their work are entitled to enjoy the fruits of their labor, and where luxury is not seen as an indulgence but as a vital motivator that drives human creativity, innovation, and progress. It is through the pursuit of luxury that humanity is propelled forward, constantly striving to improve and evolve.

Ultimately, sharing is about creating a world where resources, opportunities, and rewards are distributed in a way that benefits all members of society. It is a value that champions the well-being of the collective while recognizing and rewarding individual contributions. By embracing sharing as a fundamental principle, the Raelian Movement envisions a future where every human being can thrive, free from the constraints of scarcity and inequality, and where the collective progress of humanity is celebrated and sustained through mutual support and cooperation.

RESPECT FOR OTHERS

In the Raelian philosophy, respect for others is a foundational value that celebrates the diversity of humanity as a source of collective strength and enrichment. This value is rooted in the understanding that the differences among people—whether racial, cultural, religious, or sexual—are not merely to be tolerated, but to be actively embraced and promoted. The Raelian Movement sees the variety within humanity as a reflection of the creativity and complexity of life, each difference adding to the richness of the human experience.

Respect for others involves more than just passive acceptance; it requires an active commitment to encouraging individuals to express their unique identities fully and authentically. By promoting an environment where everyone feels empowered to live out their differences, Raelians believe that society benefits as a whole. This inclusivity fosters a culture of mutual understanding, where people learn from one another and grow through the exchange of diverse perspectives and experiences.

The Raelian emphasis on diversity also aligns with the movement's broader goals of peace and global unity. By respecting and promoting the differences among individuals and communities, Raelians aim to build a world where conflicts rooted in prejudice and intolerance become nonexistent. This respect for diversity is seen as essential for the creation of a harmonious global society, where all people can coexist peacefully, each contributing their unique qualities to the collective human tapestry.

ACCOUNTABILITY

In the Raelian philosophy, accountability is a fundamental value that emphasizes the intrinsic responsibility each individual has for their actions and decisions. This value underscores the belief that all human beings are ultimately responsible for the consequences of their actions, regardless of external pressures or directives. Even when following orders, individuals cannot *abdicate* responsibility for their behavior and must refuse to execute any order if it is contrary to his or her conscience.

Accountability in the Raelian context goes beyond mere acknowledgment of responsibility—it requires active engagement with one's conscience. If an order or action conflicts with an individual's conscience, the Raelian philosophy dictates that they must refuse to carry it out, regardless of the consequences. This principle empowers individuals to act in alignment with their moral compass, promoting integrity and ethical conduct.

This commitment to accountability is also linked to the broader Raelian vision of creating a just and harmonious world. By taking responsibility for their actions and holding themselves accountable, individuals contribute to a society where ethical behavior is the norm and where each person plays an active role in ensuring the well-being of others. This collective accountability fosters a culture of trust, respect, and cooperation, which are essential for the advancement of humanity.

ABSOLUTE RESPECT FOR LIFE

In the Raelian philosophy, absolute respect for life is a core value that underscores the sanctity and inherent worth of every human being. This principle is rooted in the belief that the life of a single, non-violent individual is as valuable as the entirety of humanity itself. To save one life is, in essence, to save all of humanity, as each person represents a unique and irreplaceable manifestation of life's potential.

This value calls for an unwavering commitment to the preservation of life, regardless of the circumstances. Even when faced with arguments or pressures that suggest sacrificing one life for the supposed greater good, the Raelian philosophy asserts that such actions are fundamentally wrong. The life of an innocent person cannot be weighed against any perceived benefits to the collective; to do so would violate the very essence of what it means to respect life.

Absolute respect for life also entails a deep sense of moral responsibility. Raelians are called to protect life in all its forms, rejecting violence and standing against any force or ideology that seeks to justify the taking of innocent lives. This respect extends beyond mere non-violence; it requires actively fostering conditions that allow all individuals to thrive and reach their fullest potential, free from fear and oppression.

In a broader sense, this value is a call to humanity to recognize the interconnectedness of all life and the ethical implications of our actions. By upholding the sanctity of every life, Raelians contribute to a world where compassion, empathy, and justice are the guiding principles. This respect for life is not just a passive stance; it is an active commitment to creating a society where every person is valued, protected, and given the opportunity to live in peace and dignity. By embracing this value, Raelians strive to build a world where life is revered and protected, and where the preservation of even a single life is seen as an achievement of the highest moral order.

FEMININITY

In the Raelian philosophy, femininity is deeply associated with love, compassion, and the nurturing aspects of humanity. It is viewed not only as a characteristic of women but as an essential quality that all human beings should cultivate, regardless of gender. The Raelian Movement believes that the development and expression of femininity are crucial for the creation of a more peaceful and harmonious world.

Femininity is intrinsically linked to love and wisdom. It's important to make this planet more feminine and to be aware that wisdom goes hand-in-hand with femininity. If all human beings on Earth were to become feminine and refined, there would be no more war. If femininity is a cure for humanity and a way to prevent its destruction, then the development of femininity is a necessity. It becomes every human being's responsibility, regardless of gender.

The nurturing and compassionate qualities associated with femininity are seen as pathways to greater understanding and empathy, which are essential for resolving conflicts and fostering global peace. The Raelian philosophy asserts that if more people embraced and embodied feminine qualities, the world would become a more refined, gentle, and peaceful place, free from the violence and aggression that often lead to war.

In this context, femininity is regarded as a cure for the ills of humanity and a vital force in preventing the destruction of our planet. It is not merely a trait to be admired but a necessary quality that must be developed and nurtured in every individual. The Raelian Movement emphasizes that the promotion of femininity is a collective responsibility, transcending traditional gender roles and stereotypes. By encouraging both men and women to embrace feminine qualities, such as love, care, and kindness, the Raelian Movement seeks to create a world where these values are central to human interactions and societal structures.

In a world often dominated by aggressive, competitive, and power-driven behaviors, the Raelian philosophy offers a vision of a future where femininity is celebrated and recognized as a cornerstone of wisdom and peace. This shift towards a more feminine and refined humanity is seen as essential for ensuring the survival and flourishing of the human race.

WORLD PEACE

In the Raelian philosophy, world peace is seen as the ultimate goal for humanity, achievable through the establishment of a unified global government that transcends national boundaries. This world government would be built on principles of respect, inclusivity, and mutual support, ensuring that every culture is represented, honored, and empowered to thrive. By creating such a system, Raelians believe that humanity can move beyond the divisions that have historically led to conflict and war.

This vision for world peace involves the dissolution of national armies, which are often a source of conflict and aggression. In their place, a global army of "peacekeepers" would be established, dedicated not to warfare, but to the preservation of peace and the protection of human rights worldwide. This force would act as a guardian of global stability, intervening only when necessary to prevent violence and uphold the principles of peace that permeate all levels of society.

A significant aspect of this idea is the reallocation of resources currently devoted to military spending. The enormous budgets that nations currently invest in arms and defense could instead be redirected towards addressing the most pressing issues facing humanity, such as hunger, environmental degradation, and poverty. By shifting focus from destruction to preservation and growth, Raelians believe that the world can make significant progress toward eradicating the root causes of conflict and suffering.

This approach to world peace is not just about the absence of war; it is about creating the conditions necessary for a sustainable and just global society. By promoting a culture of peace and cooperation, the Raelian Movement envisions a future where resources are used to uplift all of humanity rather than to fuel competition and conflict. This is in line with the broader Raelian values of love, respect for life, and the pursuit of knowledge and happiness for all.

NON-VIOLENCE

In the Raelian philosophy, non-violence is upheld as an absolute and essential principle that reflects the deepest respect for life and the dignity of all human beings. This value extends beyond the mere absence of physical violence to encompass the rejection of any form of coercion, intimidation, or harm, whether physical, emotional, or psychological. Non-violence is seen as the foundation upon which a just and harmonious society can be built.

This view emphasizes that threats of violence are as reprehensible as acts of violence themselves. A threat, whether expressed verbally or implied through actions, is considered a direct acknowledgment by the individual that they are willing to use violence to impose their will or achieve their objectives. This willingness to resort to violence, even in the form of a threat, is seen as a profound violation of the principles of peace and respect that are central to the Raelian ethos.

In this context, the Raelian Movement advocates for a society where threats of violence are treated with the same severity as actual violent acts. This approach is based on the understanding that the intention behind a threat can be just as harmful as the act of violence itself, as it seeks to undermine the autonomy, security, and well-being of others. By holding individuals accountable for their threats, Raelians believe that society can discourage the use of fear and intimidation as tools of control or manipulation, fostering an environment where peace and mutual respect prevail.

Furthermore, the Raelian commitment to non-violence is rooted in the belief that true progress and understanding can only be achieved through dialogue, empathy, and cooperation. Violence, in any form, is seen as a failure of communication and a breakdown of the human connection that should bind us together. The Raelian Movement encourages the use of peaceful means to resolve conflicts, emphasizing the power of love, reason, and compassion as the most effective tools for creating lasting change and harmony.

HUMANITARIANISM

In the Raelian philosophy, humanitarianism is a central value that embodies the profound commitment to the welfare, dignity, and flourishing of all human beings. This value is rooted in the belief that every person, regardless of their background, beliefs, or circumstances, deserves to live a life of dignity, free from suffering, and with access to the resources and opportunities necessary for their well-being and personal development.

Humanitarianism in the Raelian context goes beyond mere charity or temporary relief efforts. It is a call for systemic change and the creation of a global society that prioritizes the needs of the most vulnerable and disadvantaged. The Raelian Movement advocates for the eradication of poverty, hunger, and inequality, recognizing that these issues are not merely economic problems but fundamental violations of human rights. The goal of humanitarianism is to create a world where every individual can thrive, not just survive.

This commitment to humanitarianism is also closely linked to the Raelian belief in the unity of humanity. Raelians view all people as part of a global family, interconnected and interdependent. As such, the suffering of one is seen as the suffering of all, and the well-being of each individual contributes to the collective well-being of humanity as a whole. This perspective drives the Raelian emphasis on solidarity, compassion, and mutual support, encouraging individuals to take responsibility for the welfare of others, both within their communities and globally.

Moreover, the Raelian view of humanitarianism is deeply intertwined with the movement's broader goals of peace, environmental sustainability, and the use of science and technology. The Raelian Movement believes that advancements in these areas should be harnessed to improve the human condition, reduce suffering, and promote equality. This includes advocating for technologies and policies that address climate change, ensure access to clean water and healthcare, and promote education and economic opportunities for all.

Appendix F: International Happiness Academy: *A Journey Toward True Blossoming*

For over five decades, Maitreya Rael, guided by the wisdom of the Elohim, has invited humanity to awaken to its highest purpose: the pursuit of lasting happiness. At the heart of this transformative teaching lies the practice of Sensual Meditation—a method not only for cultivating inner peace and pleasure but for deepening our understanding of what it truly means to be human in a universe teeming with life, science, and connection.

Across the world, more than 100,000 individuals have already attended the International Happiness Academies—immersive Raelian retreats that do more than stimulate the mind. They open the heart, energize the body, and elevate our consciousness. And what's most telling? People return. Again, and again. Why? Because these are not mere workshops or spiritual getaways. They are deep encounters with the self; infused with pleasure, laughter, happiness, liberating, and profoundly illuminating.

Each six-day immersion is carefully designed to help participants recharge, reconnect, and rediscover their true potential. Through hands-on learning, group transformation sessions, and evenings filled with music, dance, celebration, and delightful cosmic mischief, people bloom into the radiant beings they were always meant to be.

The atmosphere is one of simplicity, kindness, and playful reverence. Within this space of non-judgment, participants from every walk of life— spiritual seekers, scientists, artists, skeptics, lovers, and dreamers—gather as one. Together, they explore the mysteries of the universe, of consciousness, and most intimately, of happiness itself.

What Will You Experience?

• **The Science of Happiness** – Discover cutting-edge research on consciousness, pleasure, and emotional well-being.

• **Mastering Inner Peace** – Learn accessible yet powerful techniques to cultivate serenity, clarity, and emotional resilience.

• **Cultivating Lifelong Happiness** – Uncover the keys to nurturing happiness as a lasting, lived reality—not a fleeting emotion.

Yet the Happiness Academy is not something that can be fully described. It is like a first kiss, the taste of dark chocolate on the tongue, or the hush of waves under a starlit sky. Words fall short. It must be felt. It must be lived.

And when you hear Rael himself— gentle, witty, incredibly funny, and profoundly illuminating —share the path to living with sensuality, compassion, awareness, and freedom, something inside shifts. For many, it becomes the most profound and personal spiritual experience of their lives.

The Happiness Academy is not about believing. It is about feeling. About awakening. About connecting—to yourself, to others, to life. And most of all, it is about blossoming. So come, blossom with us. In the embrace of nature, science, pleasure, and cosmic love, you may not only rediscover yourself…

You may remember the world you were born to help create.

Index

<table>
<tr><td>

</td><td>

</td></tr>
</table>

334

190, 195, 196, 197, 199, 209, 213, 216, 234, 239, 244, 280
sexual rights, xxi, 16, 53, 121, 178, 179, 183, 249, 251, 266, 269, 274, 279
sexual shame, 138, 276
Sharia, 74, 228, 240
state regulation, 80, 256
strict scrutiny, 266
Strict Scrutiny, 266, 278, 291
sustainability, 81, 164, 216, 329

T

Title V of the Welfare Reform Act, 99, 262
Torah, 31, 42, 54, 72, 111, 219, 252
transnational movements, 121, 274
Transnational movements, 274
trigger laws, 97
Trigger laws, 261
Trigger Laws, 261

U

UNESCO, 47, 124, 125, 126, 178, 232, 234, 295, 309

United Nations, 51, 61, 75, 89, 94, 125, 250, 251, 254, 292, 308, 317, 318

V

violence, viii, 2, 42, 43, 52, 53, 55, 61, 62, 70, 71, 89, 90, 92, 93, 94, 119, 126, 134, 138, 146, 147, 150, 151, 154, 155, 163, 164, 165, 168, 175, 199, 209, 213, 215, 226, 227, 229, 230, 250, 257, 259, 260, 287, 313, 315, 316, 317, 326, 327, 328, 329
voluntary childlessness, 79

W

World Health Organization, 125, 126, 251, 276, 303, 309

Z

Ziegler, 50, 237, 296